THE
Peace
MOVEMENTS
IN EUROPE & THE
UNITED STATES

edited by
WERNER KALTEFLEITER
AND
ROBERT L. PFALTZGRAFF

CROOM HELM
London & Sydney

© 1985 Werner Kaltefleiter and Robert L. Pfaltzgraff
Croom Helm Ltd, Provident House, Burrell Row,
Beckenham, Kent BR3 1AT
Croom Helm Australia Pty Ltd, Suite 4, 6th Floor,
64-76 Kippax Street, Surry Hills, NSW 2010, Australia

British Library Cataloguing in Publication Data

The Peace movements in Europe and the United States.
   1. Peace — Societies, etc. — History — 20th
   century 2. Europe — Politics and government —
   20th century 3. Peace — Societies and
   government — 20th century 4. United States —
   Politics and government — 20th century
   I. Kalte fleiter, Werner II. Pfaltzgraff, Robert L.
   327.1'72'094   JX1908.E9

   ISBN 0-7099-1576-4

Printed and bound in Great Britain by Mackays of Chatham Ltd, Kent

THE PEACE MOVEMENTS IN EUROPE AND THE UNITED STATES

CONTENTS

Contents

ACKNOWLEDGEMENT

THIS BOOK IS BASED ON A CONFERENCE
WHICH WAS CO-SPONSORED BY THE HANNS
MARTIN SCHLEYER FOUNDATION.

INTRODUCTION

Werner Kaltefleiter
Christian-Albrechts-University of Kiel,
Federal Republic of Germany

The peace movements have caught public attention in most of the Western countries in recent years. Although there is a long tradition of pacifist thinking in these countries and although there were similar movements in the 1950s and 1960s, the movements of the 1980s are closely related to a single political decision: the dual-track decision of NATO in December, 1979 to deploy new medium-range missiles in Europe in 1983 if negotiations with the Soviet Union to limit this type of weapon system were not successful. The main purpose of the peace movements in Europe was to put pressure on the respective governments; firstly, to be flexible enough to accept the Soviet proposals in these negotiations and, secondly, not to deploy the new missiles. Large demonstrations together with other unconventional happenings were organized for this purpose. The Soviet Union and other Warsaw Pact countries accompanied and supported the activities of the peace movements with various kinds of propaganda and disinformation campaigns.

The different historical and cultural backgrounds of the respective countries gave each peace movement its own national characteristic. The question is, whether beyond these national singularities there are common features. To this end, a comparative analysis is required. This was the purpose of the conference held in May 1984 at the Christian-Albrechts-University in Kiel. Representatives from Sweden, Denmark, Norway, The Netherlands, Great Britain, France, Italy, Germany and the United States presented papers on their national peace movements. In order to ensure the success of such an analysis, the speakers were asked in advance to discuss the following aspects:

1. Origin and history
2. Goals and ideology

Introduction

The idea of concentrating on these aspects comes from
a simple model of the interaction between the peace
movements and their societies. The relationship of
the peace movements to their societies is characterized first by their objectives and activities and the
effect they have achieved on the societies. This, of
course, is related to the response of the societies to
the peace movements in general, and to the support and
resistance the peace movements receive from these
societies. On the other hand, the internal structure
of the peace movements, as well as the societies, is
important. In the West German case, for example, it
is obvious that the peace movement is organized around
three circles. The innermost circle of activists is
divided into two main groups: the idealistic true be-
lievers and the communists. This innermost circle
consists of about 20,000 members but the organizational
structure is controlled by the communists. This is one
of the few cases where the German poet and Nobel prize-
winner Heinrich Boll gave strong support to the German
peace movement and participated in some of the activities and agreed with the findings of the German
Agency for the Protection of the Constitution.
    The second circle consists of about 200,000 to
300,000 people who are prepared to take part in demonstrations and other activities. The exact figures are
difficult to ascertain as the European Common Market
works at its best when it comes to the exchange of
demonstrators across its borders. Dutch and Danish
buses have been seen at demonstrations in Bonn and
German buses at similar events in Amsterdam and other
European cities.
    Finally, there is the third circle of the peace
movement which consists of people who are prepared to
vote for a party of the peace movement. This is, at
least until now, a German phenomenon: the 'Greens'
became the parliamentary wing of the peace movement.
They may be able to recruit up to 10 per cent of the
German electorate. In other countries, traditional
parties of the Left have given support to the peace
movements, which later became the case with the German
Social Democratic Party (SPD).

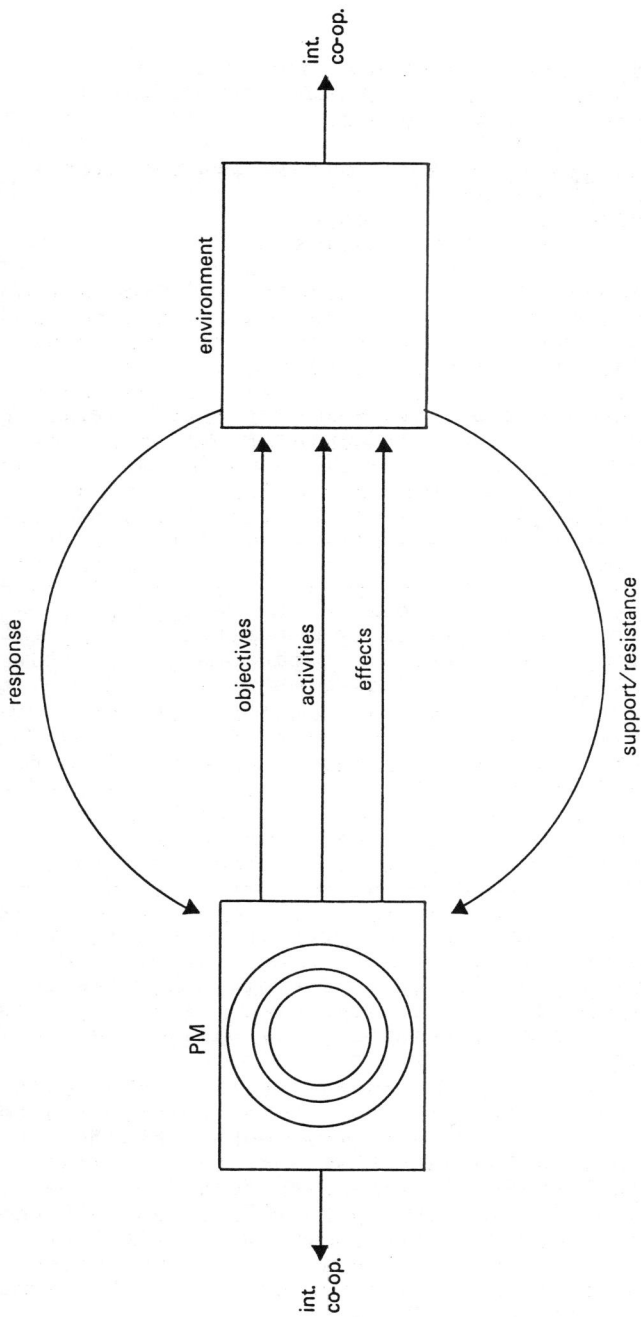

Figure 1: The Peace Movements: A Framework for Comparative Analysis

3

Introduction

With regard to the structures of societies, the political cultures of the respective countries and traditional sociological variables, for example religion, may be important. International co-operation seems to be an important variable for both peace movements and societies. In the case of societies, the Western Alliance offers a framework for this co-operation and the dual-track decision of 1979 has at least caused the revival of older groupings. In the case of the peace movements, two aspects have to be discussed: the co-ordination of certain activities and the mutual support of the peace movements; and the co-operation with the Soviet Union and/or certain proxies of the Soviets.

Of course, it is obvious that these different variables play a different role in the various countries. An overview of the results of this comparative approach is presented in a matrix in the final chapter of this book. It demonstrates a high degree of similarity despite a multitude of national characteristics.

The peace movements have played an important role in the decision-making process of the Western democracies. Although they failed to reach their final objectives, they proved to be a conspicuous force, able to influence major political parties of the democratic left. It would be too easy to call the peace movements merely an instrument of the Soviet Union, but it is obvious that the communists played an important role in the peace movements, that the Soviet Union appreciated and supported their activities, and that the objectives of the peace movements were very close to those of the Soviet Union which does not tolerate the growth of any independent peace movement within her own empire.

After the failure of the peace movements to prevent new missile deployment, the momentum they had built through 1983 collapsed. However, this does not mean that the people who supported the peace movements and the organizational framework have disappeared. Both can be reactivated for other purposes whenever another issue may arise. Therefore, it is important to understand the structure and the type of activities of the peace movements because this knowledge is the first step in successfully countering any new challenge from this end of the political spectrum. The purpose of this book, based on the papers from the Kiel conference of May 1984, is to contribute to this understanding.

Chapter One

THE PEACE MOVEMENT IN SWEDEN

Jan Andersson and Kent Lindkvist

INTRODUCTION (1)

The peace movement in Sweden functions in a situation somewhat different from many other peace movements in Europe. Many of the goals of the European peace movements have already been achieved by the Swedish peace movement. In this way, the 'Swedish model' could be described as a model which includes neutrality, non-alignment, non-imperialism, and a nuclear-weapon-free zone. While most peace movements in Europe struggle for these goals, their achievements in Sweden present a problem for the Swedish peace movement: how to be a model for other peace movements and at the same time find an identity within Swedish society.

Sweden has not participated in any regular warfare since 1814, a fact that has considerably influenced Swedish ideology concerning war and peace. It is a historical framework for the foreign policy of Sweden in its neutralist outlook. But the concepts of neutrality, non-alignment, a nuclear-weapon-free zone and non-imperialism can be interpreted in different ways. There is a consensus on the concept of neutrality, but it has been interpreted according to different ideologies, not only within the Swedish national spectrum, but also within the different ideologies of the peace movement.

Sweden's position in the world is, of course, of great importance. On the one hand, Sweden is said to be a small state, heavily dependent on international trade, investments and the supply of energy; on the other, Sweden has an intermediate position in the world system, where some countries, especially the other Nordic countries, in at least some important respects are dependent on Sweden. Sweden's technological, economic and political position is relatively independent. Its trade structure by country and by commod-

ity is quite diversified. This national position is
of importance for an explanation of the ideology, politics, structure and activities of the modern peace
movement in Sweden.
A small state could handle its external security
in different ways: 1. bilateral alliance with one great
power; 2. membership in a multinational alliance with
one or many great powers; 3. alliance with small powers only; 4. non-alignment aiming at neutrality in
every war; and 5. non-alignment, but not neutrality,
in every war. (2) The military resources of a small
state could be reinforced or weakened in all five
cases. Neutrality is not compatible with 1. and 2.
The neutrality in 3. to 5. could be pragmatic, passive
or active. The modern Swedish peace movement is predominantly devoted to 4., not to reinforce military
resources and to an active neutrality. But ideas of
3. and 5. have had and still have their adherents within the Swedish peace movement.
Attitudes towards military resources vary from
preserving the status quo to total disarmament. There
is disagreement over the extent to which Swedish neutrality needs to be defended by armed force. Active
neutrality mostly means involvement in world affairs
and some idea of a world order. But the degree of
involvement as well as the character of the peaceful
world order is disputed. There is also tension between a cosmopolitan and a national outlook. It is evident that there are divergencies of attitude from the
dominant Swedish political ideology. The alignment
policy is currently devoted to 4. which predominates
in all political camps in Sweden. In the military
resources policy, the central idea is that Swedish
neutrality needs a strong military defence, at either
existing or higher levels, but never lower ones. Only
the peace movement and some sectors of the Left want
a more modest military defence. On neutrality, there
is division between Left and Right, in that the Left
as well as the peace movement support an active neutrality, whereas the Right supports a pragmatic neutrality. If, however, we consider the peace movement
from the perspective of the last 150 years, the persistent trend is that the peace movement has been
against 1. and 2. but that all other forms of non-
alignment, military resource application and neutrality
have been represented.

ORIGINS AND HISTORY OF THE SWEDISH PEACE MOVEMENTS (3)

Pacifism as a negative view of warfare as a means in
international conflict derives from the Enlightenment

and was a part of nineteenth century liberalism. To consider the Swedish peace movement and peace ideas in the nineteenth century is to consider the directions and orientations within the liberal movement, especially from 1850 onwards. It is convenient to distinguish between two kinds of liberalism: national liberalism and Manchester liberalism. The national liberals advocated an active foreign policy. They wanted to support oppressed nations, which presupposed Swedish military intervention. On the contrary, the Swedish Manchester liberals argued that growing capitalism with free trade and investment was able to create harmony and peace between states, classes and individuals. It would promote reciprocal confidence between peoples, which would make armament unnecessary and pave the way for lasting peace. For the Manchester liberals the connection between free trade and peace was seen almost as self-evident.

In the 1860s the liberals were divided into two anti-militaristic camps. There evolved a non-interventionist wing of national liberals which proposed a reorganized defence system of a Swiss type. Opposed to them were the economic liberals who advocated strict non-alignment and a non-interventionist policy. The idea of 5. above was also advanced by the Scandinavists.

When two European peace organizations were formed in 1867, Ligue internationale de la Paix (LP) and Ligue de la Paix et de la Liberté (LPL), it revealed this division. The LP refrained from all controversial issues and was supported by the national liberals in Sweden, while the LPL emphasized democratic, republican and anti-clerical ideals and was supported by radical liberals. There also existed a third grouping, not attached to either of the two orientations, which represented Scandinavism as a bridging ideology.

The defence issue became increasingly important in Sweden and was a dividing line between the existing political parties. An initiative was given in 1869 by J. Jonasson, a representative of the Farmers' Party, which proposed that Sweden should invite other nations to take steps towards a general disarmament. This motion was rejected by parliament, but supported by pacifist adherents in different camps. The contacts between the Farmers' Party and the pacifist-oriented movement also meant an orientation to a more isolationist ideal in foreign policy. An anti-heroic concept of history also emerged in this context. The heroic projects of earlier kings were condemned. Instead, domestic development and scientific progress were considered vital.

During the 1870s and the 1880s the defence issue

dominated the yearly parliamentary sessions and divided the pacifist movement. Inspired by initiatives taken by H. Richard from Great Britain and P. Mancini from Italy, J. Jonasson of the Farmers' Party suggested that courts of arbitration should be established and treaties of arbitration be concluded between the nations. At the end of the 1870s the influential Danish retired officer and pacifist F. Bajer propagated the view that the security of a small nation was safeguarded by a formal neutralization of its territory. This idea was not widely recognized in Sweden until the issue of army organization was brought (in 1883) to a decisive trial of strength. The government's proposal was to increase the period of conscription in the army. In this situation a Swedish peace organization came into existence, Svenska freds-och skiljedomsforeningen (The Society for Peace and Arbitration in Sweden, SPAS). Most members of the Farmers' Party were not pacifists, but they were against the government's proposal on military reinforcement and increased military expenditure, due to economic interests. The creation of a peace organization strengthened antimilitaristic forces and managed to weaken the links between government and the Farmers' Party on military issues.

The susceptibility to pacifism was marked among Scandinavian popular movements, such as the labour movement, the temperance movement and the dissenting congregations. Through these channels pacifist ideas were spread all over Sweden, where local organizations proliferated. In this way, an attitude characterized by anti-militarism and aversion to a strong national defence was created, which for a long time was a distinctive feature common to the Social Democratic Party as well as the bourgeois left. A more organized peace group in parliament was formed in 1892. This fact, as well as the sharpened contradictions between Left and Right, resulted in organized co-operation between the peace and suffrage movements. However, within the Left there was a contradiction between those who advocated a nihilistic attitude towards defence and supported disarmament, and those who claimed neutrality with a strong armed force.

The increased respectability of the peace movement, heightened by the establishment of the Nobel Prize foundation and the Nobel Peace Prize, resulted in the formation of a special peace society for women in 1898. The idea of neutrality formulated by the Belgian, E. Descamp was soon adopted by Scandinavian pacifists. Neutrality was said to have a function as a peace-promoting agent. Moreover, it would be desirable for the neutral nations to unite in a federation, whose special mission would be to propagate 'pacigerance'. These ideas were quite widely accepted within the peace movement.

But at the turn of the century, the Swedish peace movement did not have a homogeneous point of view. Its members consisted mostly of liberals and social democrats. The social democratic arguments were that the bourgeois pacifist movement was deluded, since it trusted in peace conferences, arbitration and diplomacy instead of relying on international solidarity among the people and the popular movements, notably the labour movement. Only the building of democracy and a take-over of political power by the working classes could result in a lasting peace. As long as capitalism persisted there could be no lasting peace.

The crisis of the enforced union between Sweden and Norway became strained in 1895. The Norwegians protested against the Swedish regime and wanted to strengthen their independence. Militarist and conservative circles in Sweden agitated for military intervention in Norway to 'keep the Norwegians quiet'. This was a signal for mobilization of the popular movements in Sweden against war with Norway. It strengthened the connections between the popular movements in Sweden, notably the peace movement and the labour movement, and the corresponding movements in Norway. The peace movements of Sweden and Norway established close cooperation, not only at the top but also in grass-root activities such as peace tourism, pen-friend clubs, etc.

The union crisis of 1895 was something of a rehearsal for the events of 1905. The Norwegian Parliament declared in June 1905 that it did not accept Swedish royal power. The dissolution of the union was a fact. Swedish chauvinism flourished and the government mobilized its military forces against Norway. The Swedish labour and peace movements supported the Norwegian actions. However, the crisis led to arbitration between Norway and Sweden and the union was abolished without violence. This arbitrational solution gave the Swedish peace movement tremendous prestige and founded the idea of neutrality towards all political camps.

The general strike in Sweden 1909 was a serious setback for the Swedish labour movement. It was weakened on many levels, but not the parliamentary, as suffrage was extended. The weakening of the labour movement also meant a setback for other radical popular movements. The peace movement also acted for arbitration in the conflict between labour and capital. It was not supported by either of these groups. On the contrary, the peace movement lost some of its prestige in this sharpened class struggle.

The topic of military defence became increasingly important in the first decade of the new century and the peace movement had no definite idea of a national defence system. It was anti-militaristic but at the same time aware of the threat of war embedded in the Prussian spirit, in European racialism, the nationalism of expanding great powers and the aggressiveness of capitalism. Before the First World War, there was a hard struggle between Left and Right on the issue of national defence with a democratic and republican camp, and a monarchical and conservative camp. In these contradictions the peace movement had no intermediating role; it had to support the former camp. This led to the defeat of the radical popular forces. The 'crisis of the palace courtyard' of 1914 led to a reinforced monarchy and the establishment of the Hammarskjold regime, in reality a constitutional dictatorship. But Sweden stayed out of the world war, perhaps not so much because of the actions of the popular movements, but rather because of the division within the Swedish ruling classes as to foreign orientation: Germany or Great Britain. Neutrality became something of a compromise within the ruling classes, but was at the same time in accordance with the peace movement and the majority of the labour movement.

In the first decade of the twentieth century, the peace movement was supplemented by a War Resister Movement, some Christian peace organizations and a Swedish section of the Women's International League for Peace and Freedom (WILPF), which was an organization that included many prominent Swedish women. After the First World War the peace movement, with the exception of women's organizations, decreased. Of course, one reason was that there was no need for anti-war activism. But peace ideology as well as the active neutrality of the kind that the peace movement represented has no place in Swedish post-war politics. Sweden was a neutral country, whether it had pragmatic or passive neutrality. At the end of the 1920s the peace movement, notably the SPAS, increased because of the activities of the 'white general', so named because he travelled around Sweden in a large white car. During the period of social tension, he campaigned for peace, against war preparations, and a possible second world war.

In the 1930s the peace movement struggled against the arms build-up, arms trade, arms industry, militarism and war preparations. But the Machtubernahme in

The Peace Movement in Sweden

Germany made the Swedish peace movement pessimistic
and its activities were then characterized by retirement and despair by the late 1930s. The peace movement presented many resolutions against war preparations and wars such as the Abyssinian War and the
Spanish Civil War. In addition, it took part in many
activities for Spain, largely in the area of humanitarian assistance to refugees.

The labour movement formed an organization to
unite people and defence, 'People and Defence', in
which the combination of neutrality and a strong military defence was founded and accepted by broad popular groups and made into a policy for the Social
Democratic Party. Events such as Adalen 1931, where
five workers were killed by military troops, the
Machtubernahme in Germany, the struggle between the
labour movement and the military in Vienna, the fall
of the Spanish democratic republic, the Nazification
of the Swedish military, etc. were important for the
Swedish labour movement's standpoint on military
affairs. To counteract Nazi influence within the
military, integration of democratic forces and military institutions was seen as necessary.
This was a disappointment for the peace movement,
which interpreted it as a militarization of the labour
movement. But the peace movement's negativism to
military institutions was rejected by the labour
movement. Consequently, the peace movement became
quite isolated from other popular movements by the end
of the 1930s. Since that time the labour movement was
vacillated between support for the defence movement
and the peace movement. This has given rise to some
definite changes within the defence movement, notably
the acceptance of the social democratic concept of
neutrality in foreign policy conception, which has
remained to this day.
The cold war divided the Swedish peace movement.
Two new movements emerged in the post-war world: the
World Federalists and the World Peace Movement. They
took the initiative from the traditional peace movement and presented some new ideas and activities within the framework of the cold war. The World Peace
Movement, affected by communist influence, was quite
strong around 1950, when the Stockholm appeal against
atomic weapons was presented. Stockholm became the
headquarters of the World Peace Movement and the
Swedish Communist Party launched many peace campaigns
to strengthen its prestige in Sweden. The traditional
peace movement was criticized for elitism: a popular
peace movement was said to reject bourgeois pacifism.
The world Federalists also criticized the tradition-

al peace movement for its relatively nationalist orientation. Peace and communism became connected in official Swedish ideology and the non-communist peace movement as a 'third force' had very little access to Swedish opinion. This divided the peace movement, and some organizations purged alleged communists among their own members. However, the World Peace Movement lost all prestige when the Soviet Union invaded Hungary in 1956. The World Federalist Movement lost their prestige a bit later through supporting a Swedish atomic bomb as well as a Swedish hydrogen bomb.

In the middle of the 1950s it was declared that it was possible to develop and produce a Swedish atomic bomb. This led to an independent anti-nuclear-weapons movement. It was organized by about 30 intellectual personalities, who arranged rallies, debates, demonstrations and other activities. It was a single issue movement: against a Swedish nuclear weapon and to provide debate about the possibility of a conversion of military resources for constructive aims under debate.

The World Federalists claimed that the antinuclear movement was of no value for peace. Some World Federalists supported the idea of an atomic weapon as the only defence system, because it would abolish the military. And perhaps this was an accurate analysis, though completely inopportune. In fact, the military argued against an atomic weapon in 1961 because it would be too expensive and it would significantly diminish the role of conventional military forces.

Swedish nuclear weapons were not produced and the traditional peace movement was able to integrate many activists of the anti-nuclear movement in its ranks. However, the Partial Test Ban Treaty served to diminish the rise of the peace movement. It became involved in other issues such as starvation in the Third World and, later, the Vietnam issue. SPAS initiated a Committee for Peace in Vietnam, which became an organization for established political parties, the peace movement, and other traditional popular organizations. However, the Vietnam movement, essentially founded among the extra-parliamentary Left, eventually became an anti-imperialist (anti-USA) movement. For a decade this and other anti-imperialist movements held the initiative. The New Left movement, which mobilized a mass of students and white-collar workers in Sweden, was against capitalist militarism, yet was in favour of guerrilla warfare and a Swedish guerrilla defence. This divided the peace movement between radical pacifism and revolutionary anti-imperialism. The decline of the New Left after the middle of the 1970s and the

The Peace Movement in Sweden

end of the Vietnam War established some increase of
interest in the peace movement. This interest grew
even more after NATO's dual-track decision of 1979,
which led to the movement's reorganization. The rise
in interest developed mostly between 1979 and 1983,
but for the last year and a half it seems to have
stagnated.

A SWEDISH PEACE MOVEMENT OVERVIEW: 1984

The oldest among the various Swedish peace organizations is the Swedish Peace and Arbitration Society,
SPAS (Svenska freds-och skiljedomsforeningen, SFSF)
which was founded in 1883. It has about 11,600 members. It is a member of the International Peace
Bureau (IPB), the International War Resisters (WRI),
and co-operates with the European Nuclear Disarmament
(END) and the International Peace Communication and
Co-ordination Centre (IPCCC).
  The organizational structure of the Swedish Peace
and Arbitration Society is very decentralized. Local
groups, of which there are more than 100, plan their
own activities: studies, debates, demonstrations,
meetings, non-violent actions, etc. This is often
done in co-operation with other peace organizations as
well as other social, political and cultural organizations. A number of campaigns are co-ordinated nationally and/or internationally, such as campaigns
against the arms trade, the neutron bomb, the deployment of the SS-20 and the new NATO missiles, and for
unilateral Swedish disarmament.
  SPAS's programme is comprised of the following
goals:

  - international disarmament;
  - unilateral Swedish disarmament;
  - a nuclear-weapon free Europe and a nuclear-
    weapon-free zone in the North;
  - prohibition of Swedish arms export, decrease
    of international arms trade;
  - a new Swedish security policy in an alternative
    programme based on civilian defence;
  - war resistance should be regarded as a human
    right.

The Swedish Peace Committee, SPCom (Svenska fredskom-
mitten)
This movement, which was founded in 1949, is considerably smaller. It has about 2,000 members, of which

13

200 are collectively affiliated trade unions, social, cultural and political organizations. It is a member of the World Peace Council. With respect to its organizational structure, it is noteworthy that the members of the collectively affiliated organizations, for example sectors of the trade unions dominated by the social democrats, have had a formal influence on the organization. It is, however, dominated by local organizations built on individual membership and by local political branches of the different communist parties as well as some social democrats. However, some social democratic as well as some Eurocommunist organizations have left the committee during the past few years. Activities consist of meetings, study groups, roll-calls, rallies and demonstrations. The leadership of the Committee has for a long time been dominated by prominent persons from the insignificant Soviet-oriented Communist Party (Apk) as well as pro-soviet personalities within the Communist Left Party (Vpk) and the Social Democrats. However, some younger persons of the new wave in the peace movement have joined the committee leadership. The programme states that 'The Swedish Peace Committee is an anti-imperialistic front organization for peace, for the support of liberation movements against fascism and oppression. It is politically uncommitted.' The goals of the Committee are:

- disarmament;
- a nuclear-free zone in Scandinavia;
- to stop the Euromissiles;
- support for the freeze movement;
- national and international co-operation for a nuclear-weapon-free world, for detente and peace.

The Christian Peace Movement, CPN (Kristna fredsrorelsen)
This movement has its roots in the Swedish World Peace Mission, 1919 (Svenska varldsfredsmissionen) and the Association for Christian Society, 1918 (Forbundet for kristet samhallsliv). The radical pacifist sections of the two organizations merged in 1969 with the movement taking its present name in 1977. It has 3,500 individual members and co-operates with the International Fellowship of Reconciliation and War Resisters International. Its organizational structure is decentralized with local groups who organize their own activities and co-operate with SPAS in particular. According to its programme, the Christian Peace Movement is a non-violent movement, which from the gospel

of God wants to work for justice and peace, general and total disarmament and a society without violence.

The Women's International League for Peace and Freedom

The Swedish section, WILPF (Internationella kvinno-forbundet for fred-och frihet, IKFF) was founded in 1919 (WILPF in 1915) and has 2,000 individual members. The league has consultative status in UNESCO, ECOSOC, FAO, ILO and UNCTAD. Its organization is centralized and its activities include seminars and courses, and international committee work. The programme sets the following goals for the League:

- conflicts between people and states should be solved through peaceful agreement;
- the UN Declaration on Human Rights should be applied in all nations;
- to spread factual information about international matters;
- to promote understanding between peoples and peaceful co-operation between peoples and states;
- to promote general and total disarmament;
- to support the UN in its work for peace and for economic and social justice;
- to support international aid;
- WILPF works with the international STAR-campaign (Stop the arms race). The goal is to get names and economic support from one million women in every country.

The Swedish Women's Left Association, SWLA (Svenska kvinnors vansterforbund, SKV

Founded in 1914 as the League of Liberal Women, its present name was adopted in 1931. It has 1,500 members. Internationally, the association co-operates with the Women's Democratic World Federation. The organization is also a member of the Swedish Peace Committee. The association is active in solidarity work for women in Vietnam, Latin America and South Africa. The association was founded under the heading: 'Against war psychosis, for democracy and women's equality.' According to its programme, the association has the following goals:

- disarmament
- a just and peaceful society
- freedom from oppression and exploitation

The Peace Movement in Sweden

Women For Peace, WPF (Kvinnor for fred)
Founded in 1978, it now has some 3,000 members. Women
For peace exists in a number of European countries and
in the USA. Women For Peace regard themselves as a
part of the international feminist movement. The
movement has no central organization but consists of
independent groups connected with local feminist organizations. The organization aims at introducing
feminist ('new and imaginative') methods in the work
for peace. The Women For Peace seek to attain the
following goals:

- gather women in active support for peace and
  disarmament, against nuclear power and nuclear
  weapons;
- peace founded on freedom, justice and equality;
- nuclear disarmament;
- to establish a Nordic nuclear-weapon-free zone;
- to stop deployment of new nuclear Euromissiles;
- detente between East and West through popular
  and grass-root communications and solidarity.

The Physical Culture Association (Frisksportarforbundet)
Founded in 1935 with 22,500 members, this association
has no international connections. The organization
agitates against drugs and tobacco, for physical culture and a simple way of life. Its members are obliged
to abstain from drugs and tobacco. It points to the
links between environmental control and international
problems. The ground for international solidarity
lies in a just distribution of resources.

The Federation of Christian Humanism and Social Life
(Forbundet for kristen humanism och samhallssyn)
Founded in 1971, as a fusion of the Federation of
Christian Humanism and the Federation of Christian
Social Life, both of which were founded around 1910.
The Federation has 1,100 members but no forms of inter-
national co-operation. According to its programme, the
Federation concentrates on theological and ethical
aspects of a peaceful society.

The Swedish Section of the Civil Service International,
SCI (Internationella arbetslag, IAL), founded in 1943,
with about 700 members. Internationally, it co-oper-
ates with the Civil Service International and the
Co-ordinating Committee For International Voluntary
Service. Its programme contains goals in the area of

environmental control, engagement in social problems,
international work for solidarity, peace and understanding between nations and races.

**The Friends Community in Sweden, the Quakers (Vannernas
samfund - kvakarna)**
Founded in 1937, with 100 members. The goals and
ideology of this organization are rather vague. In
this respect, their programme states: 'We believe in
love as the greatest power of life, and therefore refuse to use violence to meet changes or to resist
evil. To build understanding and bridges between
opposing ideologies is important in the work for
peace.'

**The Foreign Policy Association UN-Federation (Utrikes-
politiska foreningarnas FN-forbund, UNF)**
Founded in 1950, it has no more than a few hundred
members. This organization co-operates with the international Youth and Student Movement for the United
Nations. Its goals are set forth in the programme as
follows:

- disarmament;
- conversion from military to civilian production;
- against the increased militarization of the
  Third World;
- support of NIEO;
- support of liberation movements in South Africa
  and Namibia.

**The Syndicalists (Sveriges arbetares centralorganis-
ation, syndikalisterna, SAC)**
An organization.founded in 1910, with 18,000 members
at present. The SAC is a syndicalist labour movement.
The work for peace is founded in federalism which is
intended to be carried at both international and
national levels. SAC is opposed to militarism and
military defence, and has a long history of anti-militarism. In particular, the organization supports the
right of conscientious objection.

**The Swedish World Federalists, SWF (Svenska varldsfed-
eralisterna),**
Founded in 1948, it has a few hundred members. Internationally, this group co-operates with the World

Federalist Movement and the Parlimentarians For World
Order. The Swedish world federalists work for a gradual transformation of the UN to a democratic world
parliament. They work for long-term constructive
peace politics which repudiate nationalism and military violence as a means of solving international conflicts.

NATIONAL CO-OPERATION AMONG THE SWEDISH PEACE ORGAN-
ISATIONS

The Swedish Peace Council (Sveriges fredsrad) is an
'umbrella' organization for the Swedish peace movement. It is an organization for information, discussion and co-operation between organizations with peace
and international solidarity on their programme.
Decisions are taken by consensus. For that reason,
declarations on questions of peace politics are rare,
and when they occur, quite vague. The work of the
organization is financed by the subsidies of the
organizational members. There are 13 organizations,
which are presented in the overview on pp 13-18.
    Historically the Council has its roots in the
1930s, but its activities withered away during the
Second World War. After the war, a new organization
for co-operation between the peace organizations was
founded in 1945: Centralkommitten for fredsarbete
(The Central Committee for Peace), which at the end of
the 1940s took the name of Sveriges fredsrad (The
Swedish Peace Council).
    In 1975 the Social Democratic government invited
the Swedish Peace Council (SPC) to send an 'observat-
eur' to the UN, as a member of the Swedish delegation,
SPC sent a representative, and the invitation was renewed for the next four UN sessions. In the arrangements and preparations for the UN special session on
disarmament, Sweden was one of the states to propose
that the non-governmental organizations should partake
in the preparation, realization and follow-up of the
session. The Swedish government (the bourgeois governments after 1976 made no change from the Social
Democratic policy in these matters) appreciated broad
support from the popular movements for the preparations of the Special Session. Such broad popular
support for Swedish disarmament politics was said to
strengthen the Swedish position in the international
disarmament debate.
    In 1977, SPC invited about 20 organizations for
consultations on this topic. It was essentially the
core peace organizations which were interested. In

18

1977 three organizations - the Swedish Peace Council,
the Swedish Peace Committee and the Swedish UN-Association - took the responsibility for a disarmament
campaign. It led to a constitution of a working team
for the preparation of a Swedish Peoples Parliament
for disarmament. The Parliament met in January 1978,
and was dominated by the peace movement. The Swedish
political youth organizations were represented as well
as the Church and its organizations. Some labour
movement organizations and trade unions were represented.
     The Parliament was given a double function. It
should both exhibit a broad popular support for the
Swedish government in its actions on the UN Special
Session, and express popular demands for disarmament
which are not expressed in the democratic and par-
liamentarian political process. A second Peoples
Parliament meeting occurred as a preparation for SSD
II, with even broader representation from the Swedish
popular movement; 150 organizations were represented.
On both occasions the meetings have approved proposals
for Swedish disarmament: a reduction of military
expenditure, conversion of military to civilian production as well as demands for a parliamentary committee to study the possibility of abolishing the Swedish
arms trade.
     Another umbrella organization is the Swedish
section of the World Federation of United Nations
Associations, WFUNA (Svenska FN-forbundet). Currently
the Swedish Association acts like a pressure group
with regard to UN policy questions. Disarmament questions
have not had a high priority in the Association but
today there is an active interest in disarmament
questions. A new perspective on disarmament has emerged, where it is coupled with development, resources, etc. Disarmament is also seen as a way to neut-
ralize conflicts.
     An example of this new trend in the organization
is the arrangement of the UN Forum's national conference on world disarmament. A proposal that the right
to refuse military service should be established was
rejected by a small majority. Almost every proposal
adopted was directed against nuclear weapons. The
only proposal which caused some discussion was the
Nordic NWFZ, that is the only one which touched upon
Swedish security policy.
     In 1981 the Social Democratic Party and the lab-
our unions held congresses. On both occasions proposals were raised for an increased campaign for peace
and disarmament. On this basis the Labour movement's
Peace Forum was established in 1981, with Alva Myrdal

as a chairman. When Mrs Myrdal introduced the Forum
she stated that it would work along two lines: 1. the
build-up of a stronger opinion against the arms race;
and 2. to get the superpowers to a position of new
disarmament negotiations. In this process the Forum
should serve as a data storage unit for labour movement organizations. This meant that peace organizations had to relate more directly to the Forum, if
they wanted to have an impact on labour organizations.
Peace organizations can have a small presence in the
Forum, but never dominate it. The Forum gives a basis
for labour movement activities on peace issues, a role
which it has tried to take over from the Peace Committee. The Forum tries to take the leading role in
organizing labour movement organizations for peace.
It has also tried to subdue parts of the peace movement under its organization as well as in terms of
activities related to the government and the international arena. However, it seems to be more passive
at the moment. It has not taken part in recent peace
movement projects and is not yet locally organized.

After this reorganization of the labour movement
peace organizations the other political parties related themselves to the peace issue. The Centre
(agrarian) Party formed its own Peace Forum. The
Liberal Party formed 'Liberals for Peace' and the
Conservative Party formed the organization 'Freedom
promotes Peace', arguing that the threat from the USSR
demands a strong Swedish military defence.

The pattern of co-operation within the peace
movement varies from national to local level, and from
place to place. In many places the different peace
organizations have founded an umbrella organization,
Peace Co-op (Fredsam) for the co-ordination of local
activities such as demonstrations and campaigns. In
these local Peace Co-ops professional peace groups,
environmental organizations, anti-nuclear-power
groups, local uncommitted peace groups and others co-
operate with the peace organizations of the Swedish
Peace Council. The subject of the activity is mostly
nuclear weapons, but it also can be other issues such
as a decreased military expenditure and an alternative
society. Locally, the established peace organizations
face competition from new and independent groups founded locally or one-issue groups such as the Campaign
for a Nuclear-free Europe, connected to the END.

There are two centres within the Swedish peace
movements: the SPAS and the Peace Committees. SPAS
has a much stronger position within the peace movement, but the Peace Committees have some influence in
the labour movement. There is an ideological, organ-

izational and political polarization between the two organizations. More or less connected to the Peace Committees are the Swedish Women's Left Association and the Service Civil International, while the Christian organizations (not the Quakers, who have some co-operation with the Peace Committees), the WILPF, the syndicalists, the environmental groups and the END groups are more connected to the SPAS. The Physical Culture Association is more connected to the temperance movement than the peace movement, the World Federalists are marginalized and the Foreign Policy Associations UN-federation is more connected to the UN-association. The three organizations seldom play a role in this polarization. Women for Peace is mostly dominated by the New Left branch of the women's liberation movement, and they often criticize both the SPAS and the Peace Committees. The professional groups could be seen as a field of struggle between the two centres of the peace movement.

The professional groups against nuclear weapons and/or for peace are a new phenomenon. The model derives from International Physicians for the prevention of Nuclear Weapons. The idea is that every professional group should partake in the work against nuclear weapons/for peace with its own specific knowledge and competence. Through trade union publications or their own newsletters they try to spread information. Today there are 19 such professional groups in Sweden, varying in degree of activity and number of members: physicians, teachers, engineers, artists, clergy, architects, authors, researchers, journalists, jurists, psychologists, librarians, social workers, etc. Perhaps the most impressive professional group is the Swedish Physicians Against Nuclear Weapons, which can count an absolute majority of Swedish physicians as members.

The radical pacifist tradition is strongest within SPAS and the Christian peace movement. The radical pacifists claim that 'non-violence is a way of living', and have founded a network labelled 'Non-violence' (Icke-vald), whose most spectacular manifestations so far as been the blockade of the British and Italian embassies in Stockholm in 1983,

INTERNATIONAL CO-OPERATION OF THE SWEDISH PEACE MOVEMENT

Table 1 presents a picture of the international membership of the Swedish peace organizations.
    The recent development of the peace movement has

22

Table 1: — International Memberships

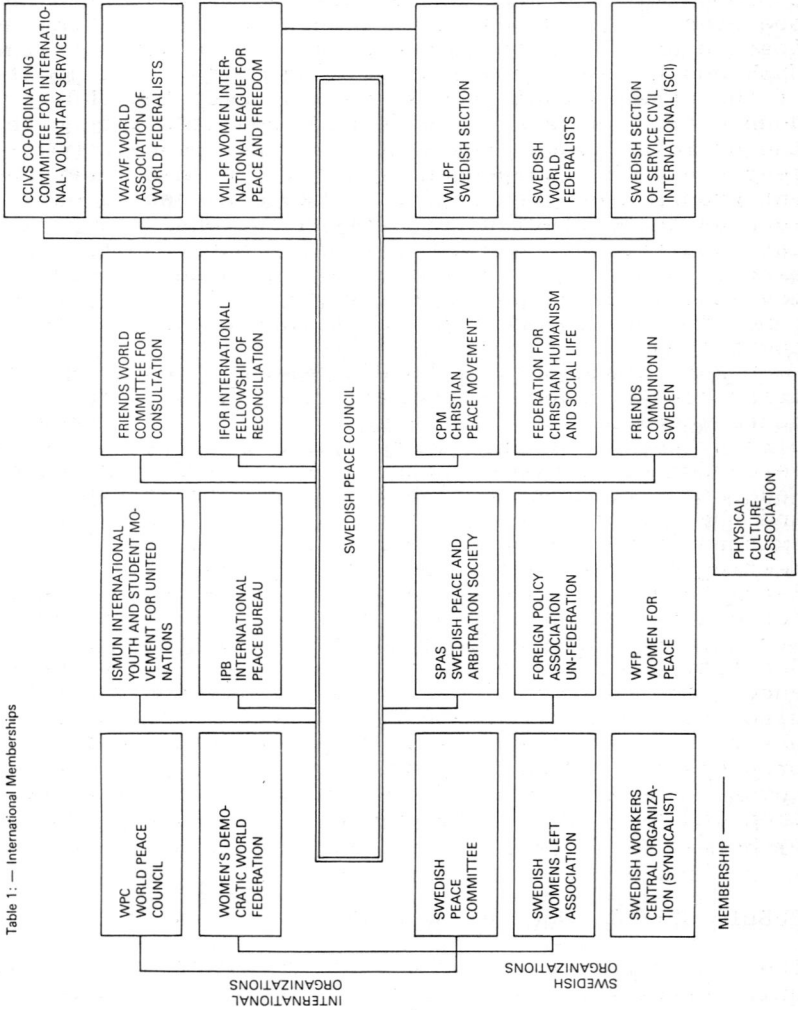

CCIVS CO-ORDINATING COMMITTEE FOR INTERNATIONAL VOLUNTARY SERVICE

WAWF WORLD ASSOCIATION OF WORLD FEDERALISTS

WILPF WOMEN INTERNATIONAL LEAGUE FOR PEACE AND FREEDOM

WILPF SWEDISH SECTION

SWEDISH WORLD FEDERALISTS

SWEDISH SECTION OF SERVICE CIVIL INTERNATIONAL (SCI)

FRIENDS WORLD COMMITTEE FOR CONSULTATION

IFOR INTERNATIONAL FELLOWSHIP OF RECONCILIATION

SWEDISH PEACE COUNCIL

CPM CHRISTIAN PEACE MOVEMENT

FEDERATION FOR CHRISTIAN HUMANISM AND SOCIAL LIFE

FRIENDS COMMUNION IN SWEDEN

ISMUN INTERNATIONAL YOUTH AND STUDENT MOVEMENT FOR UNITED NATIONS

IPB INTERNATIONAL PEACE BUREAU

SPAS SWEDISH PEACE AND ARBITRATION SOCIETY

FOREIGN POLICY ASSOCIATION UN-FEDERATION

WFP WOMEN FOR PEACE

PHYSICAL CULTURE ASSOCIATION

WPC WORLD PEACE COUNCIL

WOMEN'S DEMOCRATIC WORLD FEDERATION

SWEDISH PEACE COMMITTEE

SWEDISH WOMENS LEFT ASSOCIATION

SWEDISH WORKERS CENTRAL ORGANIZATION (SYNDICALIST)

INTERNATIONAL ORGANIZATIONS

SWEDISH ORGANIZATIONS

MEMBERSHIP ————

to some degree changed international links. SPAS co-
operates with END and the International Peace Communication and Co-ordination Centre.   In relation to the
USSR and Eastern Europe SPAS, along with the majority
of the other organizations, has followed the END
double-track strategy: to develop contacts with both
the official peace organizations - the peace committees - and the independent groups. The new independent groups are often copies of Western peace groups
such as the Christian peace organizations, the pacifists and the anti-nuclear weapons groups. With the
exception of the Peace Committee the Swedish peace
movement tries to help these groups while they, at the
same time, have communication with the official peace
committees.
     The campaign for a Nordic NWFZ has led to itens-
ified contacts and communications with the Nordic
peace movement. (4) The women's peace initiative has
already been mentioned.   Another example is the Nordic
Peace Forum. Its predecessors were the Nordic Peace
Federation founded in 1918 which existed until 1960,
and the Nordic Peace Contact Organization which
existed from 1969 until 1972. In November, 1981 a
meeting of 17 organizations constituted the Nordic
Peace Forum. The function of the Forum is as a centre
for co-ordination and information. In 1983 the Forum
arranged the Nordic Peace Movement's Conference on
Security and Disarmament in Stockholm. The conference gathered about 150 persons, mostly activists but
also some politicians and researchers. The purpose
was to present proposals on a new security policy, the
problems of nuclear weapons, the demilitarization of
Europe, the strengthening of the UN, military production and arms trade, and concrete initiatives launched
by Nordic organizations.

PUBLIC SUPPORT FOR THE SWEDISH PEACE MOVEMENT

The public support for the peace movement of today is
quite heterogeneous. It consists of 1. young people
around 20 years old, mobilized by the latest events in
armaments development; 2. a middle-aged generation,
35-45 years old with its roots in the anti-nuclear
movement around 1960, the New Left, the ecological
movement and other radical movements; and 3. old people over 60 with roots in the traditional peace movement. There is a change of leadership within the
peace movement from the old generation to the middle-
aged generation, and in some cases such as the SPAS,
there is a change to the younger generation.

Membership figures show a rise in membership as
in earlier rises in the 1880s, the 1890s, the 1910s,
the end of the 1920s, the 1940s and the end of the
1950s. On the other hand, demonstrations, rallies and
other arrangements by the peace movement mobilize
people as never before. For example, a demonstration
for a Nordic NWFZ assembled 75,000 persons in Gothen-
burg in May 1982, and in June 1982 750,000 signatures
were collected for a nuclear-weapon-free zone. In
individual membership, it seems that total peace
movement membership is not more than 25,000 and a half
of them are in the SPAS. This could be compared with
the figures of the Swedish Women's Army Auxiliary
Corps with its 56,000 individual members. The voluntary defence movement counts 700,000 members, but this
cannot be compared with 25,000 because of organizational differences. But it is quite clear that the
defence movement is far larger than the peace movement
in individual membership, if we define movements in a
narrow sense. In demonstrations and other arrangements of that kind, the peace movement can mobilize
many more people than the defence movement. On the
other hand, the defence movement works with other
kinds of activities, often connected to army organizations, in which far more people partake than in the
peace movement. This can also be seen as a question
of mobilization of different social strata. In crude
social class terms, the defence movement mobilizes the
entrepreneurs, the farmers and the conservative middle
class, while the peace movement mobilizes the radical
middle class and the working class on defence and
disarmament issues. The defence movement has no problems in mobilizing their three groups for defence
issues while the peace movement has serious problems
when they try to mobilize the working class. The
peace movement mobilizes primarily various sectors
of the middle class with radical political, social and
cultural traditions.
   If we relate the peace movement to political
parties in Sweden, we could sketch an image as follows.
The Communist Parties as well as the Environmental
Party are devoted to the peace movement wholly, just
as the Conservative Party is devoted wholly to the
defence movement. The other parties, the Social
Democrats, the Liberals, the Centre (agrarian) Party
and the Christian Democrats are in different ways
positive/ambivalent to both movements. The Liberal
Party has always consisted of entrepreneurs and is
largely middle class. Until the cold war the liberals
played a crucial role within the peace movement, but
after that their role diminished. Within the Liberal

The Peace Movement in Sweden

Party the peace movement wing was stronger than the
defence movement wing in related issues, but the situation has now been reversed. The Christian Democratic Party can be said to be in a similar situation as
the Liberal Party, but at the moment peace movement
ideas seem to be dominating that party.
The Agrarian Party, as it was reconstructed in
the 1910s after the breakdown of the old Farmer's
Party, rejected co-operation with all city-based movements for a long time, even after the co-operation with
the Social Democratic Party. At the same time the
party struggled with the Conservative Party over influence on the defence movement. In the 1950s when
the party faced a serious decrease, it opened itself
up to new ideas and co-operations, even with city-
based organizations. The party has had a strong impact on the environmental movement, but it has decreased. The middle-class connection with the party,
on the grounds of the 'green wave' and environmental
ideas, also has links with the peace movement, even if
quite weak. The core groups of the party, the farmers, are devoted to the defence movement. Most of the
people within the peace movement give their vote to
the Social Democratic Party, but that party also wants
to have good relations with the defence movement. The
party in fact dominates some branches of the defence
movement too, and many workers are engaged in defence
movement activities. This gives rise to quite a
complicated strategic and tactical situation for the
Social Democratic Party, a situation with deep roots
in the experiences of the 1930s and the Second World
War, which we shall discuss later. Within the party,
peace movement adherents probably have a stronger influence in terms of political language, but in terms
of hardware the defence (and industrial) interests are
much stronger.

GOALS AND IDEOLOGY OF THE SWEDISH PEACE MOVEMENT

The ideologies of the peace movement can be described
in several ways, but a preliminary list could be as
follows:

    1. Liberal internationalism and a negative view
    of war as a means to solve conflicts. World fed-
    eralism could be seen as a modern variant of
    nineteenth century liberalism.
    2. Religious pacifism: conscientious objection
    on religious grounds.
    3. Socialist anti-militarism: militarism is used

25

to divide the working classes and must be rejected.
4. Communist anti-militarism: anti-imperialistic
class struggle to abolish capitalism. Communist
anti-militarism and peace ideology could vary
between a Leninist, a popular front and a Eurocommunist view.
5. Feminist anti-militarism: men fight the wars
and use the weapons, therefore women must act to
stop the wars and abolish the weapons.
6. Radical pacifism: Gandhian non-violence and
secular conscientious objection.
7. Weapons pacifism: against nuclear weapons
and other weapons; for unilateral disarmament,
negotiations and arbitration.
8. Alternativism: and alternative, peaceful
society on new grounds must be formed.

These eight traditions are represented within the
Swedish peace movement today. The overall emphasis
has been struggle against war, weapons, and the conditions that create war and weapons. From early liberalism the idea evolved that it is not enough to object to war, but the means of war, that is weapons,
must be abolished. This leads to conscientious objection in personal life, and to anti-weapons organizations and a struggle for national and international
disarmament at the political level. But it can also
be said, notably with regard to the communist tradition, that it is not enough to struggle against weapons, because there are certain conditions, that is,
the capitalist system, that must be abolished. Because of the militaristic features of capitalism, and
its role as the root cause of war, weapons and militarism can only be fought by a strong military-political
organization, a communist party and a red army. Of
course, negotiations are possible, but only because
there is a strong socialist camp with strong military
forces. Alternativism also states that there are some
basic problems in the inherent construction of society,
but it attacks both capitalism and socialism, and does
not propose the same means for change as the communist
tradition.
    Five organizations of the SPC are devoted almost
exclusively to the peace questions: the SPAS, the
WILPF, the Christian Peace Movement (CPM), the Swedish
Peace Committee (SPCom) and Women for Peace (WFP).
Other organizations have a broader, social or religious orientation, or are marginalized as the world
federalists.
    Table 2 illustates the relationships between the

eight traditions of peace ideologies and the Swedish
peace organizations. The federalists represent tradition (1). The Quakers and the CFM represent tradition (2), but in the case of CFM the representation
is some kind of Gandhian tradition as in (6). The
SPAS represents traditions (6) to (8) especially. A
pragmatic pacifism dominates, but there are factions
of syndicalism/anarchism, alternativism, New Left, and
radical pacifism. The WILPF represents, of course,
tradition (5) but also (7). So does the WFP, but is
complemented by tradition (8). The SPCom represents
tradition (3) and (4) and is in principle quite negative to traditions (5) to (8), but does support them
to a certain extent. The SPCom directs its criticism
against the USA and NATO, while most of the other
movements direct their criticism to both superpowers.
The federalists as well as some of the other organizations criticize the nation state as the main cause
of war. In some cases, especially among religious
organizations, it is claimed that there is some
essential problem with human nature, which causes war
and must be remedied if the situation is to change.
Unilateral disarmament and a conversion strategy is
especially upheld by the SPAS and the CFM. There are
also some differences as to activism-institutionalism,
where the SPAS, the CFM and the WFP are more activist
and the other organizations are more institutional.
The SPCom is both activist and institutional. The
professional groups represent tradition (7) and are
naturally quite institutional, but they also partake
in the activism of other peace organizations.
      It is clearly quite difficult to link together
organizations with such different traditions, but in
the search for a common basis for action, tradition
(7) has been effective, especially from the anti-
nuclear and anti-weapon standpoints. Here it is possible to unite and it is on this basis that the peace
movement is organized in Sweden today. But it is
difficult to co-operate on other issues. The SPAS
'Programme for Peace' reflects this dilemma. It tries
to combine traditions (6)-(8)in a disarmed Sweden with
a civilian defence, and no class or other social conflicts, via an extremely democratic and decentralized
structure based on self-reliance.

ACHIEVEMENTS AND PROSPECTS OF THE SWEDISH PEACE MOVE-
MENT

The peace movement has claimed that it has had a crucial impact on a range of events such as defence expen-

Table 2: Traditions of Peace Ideology and Swedish Peace Organizations

Traditions \ Organizations	SPAS	SPCom	CPM	WILPF	SWF	WFP	Quak	UN	Wfed	Synd	SCI	Prof	Envir
1. Liberal Internationalism	x			x				x	x				
2. Religious pacifism			x				x						
3. Social anti-militarism	x	x				x					x	x	
4. Communist anti-militarism		x				x							
5. Feminist anti-militarism				x	x	x							
6. Radical pacifism	x		x										
7. Weapons pacifism	x											x	
8. Alternativism	x		x										x

diture in the 1880s, the Sweden-Norway dispute in 1895
and 1905, the fact that Sweden did not take part in
the First World War, Swedish disarmament in the 1920s
and the 1930s and the rejection of the atomic bomb in
the late 1950s. It also claims that the idea of
arbitration has been firmly accepted and that the peace
movement has been crucial for the spread of ideas of
neutrality, peace and international solidarity in
Sweden. This impact is of course very difficult to
measure. And there are other candidates that claim
their impact on the above-mentioned events. To argue
against the peace movement claims, it could be said
that the farmers' economic interests may have been
more crucial in the 1880s than the activities of the
peace organization. Without the support of the
Farmers' Party it would not have been possible to stop
the proposal on increased military expenditure. The
labour movement and the liberal movement claim the
same thing as the peace movement in the dispute between Norway and Sweden. It is evident that the peace
movement established a firm connection of solidarity
between middle-class sectors in Norway and Sweden.
But it is also a fact that the government had the option to launch a war with Norway and also prepared for
a war. The two factors of foreign policy and an
aroused popular movement were jointly crucial. That
Sweden did not fight in the First World War can be
discussed from many angles, but we see it as having
been something of a compromise in ruling circles. The
popular movements as well as parliament had no influence at the political level and their real influence
had declined since the general strike of 1909. Swedish
disarmament and the reorganization of the Swedish army
in the 1920s were supported by many groups in Swedish
society and were not due exclusively to the peace movement. In fact, it was disarmament from a position of
strength. Sweden was a strong military power in
northern Europe after the First World War. Swedish
disarmament policy tried to freeze the armament situation in northern Europe.
    Peace movement actions against the Swedish atomic
bomb had a strong impact on public opinion. The table
below shows that opinion changed remarkably; 40 per
cent of the population supported the bomb in 1957, but
only 21 per cent four years later. In 1961 the military also rejected the atomic bomb because it was realized that it was too expensive and would have some
negative effects on military organization. The Social
Democratic Party was, however, divided in its attitude
to the atomic bomb and the women's association expec-
ially played an important role within the party in its

agitation against the bomb.

Table 3: Attitude to a Swedish Atomic Bomb, (per cent) (5)

	For	Against	Don't know
June 1957	40	36	24
October 1959	29	51	20
March 1961	21	56	23

The attitude to the Vietnam War as well as the attitude to the USA was essentially changed in Sweden during the course of the war. The role of the peace
movement in the mid-1960s could be said to have been
initiatory, but then it played a very small role in the
shadow of the New Left, notably the Maoists, who played a leading role in the Swedish anti-imperialist
movement.

Today, actions of the peace movement have essentially been focused on the international arena,
European theatre forces and a Nordic NWFZ. The peace
movement has also opposed a new Swedish military aircraft, the JAS-aeroplane, an issue which was a setback
for the peace movement. In parliament only the communists voted against this aircraft; even the peace
movement adherents of other parties voted for the
eight billion-dollar project.

A Nordic NWFZ is regarded as a contribution to
detente, a confidence-building measure which would
give encouragement for other measures and other zones
elsewhere in Europe. The idea has been widely accepted, especially as Sweden is already nuclear-free. The
official standpoint, represented both by the Social
Democratic Party and the bourgeois parties, demands
the inclusion of the Baltic and parts of the USSR in
the zone arrangement, which is a problem for the peace
movement, and has partly divided it. The submarine
incidents as well as the Treholt-affair in Norway have
been something of a setback for peace movement arguments for a Nordic NWFZ. The broad aim of the Swedis
peace movement today, during a period of initial stag-
nation, is to support and influence the Swedish social
democratic government on disarmament proposals in the

international arena. However, unilateralists ideas are
growing stronger within the peace movement. If these
were to dominate the peace movement, then its basis
for support and mobilization would diminish as long as
the current world situation persists.
    To conclude, the Swedish peace movement has func-
tioned essentially as an opinion group within the
Left, the bourgeois Left and the labour movement
for ideas on peace and disarmament. In the long term,
therefore, it has certainly had an impact.

THE NATIONAL CHARACTERISTICS OF THE PEACE MOVEMENT IN SWEDEN

To describe the Swedish peace movement in its national
setting is to place it in relation to other popular
movements in Sweden, especially the labour movement
and the defence movement. Achievements, prospects,
strategies and tactics of the peace movement in Sweden
are related to these two movements in particular.
    The idea of a combined neutrality and a strong
military defence under firm parliamentary control was
launched by the social democrats in the 1930s and the
1940s. It was founded against the background of labour movement defeats in other countries in Europe and
the development of fascism. The labour movement aim
has been to object to the militarism of bourgeois
groups. A consensus on the defence issue and labour
movement influence over the defence movement have been
important features in labour movement policy. The
peace movement demand for Swedish military disarmament
has always been rejected and, at least in a short-
term, nothing would change this position taken by the
labour movement.
    There is a peculiar relationship between the
peace movement and the defence movement. There is not
exactly an open clash between them, - more of an
underground warfare of arguments and actions. The
peace movement had a mobilization peak in 1983, but the
defence movement has managed to mobilize people as
never before after the submarine incidents (notably at
Karlskrona in 1981 and Harsfjarden in 1982) and the
recently perceived Soviet threat. At the moment, the
defence movement is much stronger than the peace movement, and it is so because the peace movement cannot
mobilize 'their' social forces to the same degree as
the defence movement can mobilize their own. The
defence movement has advantages in its material activities and its connection with the army. The peace
movement does not have the same kind of relation to

the state, even if there are some minor efforts at
peace education in schools. The peace movement has no
concrete internal activity of the same kind as the
defence movement, and will therefore all the more
easily lose members just won. It was a striking problem of the peace movement in the late 1920s, when the
'white general' mobilized thousands of members into a
peace organization with no real activity. But there
is a novel development, where professional groups as
well as other organizations with concrete 'peaceful'
activities may give the peace movement a more permanent kind of internal activity.

The peace movement in Sweden has not been struggling against its government, whether social democratic or bourgeois, as have peace movements in many other
European countries. It has supported its international disarmament efforts and initiated many proposals.
There is no real clash or open contradiction between
the peace movement and the defence movement. The
Social Democratic Party balances between the two movements, keeping the peace movement out of domestic defence
policy and channelling their efforts into the international arena. There is a manifest consensus on the
Swedish model of neutrality and a strong military
defence, which would not be changed in Sweden without
some major change in world politics.

NOTES

(1)   We are grateful to Rip Bulkeley for his val-
uable comments on this chapter.
(2)   H. Wiberg: 'Security Strategies of Small
States' in Y. Sakamoto and J. Saxe-fernandez (eds),
Paris, 1982, Strategic Doctrines and Their Alternatives.
        (3)   This section is mainly based on B. Marald,
Den svenska fredoch neutralitetsrorelsens uppkomst,
Stockholm, 1974 (The Rise of a Peace Movement and the
Origin of the Doctrine of Neutrality in Sweden. A
study in ideology and public opinion from the Crimean
War to the dissolution of the Swedish-Norwegian union); and P.A. Fogelstrom, Kampen for fred (The Struggle for Peace), Stockholm, 1983.
        (4)   In 1983 a group with representatives from
the peace organizations in the Nordic countries made
a proposal on a Nordic NWFZ. The proposal claims that
a zone could serve as an example for the rest of
Europe, and be a step towards international disarmament.
        (5)   Fogelstrom, Kampen for fred, p. 261.

Chapter Two

THE PEACE MOVEMENT IN NORWAY

Sten Sparre Nilson

Origins and History of the Norwegian Peace Movement

The history of the peace movement in Norway goes back
a full hundred years. However, we do not have in
mind, when speaking of the peace movement, a single
organization but rather a number of more or less formally organized efforts to promote international peace,
a broad current within which there have been several
cross-currents.

In the nineteenth century a couple of decades of
successive wars ended when the peace conference in
Berlin was held between the great powers in 1878; and
high diplomacy was followed in the 1880s and 1890s
by peace initiatives on a more popular level, in
private associations and national assemblies. The
International Arbitration and Peace Association was
founded in the United States in 1880, arranging conferences at Brussels in 1882 and at Berne in 1884; in
1889 the first Universal Peace Congress met. That same
year was also held the first meeting of the Inter-
Parliamentary Union.

The humanitarian idea of promoting peace appealed
to Scandinavians, and sections of the International
Association were founded in Denmark, Sweden and Norway
in the early 1880s. The founder of the Norwegian
section claimed in 1884 that no less than 21,603
friends of peace were registered in Norway, a larger
number than in the two neighbouring countries. But
the figure hardly represented more than sympathy with
the idea of peace as it appeared in signatures to
petitions favouring the peace advocates' aims. Actual
organizational work proved more difficult. The following years were to witness a good deal of disagreement
between organizers of various Norwegian societies. It
did not prove possible to bring together permanently
in one organization those who were inspired by religious fundamentalism and those who were not, nor in a

later period was it easy to reconcile advocates of peace who were of a 'bourgeois' and a socialist persuasion, respectively. In this regard the Norwegian movement seems similar to that of many other nations. (1)

What gave Norway a rather special place was the activity of the country's legislative assembly, the Storting, which led to its being entrusted with the distribution of the Nobel Prize for Peace. The idea of promoting peace by the adoption of arbitration treaties was taken up within the Inter-Parliamentary Union, and as early as 1890 the Storting passed a resolution whereby it became the first national assembly to go on record as having a majority favourable to the settlement of international disputes by the orderly procedure of arbitration. The matter was assiduously pursued by the Storting during the following years.

In a certain respect this activity was somewhat ambiguous, however. Norwegians were dissatisfied with the inferior position in which their country found itself in the Union with Sweden; and among those who promoted the idea of arbitration not a few seem to have felt that it enhanced Norwegian prestige and helped in setting their country apart from Sweden, where the idea had met with less response. Some of these advocates of arbitration proved rather bellicose when relations between the two neighbours deteriorated. In 1895 it even looked for a moment as if war might break out between them. The Storting for a time had maintained an instransigent position; but eventually it backed down. At the same time, however, a rearmament process was started, clearly with the possibility of future conflicts in view. Alfred Nobel, who left his large fortune to a fund to reward achievement in the fields of science, literature and peace, wrote his last will at the end of 1895. He took a keen interest in the possibility of international arbitration, and he seems to have been deeply impressed by the political events of the year on the Scandinavian peninsula. He entrusted the distribution of the Peace Prize not to a Swedish institution, as in the case of the other prizes, but to the Norwegian Parliament. This decision probably expressed his concern about a possible armaments race and a future war between the two countries; he may have wished to encourage the conciliatory attitude of which the Storting had given an example. When the Union was dissolved in 1905, a few years after Nobel's death, it was done peacefully, and both countries were in agreement on the maintenance of a common neutral attitude during the First World War.

The Peace Movement in Norway

In the inter-war period, although no strongly
organized peace movement could be said to exist in
Norway, without any doubt the general peace mood was
a very strong one, reinforced not only through contem-
plation of the suffering brought about in the course
of the Great War, but also by the change that had
taken place in the country's situation. Military
defence no longer seemed to have any purpose. War
with Sweden had become unthinkable. Norwegian disarmament proceeded rapidly, and even the radically altered international situation in the 1930s brought about
no great change. It was assumed, not only in civilian
but also in leading naval and military circles that
the preponderant position of the British Navy in
Northern waters represented a solid guarantee of
continued Norwegian neutrality in the event of another
general conflagration. A British invasion was considered most unlikely, and also impossible to resist
if after all it should occur, while there was a widely
shared belief that the British could easily prevent
armed interference in Norway on the part of any other
power.
This complacency was rudely shattered in 1940,
when Hitler's forces invaded Norway and in the course
of a couple of months succeeded in occupying the
country. After the war the public's mood was no longer pacifist, and a rapid build-up of armed forces was
almost unanimously supported. When the cold war between the Eastern and Western powers developed it was
decided, after some discussion, that Norway would not
remain neutral but join the NATO alliance as one of
its founding members in 1949.
All through the first post-war years pacifism
seemed a dead issue. It was kept alive only in certain academic circles, where studies were made not
least of the theory of non-violent resistance, studies
inspired in the beginning by Gandhi's teachings and
practice. Though the movement remained an isolated
one, it developed considerable vigour as an intellectual force. At the end of the 1950s one of its members, Johan Galtung, founded the Peace Research Institute in Oslo, which celebrated its silver jubilee
in June 1984. On this occasion spokesmen of PRIO
pointed out that, as its English name indicated, its
activity had always been aimed at an international
public rather than a domestic one. In the course of
the years it has issued no less than 60 books and some
700 other publications, but its impact on domestic
public opinion, at least its direct impact, has been
strictly limited.
The post-war Norwegian peace movement originated in

the anti-nuclear movement which developed around 1960.
In Norway it got under way a few years after the
British Campaign for Nuclear Disarmament had been
started in 1958. Danish participants in the Alder-
maston Easter March in Britain brought the movement to
Denmark, where a demonstration march was arranged in
October 1960. Some Norwegians who participated there
took the initiative in starting a campaign in Norway
the following month.

The present-day peace movement, on the other
hand, started in Norway about the same time as in the
Netherlands, that is to say towards the end of the
1960s, somewhat earlier than in Britain, Denmark and
other countries. Apparently this is due to the existence in Norway of a group of people trained in the
organization of citizens' initiatives, who were greatly
encouraged by the victory they scored in 1972, when
a majority of No votes kept Norway outside the European Community. The name adopted by today's peace
movement, Nei til Atomvapen (No to Nuclear Weapons) is
clearly an allusion to the campaign for a No vote in
the 1972 referendum.

The earlier peace movement, which was started at
a public meeting in November 1960, called itself
'Protest Against Nuclear Weapons - The 13'. It was
usually referred to simply as 'The 13', an allusion to
the persons who signed the first public appeal and also
constituted a kind of self-appointed leadership. They
numbered 13. The figure was probably emphasized because of its sinister associations as an 'unlucky
number'. The 13 consisted of four university profes-
sors, two trade union leaders, one bishop, one medical
doctor, one engineer, one teacher, one housewife, one
writer and one architect. The latter was the secretary of the movement, who directed its daily work from
his architect's office. To some extent they could be
called a rather conservative group. One of the prof-
essors, for example, was a leading theologian. They
wanted to protest against the inhumanity of new weapons of mass destruction, and they saw to it that the
activity of the movement had a rather restrained
character. The means employed were partly demonstration marches, but more particularly a mass petition
which obtained some 225,000 signatures. The aim was
to prevent nuclear weapons on Norwegian soil being
accepted by the governing party, that is to say the
Labour Party, which then had a majority of the seats
in the Norwegian Parliament, the Storting.

Many of the movement's militants wanted to go
further, however. Some of them were ex-Communists,
who had been thrown out of their party in the early

1950s because of 'Titoist nationalism'; these were
people of leftist views and with valuable organizational experience who had for a long time been without a concrete cause to work for. A number of people
particularly from the left wing of the Labour Party
also joined as militants, partly because they were
against Norwegian participation in the NATO alliance
and saw in the anti-nuclear movement an opportunity to
gain adherents for an anti-NATO policy.

The resulting tension within the movement was visible on several occasions. In February 1961 some
persons belonging to the Labour Party left wing declared publicly that if the government were to accept
nuclear weapons on Norwegian soil there would be an
occasion for the launching of a new party 'to articulate a clear no and work for an independent Norwegian
peace policy'. The National Congress of the Labour
Party was held shortly afterwards in April and resolved to maintain its decision, adopted in the 1950s, to
the effect that nuclear weapons were not to be placed
on Norwegian territory in peacetime. The resolution
added that it was up to Norway's constitutional bodies
to decide what measures were, at any given time,
necessary to secure the independence of the country.
While 'The 13' regarded this as a satisfactory outcome and initiated the termination of the peace campaign, there were many militants who looked with suspicion upon the Labour Party statement and regarded it
as keeping open the possibility of admitting nuclear
weapons at some later date.

'Protest Against Nuclear Weapons - The 13' was
formally dissolved in May 1961. After a while some
members of the movement's left wing launched a new
campaign, and about the same time the Left Socialist
Party was founded on an anti-nuclear and neutralist
foreign policy programme. The new 'Campaign Against
Nuclear Weapons' arranged some manifestations, particularly a couple of protest marches. Only limited support was obtained, however, and after the superpowers
had signed their Nuclear Test Ban Agreement in 1963
the campaign was brought to an end. Some of its members started a campaign in 1967 labelled 'Norway Out
of NATO'; but this attempt was stillborn. There
proved to be solid support for the country's existing
security policy. Considerable opposition developed
three years later, however, when a change in the existing foreign policy line was proposed in the form of
Norwegian entry into the EEC. This idea was rejected
not only by leftists but in much wider circles, and
the 'People's Movement Against the EC' succeeded in
obtaining a 52.5 per cent No majority at the referen-

dum of September 1972.

The Left Socialist Party was very active during the referendum campaign and more than doubled its vote share at the subsequent parliamentary election of 1973, when it received some 10 per cent of the total vote. But the success was temporary. The Left Socialist share of the vote is today once more only about 5 per cent (and the Communists get less than 1 per cent), as against some 40 per cent or more for the Labour Party. Nevertheless, the Left Socialists have been seen by the Labour leadership as an ever-present menace on their flank, whose small but highly vocal parliamentary representation is particularly active in debates on foreign and security matters.

STRUCTURE AND GOALS OF THE NORWEGIAN PEACE MOVEMENT

Memories of the anti-EEC campaign are still vivid in Norwegian political circles. 'No to Nuclear Weapons' was started at the end of the decade whose opening years saw the victorious referendum campaign of a broad popular movement uniting very different elements from left and right. And 'No to Nuclear Weapons' also consists of diverse elements. In its ranks are a number of clergymen and other religious leaders as well as some feminist leaders. The organization is a loose one with a self-appointed leadership and no strict rules or regulations. There is, however, an apparently very efficient secretariat with its own office. The directing board has as its chairman and vice-chairman, a professor of mathematics and a trade union leader. Of the other nine members, five are primary or secondary school teachers, two are civil servants, one a housewife, and one an architect. The secretariat consists of two information secretaries plus a leader. The latter is a man of long experience in citizens' initiatives, having taken part in a number of these since the 1960s when he served also as leader of the secretariat of the Left Socialist Party. However, in 1969 a breach occurred between him and the party, but soon afterwards he was engaged in the anti-EEC movement. Here he directed a great deal of the work done by its secretariat for more than a year during the long-drawn-out campaign. Endowed with eminent practical sense, he knew how to arrange demonstrations and make personal contacts for all kinds of purposes, from the printing and distribution of leaflets to the purchase of office equipment - which he is said to have shown great ability in always procuring at the most reasonable prices obtainable. No

doubt he is an asset to the new movement.
    Membership figures have not been published by
'No to Nuclear Weapons', but in reply to a telephone
inquiry its office says that it estimates the total
membership to be nearly 100,000, although the movement's local subsidiaries have not been asked to
report any detailed figures. According to the latest
news bulletin, dated February-March 1984, there are
'some 300 local branches and groups'. The bulletin
poses the question, 'What can you do?', answering:

> Carry the movement's emblem;
> Discuss with friends and acquaintances;
> Be a supportive member;
> Join a local group;
> Distribute the bulletin at your workplace, in
> schools, in dwelling areas and in post-boxes;
> Start a study circle in company with others;
> State your opinion in the local press;
> Distribute our printed material to friends and
> acquaintances;
> Raise questions in organization meetings,
> discussion meetings, resolutions;
> Write to your Members of Parliament;
> Start a local branch - the branches work on the
> basis of our slogans, and you will get further
> information from our office.

'Supporting members' or 'regular contributors' are
those who give a pledge to pay 'a modest amount, such
as kr 20, 50 or 100' at fixed intervals, 'for instance
once a month'. According to the movement's news
bulletin, February-March 1984, 'our many hundreds of
contributors help us do our work'. They decide themselves how much they want to contribute. As donors
they are recipients of the movement's information
material. The August-September 1983 bulletin announ-
ces the receipt of kr 20,000 as a contribution from
one trade union and lists four other large unions that
have made contributions. At the same time 540 different clubs and organizations were said to have signed
the movement's protest against new nuclear missiles
in Europe.
    In Norwegian local elections, voters can in-
fluence the ranking of candidates on the various party
lists. 'No to Nuclear Weapons' tried to have candidates sympathetic to their cause preferred by the
voters at the nationwide quadrennial local elections
which took place in September 1983. These attempts
do not seem to have been successful, but the movement
succeeded in having a number of local assemblies pass

anti-nuclear resolutions. According to the bulletin
it has been done by eleven of the country's 19 provincial assemblies and 93 of its 445 local councils.

Beside its bulletin, which appears at irregular
intervals of one, two or three months, the movement
has produced a number of pamphlets, stickers, cards,
posters, etc. Seminars have also been arranged; in
Oslo the central secretariat arranged one that was
held on 19 and 20 November 1983. Demonstrations have
taken place on several occasions; one was arranged as
the final manifestation of 'Anti-nuclear Action Week'
in Oslo, 17 to 24 October 1983. During the summer
holidays one Peace Meeting is planned at the coast in
Southern Norway from 14 to 21 July and another in
North Norway from 9 to 12 August 1984, according to
the bulletin.

The following are declared to be the three main
goals of the movement's activity:

1. To secure a nuclear-weapons-free zone encom-
   passing the Nordic countries (Denmark, Norway,
   Sweden, Finland).

2. To contribute to a reduction of nuclear armaments both in the Eastern and the Western
   camp.

3. 'No nuclear weapons on or from Norwegian
   territory in peace or war'.

ACTIVITIES OF THE NORWEGIAN PEACE MOVEMENT

The nuclear-weapon-free zone was the main object of
activity in 1981-2, with one result to which the movement points with particular pride: the collection of
more than 540,000 signatures on a manifesto favouring
this idea. In a total population of only four million
the figure is truly an impressive one. But no further
steps of importance have followed. In a sense it can
be said that the Nordic countries are already nuclear
weapon-free. The peace movement succeeded in demon-
strating strong support among Norwegians for the
maintenance of this state of affairs. Whether or not
there was also strong support for having it confirmed
by international agreement is more uncertain. In
1981-2 there was some discussion about a proposal for
a treaty whereby a guarantee would be given by the
nuclear powers. The proposal received considerable
publicity, since it was put forward as a surprise move
at a public meeting without previous government clear-

ance by a top Norwegian Foreign Office official who
had earlier been a Labour cabinet minister, Ambassador
Jens Evensen. The treaty idea was subsequently discussed within the Labour Party as well as in the general public. A sentence which finally appeared in
the party programme displayed a compromise solution:
'Norway will work for an atomic weapon-free zone in
the Nordic area as part of the work to reduce nuclear
weapons in a wider European context.'
    Although the party thus did accept the zone idea
in principle, no steps were taken to implement it as
a separate measure. Tied to the general efforts of
European disarmament it turned out to be shelved in
practice, at least for the time being. Observers were
surprised by the ease with which the party leadership
managed after all to side-track the issue. Despite
considerable pressure from the peace movement, aided
by strong forces within the Labour Party's left wing,
no decisive breakthrough in the party's foreign policy
line was achieved, mainly perhaps because the strong
popular endorsement of the idea of a Nordic nuclear-
free zone did not imply a clear recommendation of any
particular programme of action. It could hardly be
said to give a directive to the Labour government.
Apparently what was in many people's mind when they
signed the appeal was a simple renewal of their commitment to the maintenance of the existing state of
affairs.

PUBLIC SUPPORT AND THE POSITION OF THE POLITICAL
PARTIES

In 1982-3 the situation changed. The Labour Party
lost the election of 1981 and gave way to a Conservative government. Labour was now freed from the burdens
and responsibility of office. As time went on there
seemed to be less and less prospect of the superpower
negotiations in Geneva leading to any result in the
direction of arms control, and in the event that no
agreement was reached, hundreds of new nuclear weapons
would be deployed on the Western side in response to
the continuous Soviet build-up. The idea of searching
for some other solution seemed to have considerable
appeal, as indicated by data from Norwegian opinion
polls on NATO nuclear weapons:

    a. (Norges Markedsdata). Late November 1979:

    It is said that new Soviet weapons systems have
    changed the military balance in Europe in favour

of the Soviet Union. There are consequently
plans in the NATO countries for a modernization
of nuclear weapons, one purpose being to obtain
a stronger position if disarmament talks are initiated. Do you think Norway should support the
plans for a modernization of NATO's nuclear weapons, provided they are not installed in Norway, -
or do you think Norway should go against these
plans?

Response:	%
Should support	37
Should go against	44
Don't know	19
	100

b. (Norsk Opinionsinstitutt). August 1981:

In 1979 Norway together with the other NATO
countries made a decision that 572 new nuclear
missiles should be deployed in Western Europe.
Simultaneously it was recommended that negotiations be started with a view to nuclear disarmament in Europe. Do you think that these weapons
should be deployed as planned, or do you think
it would be best not to do so?

Response:	%
Should be done	21
Best not to	71
Don't know	8
	100

c. (Norsk Opinionsinstitutt). June 1982:

A majority in the Storting recently decided to
appropriate money for preparatory work on installations to receive the new nuclear weapons
in Western Europe. The decision on deployment
of these weapons was made by NATO in 1979. Do
you think it was right or wrong for our parliamentary majority to endorse appropriation of the
amount in question?

The Peace Movement in Norway

Response: %

        Right   33
        Wrong   62
        Both/and   2
        Don't know   5
                        ___
                        102
                        ___

The peace movement reproduces the above data in its
attempt to influence Norwegian politicians. It also
points to its efforts to influence attitudes in the
East, by emphasizing the fact that such efforts have
been made from the beginning. The following are quoted as examples:

a. Telegram to Mr Breshnev, 4 November 1979:

The Norwegian Campaign against New Nuclear Weapons, whose goal it is to make Norwegian authorities avoid a NATO decision in favour of new
intermediate-range nuclear missiles in Europe,
appeals as strongly as possible to you as President of the Soviet Union to renounce further
production and deployment of SS-20-missiles in the
Western part of the Soviet Union. The time has
now arrived for the peoples to work for a gradual
disarmament and abolition of the nuclear forces
maintained in Europe by the NATO and Warsaw
treaty organizations.

b. Telegram to Mr Breshnev, 28 November 1979:

The campaign 'No to New Nuclear Weapons', which
is supported by persons belonging to the majority
of political parties and a number of organizations in Norway, will express its concern regarding the continued armaments race between the
NATO and Warsaw pacts. In recent years the
Soviet Union has deployed a considerable number
of SS-20 missiles in the Western Soviet regions.
These weapons represent an Improvement and an
Increase in the nuclear armaments of the Soviet
Union. The campaign 'No to New Nuclear Weapons',
which has lodged a telegraphic protest today to
the governments of the NATO countries against the
proposed production and deployment of Cruise and
Pershing II missiles in Western Europe, appeals
as strongly as possible to you as President of
the Soviet Union to halt the production and

deployment of SS-20. It is our conviction that a
historic opportunity now exists to stop the armaments race. This possibility can only be utilized if political leaders both in the Warsaw pact
and in NATO recognize, not only in words but also
in deeds, their responsibility to disarm, renouncing further nuclear armament.

None of these telegrams seem to have elicited
any response from their Eastern or Western addressees.
But the Norwegian peace movement was not discouraged.
It continued its public protests and marches in Norway, and also took part in marches abroad, in Eastern
as well as Western Europe, and in the United States.
Apparently, however, a good deal of its attention
has been directed towards influencing the Labour Party
leadership. In this respect a certain success was
registered in 1983. When NATO decided to deploy new
nuclear missiles in Europe at the end of the year, the
party voiced disagreement. It introduced the following parliamentary motion:

> Whereas it appears that no agreement will be
> reached in Geneva on intermediate-range nuclear
> forces, the Storting asks the government to give
> expression to the following views on behalf of
> Norway;
>
> Negotiations should be prolonged without any
> deployment taking place on the Western side;
>
> Immediate consideration should be given to the
> elaboration of an international agreement with
> the aim of securing essential reductions in Sov-
> iet intermediate-range nuclear forces;
>
> The negotiations should have a wider basis within
> the Strategic Arms Reduction Talks, based on a
> freeze as a starting-point for reductions.

The motion was narrowly defeated on 21 November 1983.
78 Members of Parliament voted against, 77 in favour.
The 66 Labour MP's voted together with the four Left
Socialists; they were also joined by seven members belonging to the Liberal, Christian Democratic and
Agrarian parties. The Liberal Party has only two MP's
and finds itself in opposition to the government. The
Christian Democratic and Agrarian parties, on the
other hand, had supported the Conservative minority
government when it took office in 1981 and had joined
it in the summer of 1983, when it was transformed into
a majority coalition government.

The Peace Movement in Norway

Those Christian Democratic and Agrarian MP's who
had publicly opposed the deployment of new missiles
before their parties joined the government were allowed to vote accordingly on 21 November. There was
still just a sufficient majority against the Labour
motion. Opposition speakers intimated that this majority may have included some members who were in reality of the opposite opinion but followed the party
line, whereupon government spokesmen retorted that
there were certainly many Labour members who found
themselves in a similar situation.

After 21 November 1983 it looked as if the general consensus on Norwegian foreign and defence policy
which had existed since 1949 was a thing of the past.
The peace movement clearly directed its strategy
towards further action at the parliamentary level.
Its bulletin had on its timetable for 1984, besides
the two summer meetings mentioned above, a 'No to
Nuclear Weapons Information Week 2-8 April', and in
addition attention was called to three prospective
debates in the Storting: one on security and disarmament,
one on the Norwegian long-term defence plan, and one
on NATO's infrastructure programme. These debates
were to take place in April, May and June.

But there turned out to be no repetition of what
had happened in November. Now the Labour Party refused to take a stand similar to that of the Left Socialists. Instead, an agreement was reached with the parties in the non-socialist government on a common stand
in matters of foreign and defence policy. Apparently
the Labour leadership is hoping for a comeback at the
parliamentary election which will take place in the
autumn of 1985. If subsequently a Labour government
takes over, it does not relish the prospect of being
in a position more or less like the one in which the
Danish government presently finds itself within NATO.

This latest turn of events evidently represented
a disappointment for 'No to Nuclear Weapons' and an
encouragement for the other side. The former secretary of the Labour Party, Haakon Lie, for three decades
a tireless advocate of unaltered NATO partnership,
declared himself 'enormously relieved' (2).

But of course 'No to Nuclear Weapons' has not
given up. As a next move it may try to focus public
opinion on what its leaders see as a vulnerable point:
the question whether Norway can be termed 'nuclear
weapon-free' in every sense of the word.

Hitherto the peace movement has received only
moderate attention from the mass media. Since there
are no nuclear weapons in Norway, it has been difficult to arrange dramatic incidents that are apt to

arouse professional journalistic interest and secure
extensive coverage in the media. But perhaps the
movement is contemplating new tactics in this regard.
A confrontation at a military airfield in south-east-
ern Norway on 11 June 1984 led to a number of arrests
and was widely reported. 'No to Nuclear Weapons' however, was not invited to this particular action, which
was directed by a number of small groups, mostly
youthful ones.

On the part of the peace movement, it is repeatedly contended that not only is the Norwegian government in a position to allow the use of nuclear weapons on or from Norwegian territory in wartime or when
war threatens; it may also be possible to direct
nuclear weapons from Norwegian territory even in
peacetime. With such eventualities in view it has
been suggested on the part of the peace movement that
the alliance agreement on Co-located Operating Bases
in Norway should be renegotiated. If implemented,
this and other demands for changes in Norwegian defence arrangements would transform the country's position within NATO, perhaps to a degree which might not
be compatible with her continued membership in the
alliance. Such may well be the ultimate goal shared
by some of the movement's members, though certainly
not by all of them.

'No to Nuclear Weapons' asks for a national referendum in case the Storting has not by the end of
1986 agreed to a complete ban on the use of such
weapons, in any circumstances, 'on or from Norwegian
territory'.

One difference between the peace movement of the
1960s and the present one should be mentioned. There
is now some discussion about strengthening Western
conventional armaments in order to reduce the need for
reliance on nuclear forces. This would clearly entail
an increase in the cost of defence. Nevertheless the
idea has received a certain amount of support, among
others from the chairman of the Christian Democratic
Party. It is also supported by those officers and
arms control specialists who regard strategies for
nuclear warfare as fundamentally unsound from a military point of view. Thus it can be said that thinking in certain military circles is reminiscent of some
of the ideas entertained within today's peace movement. But there are few signs of a convergence of
these lines of thought in Norway.

Besides 'No to Nuclear Weapons' there are some
other organizations which can be said to belong to the
peace movement in Norway, but at present they are insignificant by comparison. Some are of long standing,

such as the Norwegian section of the International
Women's League for Peace and Freedom, dating back almost to the First World War, and the group called
Folkereisning mot Krig ('People's Rally Against War'),
which has been intermittently active for a number of
years and is currently conducting an 'Information
Campaign on Norway in the Nuclear Age'. A special
organization of school-teachers, 'Teachers for Peace',
was formed in June 1982, and there are other special
groups like 'Psychologists for Peace' and 'Physicians
Against Nuclear War' as well as a separate feminist
peace organization. The latter was represented in
peace marches arranged in various countries during the
three years 1981-83, but decided to cease this form of
activity and participated instead, in 1984, at a Nordic Women's Peace Camp featuring lectures and discus-
sions, held in June/July outside Stockholm.

    Smaller groups could be added to the list. Fur-
thermore, the rather active ecologist movement, Frem-
tiden i Vare Hender ('The Future in Our Hands') deserves to be mentioned. As part of a broad programme
for the preservation of the environment it also opposes nuclear armaments. It organized support for the
Easter march against nuclear weapons from Duisburg to
Dortmund, which was joined by Norwegians leaving Oslo
by bus on 16 and 17 April 1984 under ecologist auspices.

    However, 'No to Nuclear Weapons' seems to have
more extensive international contacts. According to
Oslo newspapers it sent a representative to the United
States on 26 March 1984 for a week's conference with
Americans, Britons and Icelanders on rearmament in
Northern waters, particularly with a view to opposing
plans for making New York the base of operations of
missile-carrying naval forces on patrol in the North
Atlantic, including the Norwegian Sea. It was reported that plans for making the city of Boston the base
had been given up earlier because of local resistance.

    In Norway similar local campaigns have not taken
place, except in connection with the ongoing build-up
of stores for American auxiliary troops in Central
Norway. Local authorities and labour unions in the
locality in question took a negative attitude, whereby the progress of the operations became slower and
more cumbersome than had been originally foreseen.
Some peace organizations were involved, though only
marginally.

    Thus, there are in existence in Norway a number
of organized groups besides 'No to Nuclear Weapons',
partly competing and collaborating with it; but in the
first half of the 1980s, they all have been dwarfed in

importance by the latter organization, just as other
international issues are overshadowed by that of nuclear deterrence.

NOTES

(1) A good survey of the first 50 years of its
history is given in a book by Oscar J. Falnes, 'Norway and the Nobel Peace Prize', Columbia University
Press, New York. 1938.
(2) Interview in the newspaper, Aftenposten,
23 June 1984.

Chapter Three

THE PEACE MOVEMENT IN THE NETHERLANDS

N. H. Serry

ORIGINS AND HISTORY OF THE DUTCH PEACE MOVEMENT

The longing for peace has always occupied the hearts
and minds of people and there is therefore a long history of peace movements. This chapter, however, will
be about the 'new peace movement'; that is the movement as they describe themselves in The Netherlands
today.
     The origin of the new peace movement (the word
new will be omitted in the following) goes back to
the foundation of the Inter-church Peace Council (IKV)
in 1966. IKV is an inter-church organization which
was founded by all major churches in The Netherlands
including the Roman Catholic Church. The task given
to the IKV by the churches was:

        To study issues of war and peace and to provide:
        - information within the churches to stimulate
           awareness of these issues;
        - submit suggestions for appropriate action;
        - conduct dialogues with the government and
           other institutions in society; and
        - assist the church leaderships in determining
           their policy positions on these issues.

The guidelines call for IKV to conduct these activities on the basis of the Christian gospel and to assume
by itself responsibility for its activities. The
church leaderships are therefore not bound by the positions the IKV take.
     Eighteen years have passed since the IKV was
founded on these principles and the IKV are now the
main force in the 'peace movement' in The Netherlands
which is advocating unilateral steps for reduction of
nuclear armaments and eventual nuclear disarmament.
     The often asked question whether the IKV is still

a Church organization is answered by themselves as
follows:

> The IKV is a Council which was founded by the
> Churches. The members of the Council belong to
> and are appointed by the Churches. The Churches
> provide inspiration and the Council members are
> guided by the Christian Gospel and the feelings
> and wishes in their own Church communities. But
> it does not follow from this that the IKV as an
> institution is a Christian institution and that
> the organization for the IKV campaign is a
> Christian organization. This is not possible
> because there is no Christian consensus for the
> IKV as an institution and the organization of its
> campaign. The members of the IKV Council are
> united in their rejection of the concept of nuc-
> lear deterrence and their belief in Christian
> values is a motivation for this attitude. Later
> on the campaign, based on a political manifesto,
> was developed and added. (1)

In some of their brochures the IKV refer to themselves
as a church related peace movement.

ORGANIZATIONAL STRUCTURE OF THE DUTCH PEACE MOVEMENT

The IKV Council consists of 23 members which are
appointed by the nine founder churches. It has a
secretariat with 14 members and an unspecified number
of voluntary co-workers.
   There are some 450 'discussion groups' in the
country consisting of approximately 25 members per
group who are dedicated to IKV ideology. Their task
is to spread IKV ideology through their daily contacts
in the churches and other organizations to which they
belong.
   Liaison between the discussion groups and the IKV
Council takes place through the 'Campaign Council'
which was established in 1982. All members of the IKV
Council and a number of regional representatives of
the discussion groups are members of the Campaign
Council. The IKV co-operates with eight other 'Peace
Groups' in LOVO, which is an umbrella organization
which was set up for this purpose. The main other
peace groups are:

Pax Christi Netherlands
Church and Peace
Stop the Neutron Bomb - Stop the arms race

The Peace Movement in The Netherlands

This organization, established in 1977, gathered one million signatures against the neutron weapon in 1978.

Women for Peace
This organization also has international contacts.

Women against nuclear weapons
In this organization several women's organizations of different backgrounds are co-operating together.

Committee cruise missiles No
The IKV plays an important part in this committee which co-ordinates the peace movements' strategy to oppose deployment of cruise missiles.

The methods used by the IKV and other 'peace movements' to influence public opinion include canvassing door to door, making local political issues out of nuclear armament matters such as storage of nuclear weapons, inviting doctors, trade unions, municipalities, etc. to take a stand, writing to politicians and organizing mass demonstrations. The IKV network of 450 committed local groups plays an important part in these activities.

THE PEACE MOVEMENT AND THE SOCIAL ENVIRONMENT IN THE NETHERLANDS

Before addressing the ideology, goals and achievements of the peace movement it is necessary to make a few observations on the social environment in which the peace movement is operating. In the prosperous 1960s The Netherlands developed a social welfare system which ranks as one of the most generous systems in the world. Apart from ever increasing material benefits, much attention was also devoted by progressive intellectuals and pseudo-intellectuals to improving the quality of life. Political and social reforms were - and still are - advocated to replace the existing structures which are said to be based on wrong conceptions of human attitudes towards the essential issues for individuals and societies.

Social injustice is held to be the cause of social evils that cause innocent people to suffer. This appeals to many, especially - but not only - to the young and has provoked an anti-establishment attitude in a not insignificant part of society. For many individuals, the sense of personal responsibility and accountibility has been eroded. This section of the public can rather easily be drawn into protest activities of numerous kinds.

A substantial part of the public is only vaguely

aware of the values of the existing democratic system
and the nature of the threats to this system. They
often lack a sense of what is to be defended. Their
natural inclination is to prevent any disturbance of
the perceptions they have acquired in the 1960s and
1970s. Such individuals, and there are a good many of
them, would rather be 'red than dead' in the optimis-
tic expectation that their lifestyle would not be
materially effected. This is not altogether surprising since the establishment has not done much to ed-
ucate the public about the way East European societies
are functioning.

It would probably be wrong to accuse the peace
movement of having actively promoted the 'rather red
than dead' syndrome, but the peace movements's goals
are certainly facilitated by these aspects of the
social environment.

GOALS AND IDEOLOGY OF THE DUTCH PEACE MOVEMENT

The peace movement's (IKV) ideology rests on its res-
olute rejection of nuclear deterrence as a viable
manner to preserve peace. This was stated as follows
in the IKV manifesto in 1977:

> Nuclear deterrence is nothing but mutual hostage
> keeping and the assumption that it will be pos-
> sible to use restraint in dealing with the prob-
> lems of possessing nuclear weapons is based on
> tremendous arrogance and human self overestima-
> tion. In the long run it is most unlikely that
> nuclear deterrence will be successful whereas the
> policies of the nuclear powers and the doctrine
> of nuclear deterrence offer no hope that there
> will ever be an alternative for mutual security.
> For these reasons - but most of all - because the
> way human beings are dealing with each other un-
> der the doctrine of nuclear deterrence has sunk
> to such low moral standards that we should be
> deeply ashamed of it, the IKV demand of all people
> in The Netherlands and the Dutch Government to
> help rid the world of nuclear weapons starting in
> The Netherlands. (2)

The IKV propagates the idea that all people are
of good will and that it is wrong and counter-productive to be overly distrustful of the Soviet Union. The
Soviet Union's dominance of Eastern Europe is explained
as necessary for its security as long as the Western
European governments adhere to NATO doctrine and

accept American leadership. IKV spokesmen frequently
contend that if the whole of Europe were free of nuclear arms, there would be no need for the Soviets to
continue exercising their iron grip on the Eastern
European countries. NATO and the Warsaw Pact are seen
as the consequences of mutual distrust which should be
overcome by a policy of detente. The peace movement
argues that if the Soviets do not feel themselves
threatened anymore by the 'American inspired' NATO
build-up, they will gradually relax their tight control on Eastern Europe which will give the forces for
change in Eastern Europe more room to achieve democratic societies. In the longer run the societies of
Western and Eastern Europe could become complementary
and a 'new Europe' would emerge between the two superpowers. Suggestions that this 'new Europe' would be
under the tight control of the Soviet Union are repud-
iated as thinking only in terms of the balance of power which merely serves American interests. At the
same time IKV spokesmen maintain that the IKV are not
anti-American but that they are against US nuclear
policy and its dominance over NATO as they are also
against Soviet, British, French and for that matter
Dutch nuclear policy.
    Critics who point to the relentless Soviet milit-
ary build-up during the period of detente are told
that this is understandable since the Soviet Union
has twice had to cope in this age with aggression from
the West and that they were in the process of building
up their armaments to a level of approximate parity
with the West.
    But there is no reason, according to the IKV
leadership, to assume that disarmament steps in the
West would have no effects in the Eastern bloc countries. The main argument given to substantiate this
opinion is the existence of an official peace movement in the Soviet Union and the Eastern European
countries and that the public in these countries are
taught that socialism and communism are striving for
peace. Opponents of IKV's ideas often ask how they
can be so naive as to expect the Soviet Union not to
take advantage of the situation if the West unilater-
aly weakens itself. A reply which is often given is
that this expectation springs from IKV's Christian
beliefs.

THE ACTIVITIES OF THE DUTCH PEACE MOVEMENT

The IKV regards itself as a political movement with a
political manifesto aimed at detente and disarmament.(3)

The political orientation of the IKV is manifestly
left wing. They advised the public in a widely adver-
tised pamphlet to vote for left wing political parties
in the elections of September, 1982. This proved
counter-productive since the outcome of the elections
enabled the formation of a centre-right government to
replace a centre-left government. Moreover their voting advice created some irritation and criticism from
the churches.

According to the IKV leadership there had been no
deliberate intention to advise the public to vote for
left wing political parties but 'due to errors which
were made in the execution of an information pamphlet
on the stands of the political parties on nuclear
armaments the pamphlet turned out as advice to vote for
the left'! (4) According to polls taken at the peace
demonstration in The Hague on 29 October 1983, which
drew 550,000 people, 91.8 per cent of the participants
were supporters of the social democratic party (PVDA)
and the small left wing parties and only 1.3 per cent
were supporters of the Christian Democratic Party
(CDA). (5) It is therefore evident that in spite of
the original and still existing relationship between
the IKV and the churches that their main popular support comes from the left wing orientated part of the
public.

Although, as we have seen, the IKV does not consider itself as a Christian organization which is
confirmed by the fact that their visible support comes
overwhelmingly from the left, they do value their relationship with the churches. Firstly, because it
gives them a certain moral standing and secondly -
because of this standing - a certain extent of credibility among Christians who are not necessarily left
in their thinking.

Almost all churches have from time to time expressed their concern about nuclear arms but they had
abstained from expressing concrete standpoints regarding the governments' policies. Early in 1980, the IKV
leadership embarked on a long and patient dialogue with
the Synods of the churches with the intention of persuading the churches to express a concrete standpoint
on the IKV's political campaign for a nuclear-arms-
free Holland. The IKV leadership submitted a number
of questions and suggestions to the Synods. The most
important question was whether the Synods were prepared
to join IKV on the path they had taken with their political campaign.

In March 1984 the Synods of the two main Protestant churches agreed: After an interval of one week they
issued public proclamations addressed to the government

and Parliament in which they declared themselves to be
against deployment of cruise missiles in The Netherlands as foreseen in the NATO double-track decision of
1979.

Pax Christi Netherlands, which co-operates closely with IKV, has also tried to persuade the Roman
Catholic Church since 1980 to take a concrete stand on
nuclear arms. In June 1983 the Dutch bishops issued a
letter 'Peace and Justice' on nuclear arms. The Peace
Movement considered this letter too vague. In the
meantime the Council of Churches, in which the Roman
Catholic Church is also represented, issued a proclamation similar to the Synods' proclamations. The leadership of the Roman Catholic Church, however, has not
issued such a proclamation.

The Synods' and Council of Churches' decisions to
issue the proclamations were not unanimous. Spokesmen
for the majority members who made a decision to issue
the proclamations have stated that whilst they expect
that great moral value will be attached to the Synods'
proclamations, it does not interfere with the personal
freedom of politicians and public to make their own
choices and decisions.

The Synods of the two largest Protestant churches
were persuaded by the IKV to throw their weight in the
political arena at a very crucial moment, namely a few
weeks before the date the government had announced that
it would take a decision on the deployment of 48 cruise
missiles. More important than the effects of this
action are the long-term repercussions this will have
on society. 'The Church in politics' in 1984 is a
phenomenon on which a fundamental appraisal and reaction must and will follow.

From IKV literature it appears that in spite of
satisfaction about the results achieved so far and
these being widely known by the public, there is also
apprehension about the future if its political campaign; 'no nuclear arms in the Netherlands' does not lead
to concrete results. (6) For this eventuality the IKV
leadership have devised the following strategy:

- Continuation of the struggle by cautious involvement in civil disobedience actions and
  actions to prevent or at least to obstruct deployment of cruise missiles.
- Adding new themes to the campaign to identify
  it with the fight against social injustice.
- Internationalizing the Peace Movement on the
  basis of a concrete political campaign in
  which the promotion of a policy of detente between East and West will be the basic theme.

The IKV leadership is well aware that unlawful actions of civil disobedience may turn public opinion against them. They have a problem in this respect with the radicals in the peace movement who neither like nor believe in the need for cautiousness. The attempts of the IKV leadership to obtain back-up support from the churches for a massive popular crowd gathering of indefinite duration at the deployment site in Woensdrecht has not yet met with success. The reaction of the church leaderships to this attempt to involve the churches further in the IKV's political campaign has been ambiguous, however, and does not preclude that at some stage the churches will also be prepared to join IKV on this path of their campaign. (7)

The identification of the political IKV campaign with the fight against social injustice does not appear as yet to have been put into effect through a new revised political campaign. Interesting as an effort to this end however, is the Vancouver appeal for justice, freedom and peace which was presented, at the initiative of the IKV, to the delegates of the World Council of Churches at a meeting in Vancouver in August, 1983. A key sentence in this appeal states:

> The World Council of Churches can play a unique role in stimulating the development of a network coupling Churches and movements for peace and justice with each other in a mutual fight for safeguarding and improving the quality of life.

As a concrete starting point for the fight against social injustice IKV took the initiative for a visit of a delegation of the European and American peace movements to Nicaragua in May, 1983. As a result of this visit it was stated that the peace movement will oppose (American) interventionism and will render assistance for the country's social restructuring. (8) From the peace movement's point of view 'Sandinism' obviously deserves the benefit of the doubt. With regard to interventionism the situation in Afghanistan does not appear to worry the IKV very much. Also with regard to Poland, the IKV does not appear to have concrete plans to oppose interventionism.

INTERNATIONAL ACTIVITIES OF THE DUTCH PEACE MOVEMENT

Early in 1981 the IKV decided to make their expertise available in a more structured manner to other peace movements in Europe and the USA. Wim Bartels, as

international secretary, was appointed for this purpose. The policy consideration behind this decision
was that only an internationally operating peace movement with coherent and clearly defined political aims
can be an effective counterforce against the European
and US Governments who have NATO as the co-ordinating
organization for their defence and armament policies.(9)
    The already existing ties with Aktion Suhnezeich-
en/Friedensdiensten (ASF) in West Germany were intensified. A collaborator of ASF entered into temporary
service with IKV and acted as an intermediary between
the two organizations. With the support of the IKV,
the ASF played an important part in the organization
and the co-ordination of various peace groups which
participated in the mass demonstration in Bonn on
10 October 1981. In its contacts with peace groups
in Germany, Britain and other countries, the IKV
stressed the necessity for formulating concrete political aims and well-defined campaigns to achieve
these aims.
    In a meeting in Copenhagen in September 1981 it
was decided to set up the 'International Peace Communication and Co-ordination Centre' (IPCC). Wim
Bartels (of IKV) was appointed international secretary. Peace groups with similar aims are eligible to
join IPCC but peace groups with ties with political
parties do not qualify for membership. Communist dominated peace groups may therefore not join IPCC but
this does not preclude co-operation with them. A
number of non-communist peace groups in France founded
an organization early in 1982 under the name 'Comite
pour le desarment Nucleair en Europe' (CODENE). The
international secretary of IKV was present at the
inaugural meeting. CODENE is a member of the international umbrella organization, IPCC.
    In June 1981 Wim Bartels attended the first nat-
ional Freeze Conference in Washington and since then
the IKV has maintained close ties with the Freeze
movement. Delegations of the European peace movements
who are members of IPCC made visits to the Freeze
Organization in the USA in March, 1982 and April,
1983.
    There are conceptional differences between the
Freeze movement and the European peace movements. The
European peace movements are of the opinion that a
freeze can and should be unilaterally declared but most
of the supporters of a freeze in the United States are
of the opinion that it is not possible to build a
mass movement on the basis of a unilateral approach. (10)
A second difficulty for the European peace movements
is the condition laid down by many freeze supporters

in the USA that a freeze should be verifiable. A
third important difference is that the Freeze movement
does not unconditionally reject the doctrine of deterrence.
     The attraction of the Freeze movement for the
European peace movements, is its simplicity; i.e.
(as a first step) the containment of the existing nuclear armament levels on the basis of 'enough is
enough' added to the fact that the East European countries
have already declared themselves (without binding
themselves to verification) to be in favour of a
freeze. In view of the above-mentioned concep-
tional differences the efforts of European peace movements and the Freeze movement to devise an international political campaign on a common programme have
not yet led to concrete results. It is also not yet
clear whether and how the peace movements will be able
to internationalize their action programme on the
basis of a common political campaign for the promotion
of a policy of detente between East and West - despite
the unfavourable experiences with detente in the
recent past.
     The IKV has also for many years had contacts with
independent peace movements in Eastern Europe. One of
the oldest contacts is with the Theologische Studien-
abteilung von dem Bund der Evangelischen Kirche in
East Germany. In the last two years, however, prominent IKV officials have repeatedly been refused entry
into East Germany.
     Late in 1982 contacts were made with the 'Dialog-
ue Group' in Hungary, an independently operating
peace group which tries to operate within the
general framework of the official Hungarian peace
movement. The IKV also maintain contacts with the
official peace movements and their umbrella organizations. The international secretary, Wim Bartels,
attended the peace conference in Moscow in May 1982
but departed when it became clear that he would not be
allowed to address the delegates in a meeting at which
journalists were also present.
     In February 1984 more than 60 peace organizations
from Western and Eastern countries participated at a
meeting in Athens. The purpose of the meeting was to
explore practical ways of co-operation between the
peace organizations in the West and the official peace
organizations in Eastern Europe. No agreement was
reached and no joint final communique was issued. Some
of the Western peace organizations, including the IKV,
criticized the refusal of the Eastern European peace
organizations to express concern on the SS-20 build-
up. The chairman of the Soviet peace organization,

Joeri Sjoekov, reproved these organizations for refusing the hand of friendship extended by the Eastern
European peace organizations. (11)

THE COUNTER MOVEMENTS

The late 1970s and early 1980s have seen the emergence
of peace groups which oppose unilateral disarmament
steps and advocate negotiations for multilateral disarmament. With the exception of the 'Interchurch
Committee for multilateral disarmament' (ICTO), these
groups are virtually unknown to the public and all
suffer from insufficient organizational strength and
lack of financial means.
    A number of church members who did not want to
endorse the Inter-church Peace Council's (IKV) manifesto in 1977 formed their own local discussion
groups. In 1980 a central committee was established
to co-ordinate the actions of the local committees
(at present 70 with approximately 10,000 members) and
to formulate central policies.
    ICTO's philosophy is based on the Bible. However,
its spokesmen maintain that the Bible is not a book
for pacifists and that those in power have the right
and the duty to protect the Christian heritage, if
necessary with the use of force. ICTO is struggling
with the churches which give financial support (to the
IKV) to be treated on the same basis as the IKV with
the argument that they represent the views of a large
part of the church communities. The major view of the
the church hierarchy however, is that to recognize and
support ICTO would be to provoke polarization in the
church communities.
    ICTO has been successful to a limited extent in
becoming publicly known and is now more frequently
mentioned in the media as the leading church related
organization which disagrees with the views and policies of IKV and the majority of the churches' hierarchy.

SUMMARY

1. The Peace Movement in The Netherlands which is
advocating unilateral disarmament steps is dominated
by the IKV. The high degree of organization within
the IKV and the strategic qualities of IKV leadership
have enabled the Dutch 'peace movement' to become an
influential political pressure group.
2. The IKV has been successful after many years of

patient dialogue in persuading the Churches to come
out in open support for their political campaign.
Depending on the source, it appears from public opinion polls that 40 to 60 per cent of the public are
against the deployment of cruise missiles.
3. In order to maintain appeal for its followers the
peace movement needs definite political successes and
clearly defined political action programmes. The
strategy of the IKV leadership is based upon maximum
moral and political pressure to prevent deployment of
cruise missiles in The Netherlands and efforts to
internationalize the peace movement on the IKV concept, which may be broadened by putting more emphasis
on the fight against social injustice and improvement
of the quality of life.
4. Reactions in The Netherlands - but also in other
countries - to the churches having clearly identified
themselves with a political campaign will be of great
importance. The distinction between the responsibility of the government and politicians and the church
hierarchies on political matters will have to become
more clear to the public than it probably is at present. This is a difficult task but necessary to prevent confusion and erosion of the democratic political
system of the West.

CONCLUSION

In 1981 the term 'Hollanditis' came into fashion when
referring to the activities of the Dutch peace movement. Although different connotations were also
attached to it, it was generally used to refer to a
campaign for neutralism. Today the peace movement
refers to itself as the 'new peace movement' and it is
therefore proper to redefine the meaning of the term
'Hollanditis'.
    On criticism or questions as to how Western
Europe - if it resorted to unilateral disarmament -
can prevent itself from gradually falling under the
Soviet sphere of influence, the 'new peace movement'
has no convincing answers. The new peace movement
puts its trust in the emergence - as a result of unilateral disarmament steps - of a 'new Europe' in which
the present controversies between East and West Europe
will no longer exist. In the absence of concrete
arguments which could give credence to this expectation, the IKV leadership puts its belief in Christian
values as justification for this expectation.
    This attitude is the 'new Hollanditis', namely
'putting the moral values of the Christian heritage

in the service of political campaigns which open the road to the system of East European State Socialism.

This I would term a 'disease' - the beginning of decay in the Western democratic system based on the Christian heritage. It is infectious and is spreading. To stop it, more is required than to determine its existence and to debate it.

NOTES

(1)   Wat is en hoe werkt het IKV? (IKV brochure.)
(2)   Vredeskrant, 1977, p. 3 (IKV Peace journal.)
(3)   Zes jaar IKV campagne, (IKV Peace Book no. 2) p. 15.
(4)   Zes jaar IKV campagne (IKV Peace Book no. 2) p. 38.
(5)   Atlantisch perspectief, 1983, no. 5-6 p. 2.
(6)   Kernblad, December, 1983, p. 10, Ch. C.
(7)   Verklaring Ds. Roos NRC, 14 February 1984.
(8)   Zes jaar IKV campagne (IKV Peace Book, no. 2) p. 67.
(9)   Zes jaar IKV campagne (IKV Peace Book, no. 2) p. 52.
(10) Zes Jaar IKV campagne (IKV Peace Book, no. 2) p. 63.
(11) Eindhovens Dagblad, 10 February 1984.

APPENDIX

Decision of the Dutch Government Announced on 1 June and Approved in the Second Chamber on 13 June 1984 on Deployment of 48 Cruise Missiles

1.   Deployment of 48 cruise missiles in The Netherlands in 1986, as foreseen in the NATO double-track decision of December 1979, is postponed till the end date under the total NATO deployment scheme, that is, December, 1988.

2a. If no agreement has been reached on reductions of intermediate missile deployment between the USA and the USSR on 1 November 1985 and if the Soviet Union has then deployed more SS-20 missiles than in place on 1 June 1984, The Netherlands will deploy all 48 missiles before December 1988. The treaty with the USA for the deployment of the missiles will then be presented in November, 1985 to the Second Chamber.

b.   If before 1 November 1985 agreement has been reached between the USA and the USSR on mutual

reductions in deployment of intermediate missiles, The Netherlands will deploy its reduced share
of the missiles to be deployed by the NATO
countries.

c. If, however, the USSR has not deployed more SS-20
    missiles on 1 November 1985 than in place on
    1 June 1984, The Netherlands will not deploy any
    cruise missiles.

3. Since the Second Chamber accepted the Governments
    proposal on 13th June 1984, there will be no vot-
    ing in November, 1985 on deployment of the 48
    cruise missiles if the Soviet Union has by then in-
    creased the number of ss-20's deployed and no
    significant changes have then occurred in the
    international situation.

4. It is certain, however, that the opposition will
    try to reopen the debate in the Second Chamber
    in November 1985 on the argument that new facts
    warrant a reappraisal of the decision taken on
    13 June 1984.

Chapter Four

THE DEVELOPMENT OF THE PEACE MOVEMENT IN BRITAIN

Peter Byrd

ORIGINS AND HISTORY OF THE BRITISH PEACE MOVEMENT

The peace movement has become a major force in Britain
since about 1980 in terms of size of membership, impact on the national political culture, and ability
both to stage major demonstrations and also to sustain
long-term direct action. On the other hand, this
chapter will argue that it has succeeded only partially in capturing public opinion, while it has manifestly
failed to force changes in government policy. The
peace movement nevertheless presents an extraordinary
phenomenon. In many ways of course it is similar to
continental peace movements. Two distinguishing characteristics of the British movement should be noted,
however. The first is that the existence of British
strategic nuclear weapons under national control has
led to the movement to emphasize unilateral national
renunciation of nuclear weapons. The peace movement
in Britain in its first phase in the late 1950s and
early 1960s was, and, though to a lesser extent, remains national in orientation. The second is that
the anti-Americanism represented by the peace movement
strikes at very deeply-rooted aspects of the political
system because of the close integration of British
and American security policy since 1940. The peace
movement challenges the consensual nature of British
defence head on and without the benefit of an anti-
American or non-American tradition in defence on which
to draw.
        In Britain the peace movement has been based on
the Campaign for Nuclear Disarmament. CND embraces
pacifist opinion but extends beyond pacifist opinion
which is not strong in Britain and is not discussed in
this chapter. CND campaigns for nuclear disarmament,
beginning with the unconditional and unilateral renunciation of British nuclear weapons and of American

63

nuclear bases in Britain. (1)

CND enjoyed its first phase of support in the late 1950s when three factors contributed to its growth. The first was the re-emergence of a cold war atmosphere with the international crises and confrontation over Berlin (1958) and the U-2 (1960). The second was increasing fears about the consequences of nuclear testing in the atmosphere which led CND to rally support for a complete halting of tests. The third was the development of British nuclear power with the testing (in 1957) and then deployment of thermonuclear weapons, together with the development of modern delivery systems. The failure of the ballistic missile, Blue Streak, and then the American cancellation of its chosen replacement, Skybolt, led to widespread concern about Britain's inability to remain a nuclear power of the first rank.

CND probably reached its first peak in 1960 when the Labour Party narrowly adopted a resolution calling for the abandonment of British nuclear weapons and the removal of American nuclear bases. However in 1961 the parliamentary leadership of Hugh Gaitskell succeeded in re-establishing a multilateralist policy at party conference. CND's strategy had placed great reliance on gaining power through the Labour Party and there was inevitably an internal debate. Although CND sympathizers continued to work within the party the organization itself divided into a majority who favoured the original campaign of persuading public opinion by propaganda and peaceful demonstration and by work within existing groups (trade union, churches, the Labour Party, etc.) and a minority which favoured direct action against the public authorities by tactics of 'sit-ins', occupations and non-violent civil disobedience. This minority led by Bertrand Russell in the Committee of One Hundred alienated public sympathy with the unilateralist cause. Moreover, the political climate which had given rise to CND became less favourable. In 1962 the successful resolution of the Cuban Missile Crisis appeared both to vindicate the American policy of deterrence and to usher in an era of detente. The Partial Test Ban Treaty of 1963 resolved the main problems created by nuclear testing. So far as British nuclear power was concerned, the Nassau Agreement of 1962 provided for the replacement of Skybolt by Polaris and a period of stability was ushered in for the British deterrent - albeit now provided by American technology which called into question the whole concept of a national deterrent.

In the 1964 election nuclear disarmament was not a major issue. The Labour manifesto was opposed to the Nassau Agreement but the leader, Harold Wilson, played down the whole question and when in office simply ignored the manifesto commitment. CND melted away as a major political force and the energies of the peace movement were expended on the Vietnam War and the student movement.

The re-emergence of the peace movement in the late 1970s can be traced to a number of developments, all now well-known, and applying in most cases to the continental developments. They can be simply listed here: the 1977/8 on/off decisions about the neutron bomb; the collapse of detente and the rapid deterioration of Soviet-American relations; the shift in American deterrence doctrine away from MAD towards a counter-force war-fighting strategy; the increasing hawkishness of American foreign policy under Reagan; above all, the twin track decision of December 1979, the failure of the INF talks and the consequent deployment of cruise and Pershing 2. In Britain's case, the peace movement has also argued that the Americans do not contribute directly to national defence, for instance by deploying air defence weapons, but rather use Britain as a base from which to deploy long-range offensive weapons (Poseidon, Fl-11, cruise) - Britain thus has to assume the role of America's unsinkable aircraft carrier. More important, in Britain the question of national nuclear capability re-emerged as a major topic of public debate after nearly two decades of obscurity and apathy. In January 1980 the new Conservative government revealed that its Labour predecessor had secretly spent £1 billion on modernizing the Polaris force, the Chevaline programme, despite the 1974 and 1979 election manifesto commitments not to develop a successor system to Polaris. Secondly, in July 1980 the government concluded an agreement with the Carter administration to purchase Trident C4 missiles to replace Polaris/Chevaline in the 1990s. This agreement was modified in 1982, and made much worse so far as the peace movement was concerned, by specifying the more powerful Trident D5 system.

Thus, as in the 1950s, the peace movement was stimulated partly by national decisions about weapons procurement and partly by broader international developments which were interpreted as exacerbating the arms race and making war more likely.

This chapter is organized into four main sections. The first discusses CND, groups and protests related to CND, and the impact of CND on two sets of institutions - the churches and the trade unions. The second analyses the situation within the Labour Party which has proclaimed itself as in the vanguard of the peace movement. The third analyses some of the ideas thrown up by the peace movement for an alternative and non-nuclear defence policy. The fourth discusses the impact of the peace movement on public opinion.

THE CAMPAIGN FOR NUCLEAR DISARMAMENT

CND remained alive throughout the 1960s and 1970s and benefited from an enormous explosion of membership from 1979 when it assumed its role again as the un-challenged base of the peace movement in Britain. Membership is difficult to measure precisely because most members enrol in local CND groups rather than the national organization.

Table 4.1: National Membership (in October) (2)

1979	1980	1981	1982	1983
4,267	9,000	20,000	41,000	52,000

National membership is now estimated at about 90,000. The number of local groups directly affiliated to CND has grown:

Table 4.2: Local Groups Affiliated to CND

1979	1980	1981	1982	1983
150	300	700	900	1,100

Membership of local groups is now estimated at at least 250,000 and, even allowing for a degree of double-counting, these are very impressive figures. For instance, the Labour Party's membership stands only just above this figure and probably includes a higher pro-portion of inactive members.

CND has developed a capability of organizing mass demonstrations. Its October 1980 rally marked the revival of the peace movement in the aftermath of the twin-track and Trident decisions, and 60,000 attended. In its subsequent October rallies the attendance has been estimated at 250,000, 250,000 and 400,000. The 1983 demonstration was given special emphasis in order to sustain the movement's momentum after the set-back of the Labour Party's defeat in the June election. In addition to the national demonstrations, smaller demonstrations have been held in many areas, and local groups organize a wide variety of other activities.

A number of careful surveys have been taken of CND membership by one of its members, Peter Nias, who is a professional market researcher. The following analysis is drawn from his work. (3) In August 1982 about 50 per cent of CND national members were employed in non-manual, mostly professional, jobs, and only 5 per cent in manual jobs. Nearly 20 per cent were students, and hence future professionals, and membership as a whole was younger than the national population. Members were geographically concentrated in the south-east (about 50 per cent) and over 90 per cent had joined since 1980. Nearly 70 per cent were Labour voters and 12 per cent Liberal-SDP Alliance voters. Nearly half the national members belonged also to a local CND group and 20 per cent considered themselves 'active' in that group. Being middle class in Britain as CND overwhelmingly is, and Nias' analysis indicates that if 'housepersons', retired and unemployed, were classified in class terms then the membership would appear as practically totally middle class, means that CND is also white. Sanity, the organization's magazine, regretted in December 1982 the failure to penetrate Britain's black communities.

These membership profiles are not surprising. They confirm an overwhelming impression of well-educated and sincere people, many supporting other worthy liberal causes, who share some of the characteristics of a model of post-industrial society. For instance. only a third of CND members belonged to a trade union and only a quarter to a political party - two of the major institutions in models of industrial society.

This sort of membership is similar to that found almost 20 years earlier in Frank Parkin's classic study of CND. (4) Parkin elaborated the concept of 'expressive politics' to fit middle-class membership of CND into a wider set of radical middle class values which emphasized the promotion of principles (often in the area of defence and foreign policy) and the benefits and satisfaction gained from that promotion rather than the achievement of specific materialist goals. (5) To use a slightly different language of analysis, expressive politics lies at the idealist pole of the idealist-realist dichotomy. Parkin found CND membership dominated by an educated middle class employed in welfare, teaching and social work rather than commerce and industry. (6)

In Nias's survey, CND members, middle class and

Labour voting, wanted much more radical disarmament
than abandonment of cruise and Trident, the two principal foci of CND's public campaign. Members are unilateralist, wishing substantial unconditional disarmament. The survey found that 99 per cent wanted all
American nuclear bases removed, 77 per cent wanted all
American bases removed (the distinction might in prac-
tise be conceptually difficult to make), and 74 per
cent wanted Britain to leave Nato. In the second two
issues the considerable, less radical minority was
dominated by members who supported the Alliance rather
than the Labour party. A total of 63 per cent opposed
Britain having more conventional weapons if all nuclear weapons were abandoned. This figure might be
taken to confirm the impression of idealistic expressive politics. On the other hand, 18 per cent supporting conventional rearmament and 19 per cent not
knowing might be interpreted as rather high in an
organization dedicated to disarmament and a reflection
of a degree of sophistication or realism about alternative defensive strategies.

In terms of future strategy, the two most important activities were seen as education and 'big public
events'. Non-violent illegal direct action (activity
similar to that pursued by the Committee of One Hundred)
was seen as the most important activity by only 7 per
cent of members and 33 per cent said they would not
wish to participate in activity of this sort.

Nias obtained similar results in a survey of
marchers on a demonstration in London in June 1982;
65 per cent belonged to no political party, 25 per cent
to the Labour Party, with the Alliance at under 3 per
cent less than the Communist Party and barely above
the Socialist Workers' Party and the Ecology Party.
This bias to the left in a march is unsurprising.
Nineteen per cent of marchers described themselves as
practising Christians, twice as great as the national
population. Eighty-eight per cent opposed British
policy in the Falklands War then going on, a tremendous contrast with the 89 per cent support from the
general public in a poll taken at about the same time.

CND holds an annual conference which determines
policy and elects a national council and executive
committee to carry out the policies of the conference.
In 1982 the annual conference appeared to shift to the
left. Hitherto CND had pursued a rather distant policy
towards direct action groups but at conference five
members of the Greenham Women Peace Camp were elected
to the council and direct action was given greater
prominence alongside the existing strategies of edu-
cating and mass demonstrations to influence public

opinion. The 1982 conference also voted by 680 to 642
to campaign against Nato membership, against the wishes of some senior public figures in the movement such
as E.P. Thompson who argued in favour of concentrating
on the more immediate and popular goals of opposing
cruise and Trident. However, despite its left-wing
membership and policies, the organization has taken
severe action against splinter groups and Trotskyist
groups who had penetrated some branches of CND or
organizations like Youth CND. The Trotskyist slogan
of 'Jobs not Bombs' has not officially been taken up
by the organization although some local groups with
Trotskyist members use it. On the whole CND has been
careful not to allow itself to become a trojan horse
for the extreme left, although opponents have pointed
to communist members on the national council. The
mere presence of Monsignor Bruce Kent as general secretary has helped to resist charges of left-wing ex-
tremism.

Despite the 1982 decision on Nato, CND propaganda
continued to argue for unilateral nuclear disarmament
in terms of British nuclear weapons and American nuclear bases and weapons in Britain. Nato membership
and the difficult problem of defining a nuclear base
were played down. In the 1983 general election CND
campaigned actively against cruise and Trident, although without giving overt support to the Labour Party
(because of electoral laws). The July 1983 edition of
Sanity, naturally depressed by the crushing defeat
suffered by the Labour Party, rather unconvincingly
blamed the Labour Party for not fighting more strongly
and convincingly the unilateralist case. There is
absolutely no evidence to support this case. The truth
is that unilateralism is unpopular with British electoral opinion, despite great concern (discussed below)
about nuclear weapons.

CND has become a big organization with large resources. It employs professional bureaucrats and
organizers. In addition to a monthly magazine for
activists (Campaign) listing various events, it
publishes a glossy monthly magazine (Sanity) which
sells by subscription and directly through retailers.
Sanity contains serious articles on various aspects
of the arms race and is generally written to appeal
to an educated readership. Its advertisements reveal
how far opposition to nuclear weapons has penetrated
middle-class values and culture. Advertisements
appeal not only to ecologists, vegetarians and feminists of the loonier variety, though they do appeal to
these, but also to the prosperous middle class with
plenty of cash to spend and a self-consciously radical

chic image to sustain. A full-page costs an advertis-
er £500. Sanity reveals the strength of the peace
movement compared with the 1960s when CND activists
considered themselves to be on the fringe. Whether
the current vogue for anti-nuclearism will be strong
enough to sustain CND through several more years of
Conservative government is uncertain, but conservatives and Atlanticists would be ill-advised to assume
CND will wither away following Labour's electoral
defeat.

Another indication of the success of the peace
movement in establishing itself in middle-class values
is the enormous success of publications about the
peace movement itself and the issues in nuclear disarmament. In Britain this success has been enjoyed
not only by established publishers, practically all
of whom have sections of their catalogues devoted to
the causes of the peace movement, but also by left-
wing publishers who have multiplied and grown successful. Pluto Press is perhaps the best known but there
are others, Merlin for instance, and a host of local
co-operatives, workers' presses, etc. Modern technology has obviously helped this development. The
peace movement, and feminism, have become big business.
There is a readership to cultivate and satisfy. All
this stands in clear contrast with the 1950s and 1960s
when the peace movement was synonymous with fringe
publications labouring under enormous commercial hand-
icaps.

Operating under the CND umbrella are a large
number of more narrowly-based peace groups. Among the
more prominent are: Lawyers for Nuclear Disarmament;
Scientists against Nuclear Armaments (led by Professor
Michael Pentz who is a leading CND spokesman and a
national vice-president); Christian CND; Clergy
against Nuclear Armaments; the Medical Campaign against
Nuclear Weapons (a group consisting of doctors which has
publicized the British Medical Association's report on the
consequences of nuclear war); Journalists against
Nuclear Extermination. There are also groups based on
women's groups and gay groups. Fringe groups have
included Babies against the Bomb, inevitably located in
the most progressive and affluent London suburbs, and
Ex-Service CND. CND has given some prominence to this
latter group in order to help combat CND's left-wing
and pacifist image. Ex-Service CND is a small group
whose chief achievement has been to gain permission to
participate as a group in the national annual remem-
brance day parade in London. In contrast with military involvement in some of the continental peace
movements, for instance The Netherlands, Ex-Service

70

CND appears to be composed of former 'other ranks'
rather than officers.
   In addition there are party-based CND groups of
which Labour CND is by far the largest, holding its
own large annual conference. The president of CND,
Joan Ruddock, is a former Labour parliamentary candidate, though the national leadership of CND plays
down party affiliation. There is a well-established
liberal CND which has helped unilateralist policies to
dominate the annual Liberal Party Assembly. The
parliamentary leadership of the party, however, while
hostile to both cruise and Trident, is not unilateralist. There is a much smaller SDP CND which is rather
unimportant within the party. The original leaders
of the SDP in the 'gang of four' included two of the
most committed Atlanticists from the Labour Party,
David Owen and Bill Rodgers, who had written pamphlets
in 1980, while still in the Labour Party, in favour of
cruise. Owen's pamphlet was published by the Campaign
for Labour Victory, a right-wing pressure group within
the party which largely went over to the SDP in 1981.
Rodgers' pamphlet was published by the Labour Committee
for Transatlantic Understanding, a loose grouping of
right-wing trade unionists funded by Nato. The establishment of the SDP considerably weakened the anti-
unilateralist factions within the Labour Party and
weakened the strongly pro-Nato group of MPs both numerically and in terms of their general displacement
within the party. The peace movement is not represented of course within the Conservative Party, though
the right wing of the party contains 'Little England
ers' who are strongly anti-American and favour a
Gaullist policy. A group known as Tories against
Cruise and Trident has attempted to establish itself
but its support appears to be tiny and the offical
party apparatus is hostile to its existence. There
has developed a good deal of criticism of existing
alliance strategy from within the Establishment.
Lord Carver, a former Chief of the Defence Staff, has
argued consistently against independent British nuclear
weapons. (7) Many soldiers and strategic thinkers are
opposed to current reliance on early use of nuclear
weapons, however their prescriptions, which involve
up-grading conventional defences and retaining nuclear
weapons as weapons of last resort, do not fall within
the ambit of the peace movement. However, it is a
measure of the success of the peace movement that it
has contributed to a major debate about strategic
doctrine and defence deployments.
   Three further alignments within the peace movement deserve slightly fuller consideration. These

are: nuclear free zones; the peace camps; European
Nuclear Disarmament.

Nuclear Free Zones

After 1980 many Labour-controlled local authorities
declared themselves to be nuclear free zones, primarily to raise public consciousness about disarmament.
By October 1983 155 councils had so declared themselves, including every Welsh local authority some of
which are not Labour-controlled. Most Labour authorities have now made this declaration. They have formed a national conference to co-ordinate activities.
The Greater London Council led by Ken Livingstone has
been the most prominent. It declared 1983 to be
'Peace Year' and spent £400,000 of its budget campaigning for CND and against civil defence. Sheffield
City Council appointed a disarmament co-ordinator in
place of a civil defence organizer and most of these
authorities have refused to carry out their statutory
civil defence responsibilities. In 1982 they forced
the government to abandon its major civil defence
exercise, Hard Rock, which was probably the biggest
single success of the peace movement. All these
authorities support the CND campaign against civil
defence on the grounds that it is both a cruel deceit
of the public and a preparation for nuclear war, although some authorities such as Coventry pursue the
apparently contradictory policy of both denouncing
civil defence and declaring itself a nuclear free zone
while at the same time carrying out statutory duties.
In 1983 the Home Office tightened up civil defence
regulations and a major confrontation is thus likely
when the next major national exercise is to be held.
    The nuclear free zone concept has become a pop-
ular device for CND. Within the Church some parishes
have even declared themselves to be nuclear free.

The Peace Camps

The Greenham Common camp began on a permanent basis in
March 1982 after a series of earlier demonstrations
and vigils. It has of course attracted great attention on an international front. Several other nuclear
bases in Britain, including Molesworth, the second
cruise site, have attracted permanent peace camps.
The camps have been composed entirely of women,
and they have helped cement the alliance between
the peace movement and the women's movement into
one of the most interesting contemporary social movements. The camps at Greenham, for there are in fact

several, one on each gate, have survived many attempts
at removal by the authorities, and the women have displayed great ingenuity in maintaining their presence
despite harassment and being dispossessed by bailiffs.
For most of the time there are relatively few women
present, perhaps a hundred, but they are regularly
reinforced at times of crisis and for major rallies.
In December 1982, for instance, 30,000 women attended
to 'embrace' the camp. The peace camps appear to
observers to be completely unbureaucratic and to be
supported by informal lines of communication to groups
of supporters in the country. On the other hand, the
exclusion of men has aroused some opposition from men
within the peace movement, and the press, after treat-
ing the women rather favourably at first, is now in
clined to portray them as fanatical 'wierdies' (the
Guardian excepted). The increasingly desperate tactics employed by the women to survive against the
authorities may also have alienated public support.
The Greenham camps have also failed to prevent the
installation of cruise (the hardware was flown in by
the Americans) and the successful completion of recent
training exercises outside the base. National CND
has been dragged along by these direct actions which
verge permanently on the illegal and stand in contrast
to the ordered and bureaucratic nature of CND as a
major national pressure group.

European Nuclear Disarmament
END was launched in a declaration in April 1980, inspired primarily by E.P. Thompson, a social historian
and Marxist who had become a major CND national figure. (8) END is, so far as Britain is concerned, a
unilateralist grouping, closely allied with CND and
with an overlap of membership and national leaders.
Its campaigning, however, has developed two distinctive characteristics. Thompson has developed an extended critique of deterrence theory, alliance blocs
and what he terms the mentality of exterminism. (9)
END's programme thus extends beyond nuclear disarmament to a call for a reconstruction of the states-
system. Secondly, Thompson argues that the goals of
END can be achieved only by popular movements against
governments co-ordinated on an international basis.
Thus END emphasizes the international nature of the
peace movement, with specific emphasis on the campaign
against cruise and Pershing, and concentrates less on
the specifically British issues emphasized by CND.
END's immediate goal is the establishment of a nuclear
free zone stretching from Portugal to Poland. Thompson

thus places more emphasis than CND on the development of a peace movement in Eastern Europe which would influence the policy of the Soviet Union. Opponents of END have thus been at pains to point out the difficulty of locating and nurturing unofficial peace movements in the East and the events in Poland, which appear to have had virtually no impact on CND's membership or propaganda, are a setback for END which has taken a pro-Solidarity line.

Thompson strongly opposed CND's 1982 decision to campaign against Nato membership. The continental peace movements, with whom he is in close touch, have either not seen Nato membership as a critical question or, more generally, have argued in favour of changing Nato from within. Thompson was, perhaps, quicker than other CND leaders to recognize the importance of articulating alternative defence strategies and he has undoubtedly been influenced by his experiences as a junior army officer in the Second World War participating in a popular struggle against fascism.

END's membership, analysed by Peter Nias, is remarkably middle class and highly educated. In contrast with CND membership its membership is rather older, male dominated and excludes communist and left-wing fringe party members. Forty per cent of members had studied as post-graduates and about half belonged to a political party. Notwithstanding Thompson's European-wide policy, 73 per cent wanted Britain to leave Nato (virtually identical with CND) but only 38 per cent favoured British withdrawal from the European Community, a slightly lower figure than the national average. Although END's supporters (now members) are numerically slight compared with CND, the organization constitutes the intellectual base of the British peace movement and represents its place within a broader European movement. (10)

END has also been important in extending the debate from a concern with policy to the role of the state itself. Given the intellectual disinterest in the state in Britain, this is no mean achievement. Clearly nuclear weapons do raise interesting questions about the state and the peace movement has challenged the state in three areas: firstly, the procedures for deploying nuclear weapons; secondly, the 'authoritarian' measures adopted by the state to protect its nuclear weapons from protest; thirdly, the territorial sovereignty of the state in terms of the status of American bases within Britain. (11)

THE CHURCHES AND THE TRADE UNIONS

The churches and the unions are the two sets of
national institutions, outside the parties, in which
the peace movement has been most successful, excluding
the women's movement which has not assumed institutional form and is now in any case very closely enmesh-
ed with the peace movement.

The churches have naturally debated the ethics
of nuclear deterrents and nuclear war-fighting within
the classical framework of the just war. Individual
Christians have been prominent in CND, mostly notably
Monsignor Bruce Kent who has received leave of absence
from his pastoral responsibilities to assume the role
of general secretary of CND. The churches have not
been as active in the peace movement, however, as have
been some of the continental churches, and there is
no real equivalent, for instance, of the Dutch Inter-
Church Peace Council.

The Church of Scotland, the largest church in
Scotland and enjoying more or less the status of the
established church, and the United Reformed Church in
England and Wales are firmly unilateralist. The
Methodist Church is very close in its policy to unilateralism. The Roman Catholic Church has not officially advanced beyond the Pope's opposition to the
arms race and extremely reluctant endorsement of deterrence as a short-term lesser evil. Individual
Catholics, however, are active in the peace movement
in Pax Christi.

The most interesting and full debate has occurred
within the Church of England. The Church enjoys priv-
ileged status as the established church in England
(not in Wales or Northern Ireland) with the Queen as
its temporal governor. The Prime Minister appoints
bishops and archbishops on the advice of the church.
The church plays an important role in English society,
although most people of course do not actually attend
its services, and historically the church has been
associated, though not exclusively, with conservatism.
In 1963 the church played a major role in a report
produced by the British Council of Churches (consisting of all the churches except for Roman Catholicism)
on the British nuclear deterrent. The report came to
no very clear conclusions but implied its support for
the abandonment of British independent nuclear weapons
and for larger conventional forces to help raise the
nuclear threshold (plus ca change...) (12)

In 1979 the Church of England Synod, the governing body of the church representing clergy and laity,
requested, through the Board for Social Responsibility,

a full report on nuclear weapons. The report became
a best-seller and a major contribution to the peace
movement and the broader national debate about defence
strategy. (13) The report offers a serious and sustained analysis of the arms race, deterrence theory
and Nato strategy. It concludes that no nuclear war
could meet the criteria required by a just war and,
more controversially, that nuclear deterrence was
morally unacceptable because it required a conditional
intention to wage nuclear war. The report recommended
abandonment of Britain's nuclear weapons which it
argued might breathe new life into the cause of non-
proliferation and would eliminate the destabilizing
consequence of 'Britain's ambiguously separate centre
of decision making on the use of nuclear weapons'
(p. 160). The report also recommended the removal of
American nuclear bases but favoured continued membership of Nato and accepted as inevitable the continuation of nuclear deterrents between the superpowers
for the foreseeable future. The report thus favoured
a number of unilateral British steps to advance what
was seen as a multilateral process of arms reduction.
It stressed the need for consultation and was sensi-
tive to the dangers of instability created by precipitate action. Unilateralism would be implemented
cautiously and in stages.

Synod rejected the report by 338 votes to 100
after the Archbishop of Canterbury (an ex-officer
decorated for gallantry) argued that unilateral disarmament would not assist negotiations for multilateral reductions and might undermine peace by destabilizing Nato. Synod agreed by 275 votes to 222 to a compromise motion proposed by the Bishop of Birmingham
which opposed first use of nuclear weapons but accepted the imperative of maintaining deterrence and in
particular of preventing nuclear blackmail. (14) The
chairman of the working party, the Bishop of Salisbury, has continued to argue his case and the matter
is by no means permanently settled.

Trade unions were responsible for the shift in
Labour party policy in favour of unilateralism in 1960
and back to multilateralism the following year. In
1958 a unilateralist motion was defeated at the Trade
Union Congress by five and a half million votes to one
million. In 1959 the largest union, the Transport and
General Workers' Union, under a new left-wing general
secretary Frank Cousins, decided by a tiny majority
at its biennial conference in favour of unilateralism.
It has since persistently supported CND. By 1960
enough unions had switched to unilateralism to defeat
the strongly Atlanticist policy of the leader Hugh

Gaitskell at the party conference. However, it is important to place this particualr policy issue in the context of a broader inner-party struggle between Gaitskell and his supporters, the 'revisionists' and the left wing following the third successive general election defeat in 1959. Three of the unions which switched policy in 1960, the miners, the railwaymen and the shop-workers, reverted to multilateralism in 1961 and Gaitskell regained control of party conference. CND supporters who were not party activists were appalled by the way in which defence was simply used by protagonists on both sides of the debate as part of a struggle for power within the party. Moreover the failure of the Labour Party to sustain its unilateralism led CND to distrust the party as a vehicle for its strategy. This distrust was confirmed in 1964 when the party's manifesto commitments on defence were ignored by the Labour government. CND has of course been active inside the party since 1964 but it has never relied entirely on the party nor trusted the party to carry out in office its defence policies enunciated in opposition.

Throughout the 1960s the TGWU carried the unilateralist cause within the TUC, supported by a few small craft unions and two left wing unions, the public employees and the firemen. In the 1970s other unions moved towards unilateralism and in 1972 and 1973 succeeded in carrying motions at both the TUC Congress and party conference. During the second Wilson/Callaghan government the unilateralist cause declined slightly, though less in the party than in the TUC, but in December 1979 the general executive committee of the TGWU decided to press once again for a concerted unilateralist campaign. In 1981 at Scarborough the TUC adopted a unilateralist stance and this was consolidated in 1982 when the unions were responsible for the Labour party adopting by a two-thirds majority a commitment to pursue an 'unequivocal' unilateralist policy. The unions of course command about 90 per cent of the votes at party conference and are thus critical in achieving the necessary two-thirds majority for any policy to become part of the party programme from which the election manifesto is drawn. In 1982 the party conference appeared to swing back to the right as the unions determined to halt the leftward drift of the party. However, the commitment to unilateralism was unaffected because the 'soft left' was as strongly committed to unilateralism as the 'hard left'. By 1983 only three major unions remained hostile to unilateralism; the second largest union, the engineers, under strong right wing control; the

General and Municipal which is centrist and hostile
to cruise and Trident; the smaller electricians' union
which is under ultra-rightist leadership.
     However, the support of the trade unions for the
peace movement remains rather eqivocal. Working-
class participation in CND is extremely limited as we
have seen, and a contrast must thus be drawn between
the official policies of trade unions which are made
by leaders and activists, who stand to the left, and
ordinary members, only 39 per cent of whom for instance voted Labour in 1983. To the extent that CND
is a middle-class pressure group enunciating post-
industrial values, its appeal to the working class is
limited. A necessary condition for broader CND pen-
etration of trade unions is almost certainly much
wider understanding of, and support for, policies of
industrial conversion through which employment in
armaments would be converted to employment in produc-
ing 'socially useful commodities' (to employ the
left's jargon). The cause of industrial conversion
has made some progress on the left of the Labour
party where the plans of the Lucas aerospace shop-
stewards have received most attention. But specific
proposals with management support have got virtually
nowhere. While CND is widely perceived as campaigning
for disarmament, and hence job losses, trade union
support is bound to be problematical. In 1983 Ron
Todd who is a national officer of the TGWU and the
doyen of trade union unilateralists was elected to the
vice-presidency of CND, and this may herald a renewed
effort to gain support for CND among trade unionists. (15)

THE LABOUR PARTY

The 1964-70 and 1974-9 governments were strongly Atlanticist. There was a strong commitment to working
closely with the United States (despite party conference resolutions in the 1960s opposing the Vietnam
War) and, after the abandonment of the 'East of Suez'
policy a concentration of military deployment within
the Nato area. There was an equally strong commitment
to maintaining the independent nuclear deterrent. The
governments recognised no inconsistency between Atlan-
ticism and independent nuclear power. Whilst it might
be argued that, whatever doctrinal subtlety is employed (the trigger argument, second centre of decision-
making argument, etc.) these two positions sit un-
easily together, in practice the two positions could
not be interpreted as inconsistent because the United

States was necessary for Britain to remain a nuclear power with modern long-range delivery systems.

The 1964 manifesto's opposition to the Nassau agreements was ignored after the failure of desultory negotiations over the MLF and the Atlantic Nuclear Force. American Polaris submarines operated out of Holy Loch and British Polaris submarines were built. As early as 1967 the government gave preliminary consideration to modernizing Polaris to cope with improved Soviet ABM systems. (16) In 1969 70 American Fl-11 long-range bombers, the government agreed, would be based in Britain to strengthen the theatre nuclear element of Nato's flexible response.

In 1972 and 1973 resolutions against American nuclear bases and reliance on nuclear weapons were carried at conference against the wishes of the leadership. Both 1974 election manifestos committed the party to removing the American Polaris base and disowned any intention of acquiring a new generation of British nuclear weapons. (17) Nevertheless, the Wilson/Callaghan governments carried through the Polaris improvement programme (Chevaline) on which the Heath government had incurred only minimal expenditure, despite enormous cost escalation after 1974. The programme was kept secret from Parliament (though there are coded references in the government defence white papers) (18) and, if not contradictory, was hardly consistent with the manifesto commitment. Moreover in 1978 the government began preliminary consideration of a replacement system for Polaris in the 1990s and by the time of the election defeat considerable progress towards a positive decision had been made. (19) The 1979 election manifesto thus considerably weakened the 1974 commitment. (20) Likewise, the commitment to seek the removal of the American Polaris base was ignored and American Polaris submarines were replaced by Poseidon which carried a Mirved warhead.

The government strongly defended alliance strategy, in particular flexible response including the use of British battlefield nuclear weapons with American warheads and American long-range theatre nuclear weapons. Battlefield and theatre weapons were seen as essential links between Nato's front-line conventional strength and the American strategic nuclear forces which guaranteed the alliance. The government also supported the shift of American targeting policy away from the counter-value and towards counter-force targets so that 'Nato can, therefore, use its nuclear weapons in a controlled and effective way'. (21) In May 1977 it supported the 3 per cent improvement programme to begin in 1979 and participated in, and endorsed, the report of the High Level Group which in May 1978 produced the long-term defence programme. This programme included among a variety of improvements the continuation of long-range theatre nuclear weapons which would be 'modernised as necessary'. (22) As part of the enhancement of the American theatre capability, the government agreed in 1977 to an increase in the deployment of Fl-lls from 70 to 160.

Government defence white papers warned of the increasing threat posed by the Soviet rearmament programme which exceeded legitimate defensive requirements and undermined the spirit of detente. At the same time financial constraints were tightening and a major review of policy in 1974 by defence secretary Mason led to decisions in 1975 to reduce further deployments outside the Nato area (South East Asia, Simonstown naval base South Africa, the airportable brigades) and in the Mediterranean. On the other hand the government continued to support a large surface fleet and maintained a naval maritime capability by building three anti-submarine warfare cruisers or mini-carriers. The left of the party criticized this decision in particular as a reversal of the 1966 decision to abandon aircraft carriers. Moreover, other than by cutting away at the most peripheral commitments, the government opposed any major structural reform of the defence effort. The government pledged itself to maintain its four distinctive Nato roles: in Germany (a standing army of over 50,000 plus a tactical air-force), the eastern Atlantic (naval and air deployments), defence of the UK base itself, Polaris.

The government's ultra-orthodox policy was entrusted to strongly committed Atlanticists; Roy Mason and Fred Mulley as secretaries of state, Bill Rodgers and John Gilbert as ministers of state. By 1979 expenditure was rising again with the 3 per cent programme and conflict growing with party conference.

The first sustained attack on government policy was mounted by the Defence Study Group appointed by the National Executive Committee in 1974 (23) The group was chaired by veteran unilateralist Ian Mikardo and completely captured by unilateralists critical of the government. It not only challenged the fundamentals of government policy but sketched the outlines of an alternative defence policy. The report rested on two premises. The first was that there was no Soviet threat, whether judged in terms of Soviet intentions (which in Europe favoured maintaining the status quo), Soviet interests, or Soviet capabilities. The second was that British expenditure was far too high, a prime

source of economic weakness and should be reduced over
five years from 5.2 per cent of GNP to 3.2 per cent -
a massive cut. The 'cost approach' to defence dominates the report and a number of options were discussed. These included abandoning Polaris (which the
group favoured although - in ignorance of Chevaline -
the savings were slight), reducing the surface fleet
and in particular abandoning the three anti-submarine
warfare cruisers, halving the army in Germany (which
would only, it was claimed, reduce Nato's strength to
north central Europe by 3.9 per cent), abandoning the
multi-role combat aircraft in favour of existing aircraft, using precision guided munitions to enhance
Nato's defensive power.
     The report is equivocal on arms reductions in
Europe. At one moment defending them as a unilateral
gesture to the Soviets, at another arguing that Germany could fill the gaps, at another warning against
an increased German defence effort.
     The defence policy of the reformers thus emerges
as non-nuclear defence within Nato with Britain giving
up all her nuclear weapons and removing American nuclear bases. The alliance would adopt a policy of
'no first use' of nuclear weapons. The strategic
doctrine can be characterized as 'defensive deterrence' based on a denial capability, maximizing the
defensive advantages claimed to flow from precision
guided munitions, without a reprisal capability. The
report also stressed the negative consequences of high
levels of research and employment in defence and argued
the desirability and practicability of transferring
research and employment to socially useful activity.
By the 1980s the conversion of employment had
become a standard component of alternative defence
strategies.
     The response of Labour defence ministers to the
report was hostile with virtually no common ground
with the reformers. (24) On employment, they argued
that the million-plus in defence-related activities
were not readily replaceable and were in any case
socially useful in defending the social fabric. On
the Soviet threat they adopted a classic realist position. The threat should be assessed in terms of high
defence spending, the brutality of their policies
within Eastern Europe and foreign policy intentions
which, while difficult to judge with certainty given
the closed nature of Soviet society, 'in Western
Europe and the rest of the world they remain firmly
attached to revolutionary change'. The ministers
defended each of Britain's defence roles, implicitly
rejecting the possibility of further economies, opposed

a major expansion of the German defence effort, and
warned that any reductions of effort by Britain could
easily precipitate a general 'unravelling' of Nato.
    The publication of the NEC study and the govern-
ment's hostile response mark the beginning of a major
sustained conflict within the party over defence policy. In 1978 conference adopted a resolution against
basing American cruise missiles in Britain, in direct
opposition to the government's support for the long-
term improvement programme and the modernization of
theatre nuclear weapons. In the 1979 election manifesto Callaghan attempted to contain opposition to
defence policy by obscuring the question of Polaris
replacement and defusing the defence problem by rele-
gating defence to a minor part of the manifesto itself - an old device for managing defence within the
party. But by this time the general conflict between
the leadership and conference was becoming acute.
The leadership had failed to meet the wishes of conference in several key areas since 1974, incomes
policy, industrial policy, expenditure policy, defence
policy, and there was widespread opposition to the way
in which Callaghan controlled the process of drawing
up the manifesto. Conflict between the conference and
the parliamentary party, in particular the parliamentary leadership, expressed itself in a bitter debate
about reform of the party's structures to increase
accountability of the parliamentary party and leadership within a framework of greater intra-party democracy. In the struggle over party democracy, which
began as early as 1974, escalated in 1977 and reached
crisis levels from 1979-81, defence was perhaps the
policy area most-often cited by the reformers.
    At conference in 1980 defence was the major polic
issue. The peace movement was growing rapidly and the
campaigns for unilateral British and European nuclear
disarmament had captured the hearts and minds of delegates. Resolutions were passed opposing American
nuclear bases, cruise, Polaris, Trident and any defence policy depending on the threat to use nuclear
weapons. In 1981 and 1982 further resolutions were
passed reinforcing and expanding these policies and
culminating in a unilateralist resolution adopted by
a two-thirds majority which thus became part of the
party's programme from which the election manifesto
would be drawn. Party propaganda for external con-
sumption stressed the party's leading role in the
European peace movement. Most of the anti-unilateral-
ist vote in 1982 came from just two unions under strong moderate leadership, the Engineers and the General
and Municipal. The question of Nato membership was

not given prominence and resolutions in favour of
withdrawal from Nato (which would of course have put
multilateralists in an impossible position) were heavily defeated. Unilateralists and the Left stressed a
policy of minimal participation in Nato based on the
Danish, Norwegian and, increasingly, the Greek model.
   The split with the SDP in 1981 weakened the position of Atlanticists and multilateralists inside the
Labour Party and encouraged the Left to pursue its
unilateralist line. Increasingly, anti-unilateralism
was confined to the right-wing of the party as the
balance of power shifted.
   The position of the parliamentary leadership was
inevitably also shifting. Callaghan maintained his
Atlanticist commitments but his position had become
impossible and in the autumn of 1980 he resigned. The
leadership contest was won by Michael Foot, a life-
long unilateralist and disarmer, who defeated Denis
Healey who was as strongly identified with Nato and
a realist position. Foot's victory reveals the growth
of unilateralism within the parliamentary party although it is clear that he gained votes from non-uni-
lateralists who saw in him a more credible leader to
cope with the demands for greater democracy within the
party. In the subsequent election for deputy-leader,
conducted under new rules providing for a broader
electoral college including trade unions and constit-
uency parties, Healey was faced by two unilateralists,
Tony Benn and John Silkin. Benn supported the full
conference policy on defence (notwithstanding his
membership of the Callaghan government) while Healey
opposed both Trident and the twin-track decision on
the grounds that American nuclear weapons were already
adequately committed to the alliance, while cruise and
pershing were strategically unnecessary, escalatory,
and invited a Soviet pre-emptive attack. The deputy-
leadership contest ensured that defence remained a
major issue in the party throughout 1981 during the
period of the SDP defections. Callaghan and, more
surprisingly, Foot's defence spokesman was Bill Rodgers
until his defection to the SDP. Rodgers was a strong
supporter of the twin-track decision. Foot replaced
Rodgers with Brynmor John, considerably less hawkish
but a strong supporter of Nato. At conference in 1981
John was prevented from speaking on behalf of the parliamentary party and Foot almost immediately replaced
him with Silkin whose views were much less clearly defined but considerably more sympathetic to the unilateralist position. By the 1982 conference the multilateralists were thus in a difficult position, forced
to maximize the significance of Healey's role as

deputy-leader, of the conference's votes against withdrawal from Nato and of the inevitable ambiguity of a
unilateralist stance together with support for an alliance whose doctine remained wedded to the early use
of nuclear weapons.

The fullest statement of Labour's revised defence
policy was contained in Labour's Programme 1982, a
general statement of policies approved by the NEC and
conference as the basis of the election manifesto. It
marks a radical departure from previous policy in its
even-handed treatment of American and Society policy.
The Atlanticist assumption of an automatic and extensive community of interests with the United States was
absent.

> The erosion of detente since the failure of the
> United States to ratify the Salt II agreements,
> with the role of the United States in El Salvador
> and the Soviet Union in Afghanistan and Poland,
> linked with the emergence of the new generation
> of nuclear weapons, has considerably increased
> the risk of potential conflict.
> While the United States is equipping a Rapid
> Deployment Force to impose its will anywhere in
> the globe, the Soviet Union has intervened dir-
> ectly in Afghanistan and is actively involved in
> the Horn of Africa. Such interventions are a
> violation of the rights of the peoples of the
> world to self-determination...

Labour's defence policy was presented as nuclear unilateralism. It strongly endorsed the peace movement's
analysis of the superpower confrontation which was
directly threatening to Britain in particular and to
Europe in general. The question of Nato membership
was given little prominence either in terms of support
for membership or withdrawal. The report emphasised
non-nuclear, defensive strength within a concept of
defensive deterrence. All nuclear bases in Britain
would be closed as the first step to a European nuclear weapons free zone, the 3 per cent improvment
programme abandoned and expenditures reduced to European levels. On structural reform within Nato and
reduction in the number of separate British defensive
roles the report was vague. The report admitted of no
possible contradiction between defensive deterrents and
reduced conventional expenditures.

The leadership remained under intense pressure
from the party to live up to these unilateralist commitments, and the position of Healey in particular had
become very difficult. The leadership's support for

The Development of the Peace Movement in Britain

the government in the Falklands War increased tensions
with party activists. Foot was regarded by conference
with suspicion for accommodating the multilateralists in the shadow cabinet. The election manifesto
itself gave the unilateralists perhaps 95 per cent of
their demands, though some of the commitments were
clothed in language opaque enough to allow the multilateralists to minimize the real concessions they had
been forced into yielding.
     Within the manifesto there were seven major
commitments on defence (25) Four can be identified as
reflecting a consensus within the party: oppositon to
the twin-track decision and cruise deployments in
Britain; cancellation of Trident; a nuclear freeze;
a shift towards conventional and defensive deterrents.
Fifthly, the party would reduce expenditure to bring
it 'into line' with the major European states 'without
increasing the reliance on nuclear weapons'. Two
further policies produced the most difficulty for the
party. The first was the unilateral scrapping of Polaris. The manifesto was especially vague here by
arguing both that Polaris should be 'included' in
nuclear disarmament negotiations and that a non-nuclear policy would be achieved within five years. This
confusion of multilateral and unilateral disarmament,
that is of conditional or negotiated reductions and unconditional reductions, inevitably failed to paper
over the cracks. Callaghan, Healey and Shore attacked
the manifesto during the campaign and argued that
abandonment could only be in return for Soviet concessions. What these multilateralists failed to
identify was the sort of Soviet concessions that would
satisfy them. Given their assumption that Polaris
made a significant contribution to national security,
it becomes difficult to imagine the sort of concessions the Soviet Union could make that would justify
the complete abandonment of a national deterrent
force. The only interest the Soviet Union had shown
in the British force was as part of an offer to reduce
SS-20 deployment to the level of British and French
nuclear forces excluding any American missiles. From
a Western European Nato perspective, British deterrent
forces could only complicate the process of arms negotiations with the Soviet Union. From a German perspective, Britain's Polaris force balanced against SS-
20s was an inadequate substitute for American missiles. The position of Labour multilateralists on negotiating away Polaris appears therefore to be rather
ill-thought out and inconsistent. The truth, one sus-
pects, is that Callaghan, Healey and Shore were gen-
uinely attached to Britain retaining an independent

strategic nuclear capability.

Similar confusion surrounded the other policy commitment, namely the removal of all nuclear bases within five years in order to achieve a non-nuclear defence. The multilateralists obtained a small concession in the manifesto's admission that the bases could not be removed 'at once' and 'the way we do it must be designed to assist in the task to which we are all committed - securing nuclear disarmament agreements with other countries and maintaining cooperation with our allies'. However, such was the difficulty of obtaining internal party agreement that the manifesto here conflated two quite separate problems, namely securing agreements with potential adversaries on the one hand, and maintaining co-operation with allies on the other. The manifesto also failed to identify what it regarded as a nuclear base, because beyond the obvious cases of Poseidon, Fl-11 and cruise bases all 102 American bases and installations had (potentially) a nuclear role because they were related directly or indirectly to American nuclear deterrent forces.

Three general comments might thus be made on the manifesto. The first is that it failed to face up to all the problems of a non-nuclear policy while at the same time remaining at Nato, although the manifesto could be interpreted as reflecting accurately the new conventional wisdom on the need to reduce the emphasis on nuclear weapons in Nato's strategy. The second is that the manifesto appears less a set of consistent policies directed at the outside world than an attempt to compromise fundamental internal differences on defence. Apparent agreement on some specific policy issues, for instance opposition to cruise, barely masked underlying differences of approach, in this instance between those who considered the United States was already adequately coupled to European defence and those who wished to uncouple the United States from Europe. The third is that whereas previous manifestos had performed a balancing act by offering some concessions to unilateralists, in 1983 it was the multilateralists who were clinging precariously and unconvincingly to the party line. Moreover, defence had become so salient that it was more difficult to camouflage differences or, as Roy Hattersley repeatedly attempted, to point to the policy issues on which the party was united.

It is possible to identify three main groupings of opinion in the party on defence. The groupings are neither completely exclusive nor internally cohesive but they reflect fairly accurately current thinking on defence and attitudes to the peace movement.

The Development of the Peace Movement in Britain

High Profile Atlanticists. This group, largely confined to Parliament though with a weak organization in
the extra-parliamentary party (the Labour Defence and
Disarmament Group chaired by John Gilbert), is the
remnant of the group once dominant in the leadership
and the parliamentary party. It is now reduced to
about 30 MPs. It was never dominant in the constit-
uency parties but until recently it was able to control, manipulate or ignore conference. It contains
those who have dominated defence decision-making in
government including Callaghan, Healey, Mason, Gilbert
and Duffy. Members of this grouping have criticized,
at least publicly, aspects of the twin-track decision,
but strongly support the retention of American bases
in Britain. They also favour retention of a British
nuclear deterrent, though not necessarily Trident.
        A full statement of this position is contained
in the minority report of the House of Commons' Select
Committee on Defence report on Strategic Nuclear
Weapons Policy (26) by John Gilbert, Bruce George and
Bernard Conlan (two leading Labour moderates, of whom
George is a specialist on defence) together with John
Cartwright who had just defected to the SDP. The
report favoured retaining Polaris/Chevaline into the
next century with new submarines, or failing that, a
cheaper deterrent than Trident. It acknowledged that
independent use by Britain was a questionable assumption but considered that Polaris made a contribution
to the alliance. However, it is doubtful whether a
British minimum deterrent (counter-value deterrent)
does meet alliance requirements. Trident C4 was crit-
izied as excessive for a minimum deterrent and the
construction of the necessary submarines as very dam-
aging to the SSN construction programme. Trident D5,
the minority concluded, would be ever more inapprop-
riate, a conclusion with which the majority conservative report concurred.
        The only concession made by these high profile
Atlanticists to the peace movement has been to oppose
battlefield nuclear weapons. (27) Here, of course,
they are virtually pushing at an open door.
        The new deputy leader of the party, Roy Hatters-
ley, associated earlier in his career primarily with
Europe, supports this high profile Atlanticist position which thus retains a toe-hold in the leadership of
the party.

Non-Nuclear Nato. This position represents official
party policy and is espoused by the new leader Neil
Kinnock. The emphasis is on defensive deterrents

through strong denial capability with the removal of
nuclear bases. However, on his recent trip to the
United States Kinnock stressed the importance of retaining conventional American bases. He has also
sought to re-establish the credibility of Labour's
defence policy with public opinion by tacitly dropping
the commitment to reduce defence expenditure, emphas-
ising instead additional spending on conventional
forces within a Nato framework which includes the forward defence of Germany. Kinnock's policy has thus
moved considerably away from the position of CND and
possibly of party conference. In the CND demonstration of October 1983 he was also extremely circumspect
in his remarks on abandoning Polaris, appearing to
favour negotiation with the Soviet Union. (28)
     It may well prove to be the case that within the
Labour party there is a minority strongly committed
to an Atlanticist position, perhaps a majority of the
party conference who favour moves to disengage from
Nato (see section below) and that the current 'official' policy has rather little support.

Disengagement from Nato. The left of the party emphasizes minimal participation in Nato, conditional participation in Nato, and non-alignment (the policy of
CND). Conditional membership means membership conditional on Nato becoming non-nuclear which, given the
objections of other states and the impossibility of
Britain alone determining alliance strategy, in practice this means withdrawal and non-alignment.
     Conference has come close to advocating disen-
gagement. In 1983 it approved a resolution which went
further than the 1982 unilateralist motion in opposing
all foreign military bases and membership of an alliance dominated by the Pentagon and committed to
possible first use of nuclear weapons. This emphasis
on conditional membership, for this in effect is the
meaning of the motion, will make it difficult for
Kinnock to defuse the defence issue within the party
and at the same time to steer the party policy in the
eyes of the public back towards a more centrist position.

ALTERNATIVE NON-NUCLEAR DEFENCE (35)

The peace movement has naturally concentrated on disarmament and in particular on opposing the twin-track
decision. During the same period there has been a
growth of criticism of Nato strategy from a broad

spectrum of opinion, running from those who stand quite
close to the peace movement at one end to those at the
other who fear the lack of political and military
credibility in current strategy. (29) What is common
among all these critics is opposition to the emphasis
on early use of nuclear weapons by Nato. Barnaby and
Boeker have proposed defensive deterrents based on
high technology and Booth has proposed 'heavy' conventional forward defence in Germany (requiring conscription to increase the British contribution). (30)
The fullest statement of an alternative strategy is
the report of the Alternative Defence Commission which
included a strong Labour party membership including
two leading members (Mary Kaldor and Dan Smith) of the
Labour party report Sense about Defence.(31) The report was written by unilateralists supporting CND,
although the convener of the group stands in an unus-
ual position of being a pacifist advocating non-violent
civil disobedience as the only acceptable form of
defence policy. CND has never endorsed the report but
it nevertheless comes closest to a statement of the
defence policy of the peace movement even though in
advocating conditional membership of Nato it does not
follow CND policy. On the other hand its emphasis
throughout on problems of national defence, with rather
little to say about co-operation with the European
peace movement, places it firmly in the tradition of
British unilateralism.

Although the report states very clearly and convincingly the case for Nato membership from an orthodox perspective (making a strong argument about a
potential Soviet threat), the report nevertheless
concluded in favour of membership of Nato conditional
on Nato adopting a non-nuclear strategy. This en-
tailed:

- a policy of no first use of nuclear weapons (to
  be achieved in one year);
- withdrawal of battlefield nuclear weapons;
- withdrawal of long-range theatre nuclear
  weapons (both to be achieved in three to four
  years);
- decoupling from the American strategic nuclear
  deterrent.

The last aspect of 'denuclearization' is the most
difficult and the one that the Labour Party had failed
to resolve. Some members of the commission argued that
complete decoupling was logically inconsistent with
American membership of Nato and they therefore favoured British withdrawal. The majority who rejected this

view must presumably accept that decoupling cannot be
absolutely guaranteed, given that the Americans would
presumably retain under this rather implausible scenario well over a quarter of a million 'non-nuclear'
troops in Europe.

The military strategy favoured by the commission,
and discussed in considerable detail, was one of conventional forces constituting a strong defensive deterrent power, preferably deployed so as to offer forward defence to save Germany from the fighting in a
conventional war, and extracting a 'high entry price'
from any Soviet aggression. The commission favoured
a defensive war-fighting strategy that would, so far
as possible, avoid taking the war into Eastern Europe.
Such a strategy might separate the Soviet Union from
its doubtful allies in Eastern Europe. Taking the war
into Eastern Europe would reinforce Warsaw Pact solidarity, the absence of which the report argued, constituted in itself a deterrent to the Soviet Union. Nato
would thus have to fight without forward attacks on the
enemy's bases and advancing columns, using short-range
defensive weapons including anti-tank weapons and air
defence fighters but eschewing long-range bombers and
all but a limited number of tanks for tactical battlefield advance or recovery of lost ground. The commission was attracted by the potential advantages for the
defence offered by precision guided munitions though,
unlike the Labour Party, was guided by a cautious
realism about their practical consequences.

The report examined in detail a number of different deployments to pursue such a strategy but was
obviously worried about the very large numbers of
forces required to sustain a forward defence of Germany. It concluded by abandoning forward defence in
favour of in-depth dispersed territorial defence of
Germany requiring mobilization of greater numbers of
German reservists and, at least in the short-term, a
limited increase in the size of British ground forces
in Germany.

The commission was attracted to a general policy
of territorial defence in depth employing large numbers of volunteers or conscripts but recognized the
difficulties confronting isolated and demoralized
troups, the unfavourable terrain and the risk of re-
prisals against civilians. The commission likewise
rejected the idea of partisan or guerrilla warfare as
extensions of territorial defence and, for similar
reasons, defence by the threat to adopt non-violent
civilian disobedience.

These proposals, interesting though they are and
despite the interest shown by one or two smaller Nato

governments in unconventional defence, are unlikely to
be approved by Nato. The report concedes this and
discusses in some detail a strategy for British defence outside Nato. Here it favours a strategy based
on high technology to exact a high entry price from
any external attack, the Swedish rather than the Swiss
or Yugoslav model. There would be strong coastal and
air defence with a residual territorial defence and
civil defence. British forces would be larger than at
present though professional forces would be smaller
and concentrated in the Navy and Air Force with the
Army providing mobile forces to supplement territorial
defence provided by an expanded territorial army and
home guard. Such a policy would be expensive. The
report noted that Sweden is gradually abandoning high
technology frontier defence for cheaper territorial
defence. The estimates for costs given suggest the
possibility of economies but the main thrust of the
report is not to cut costs but to provide for credible
defence without nuclear weapons.

The report considers whether conscription is
necessary to give the manpower required for its policies both within and without Nato. It rejects the
idea, although the concluding remarks (p. 272) are
rather ambivalent.

A number of problems emerge from the report which
are worth considering because they are probably im-
plicit in any alternative strategies that the Labour
Party in office might adopt. The first is that defence is conceived very narrowly to preserve merely
the territorial sovereignty of the state against external attack. Such a policy, relying entirely on
defensive denial power, would be useless against any
sort of pressure that fell short of actual invasion.
Moreover it might be argued that such a policy actually encouraged pressure short of invasion. For Britain
outside of Nato the report must assume either a rosy
view of a stable world or of Britain enjoying the
benefits of collective defence without incurring the
costs - this is the free rider argument which, the
report itself admits, could be applied to Swedish
neutrality.

The second problem is that although the report
repeatedly concedes the situation of Germany as the
most exposed front-line state, it nevertheless recom-
mends a policy of dispersed defence which is considerably more attractive to a state in the second-line,
such as Britain, than it is to Germany. Moreover,
although the report warns of the dangers posed by a
strong German-American axis following British withdrawal from Nato, the report's recommendations would

be bound to increase the attraction to Germany of rearmament plus an enhanced alliance with the United
States.
        The third point is that the argument for defen-
sive deterrence is attractive and the dangers of reliance on battlefield nuclear weapons now widely
accepted (even if one ignores the fact that most of
these weapons would explode on West Germany and thus
their use is to a large extent 'self-deterring'). On
the other hand, the threat of first-use both complicates Soviet force planning and complicates enormously
calculations about risk. But a purely defensive
strategy risks defeat by gradual attrition. Perhaps
more serious is the threat of Soviet nuclear blackmail
to coerce Nato into surrender. The report repeatedly
turns to this problem, acknowledging its force, and
failing to give a thoroughly satisfactory answer. It
argues that a policy of partisan or dispersed defense
reduces the risk of blackmail - in Clausewitzian terms
this might be regarded as shifting the centre of grav-
ity of the defence away from the armed forces or the
capital city. However, the report does not pursue a
policy of partisan warfare and only a partial form of
dispersed defence. In any case, against the threat of
nuclear blackmail the centre of defence is surely likely to be the general sanctity of civilians, and thus
the report is unconvincing here. The report concludes
that there may be no defence against a state determined to engage in nuclear threats but argues that the
possibility of employing nuclear blackmail as a threat
may have been overstated - an argument developed at
length elsewhere by one of the members of the commission. (32) Nevertheless, the report's conclusions on
nuclear blackmail remain a weakness given that in a
conventional war in Europe nuclear blackmail is possible and a nuclear retaliatory capability <u>might</u> deter
it.
        The fourth problem in the report concerns British
(and indirectly other Nato) reserve forces. If conscription is rejected, then the report's proposals
demand much larger reserve forces both at high levels
of training (equivalent to the Territorial Army) and
much lower levels for purely local duties (equivalent
to the government's 1981 home guard). But since 1957
the nation has relied on increasingly small professional forces (now about 330,000) and it is difficult
to imagine a consensus for reversing the present policy. 1940 is the only precedent for the sort of forces favoured by the report. It is particularly difficult to imagine support from the Left for such a
policy which would surely be damned as involving a

'militarization' of society. On the other hand, the
case for large reserve forces is probably greater for
Britain within Nato than without because a non-aligned
Britain would depend primarily on highly skilled professionals at the frontier and the role of the citizen
soldier would be limited.
     The fifth problem is cost. The report does not
regard cost as the overriding factor but still hopes
to reduce costs. Sweden, on which much of the argument is based, only spends 3.4 per cent of GNP on
defence, to be offset against much greater wealth per
capita but a more difficult terrain to defend than
Britain (close to the Soviet Union and a large land
area in terms of population). Certainly the report's
case holds out only qualified hope for those who
favour massive cuts in defence expenditure, and would
not be acceptable to those in CND who oppose any conventional rearmament to replace nuclear weapons.

PUBLIC OPINION

A large number of polls reveal considerable consis-
tency of opinion towards cruise deployment, American
bases and British nuclear weapons. A possible paradox
emerges in the sense that opinion is sympathetic to
some of the specific goals of the peace movement yet
hostile to the movement's broader self-proclaimed goal
of unilateral nuclear disarmament. Polls also suggest
that the peace movement is seen as hostile to defence
per se and that unilateralism is interpreted to refer
to general unilateralism rather than specifically
nuclear unilateralism.
     Opinion has been consistently hostile to cruise
with no majority ever found in favour of deployment.
Hostility is increased by reference in questions to
sole American control and has also increased after
Anglo-American friction, for instance over Grenada.
A series of polls in the Guardian has asked the same
question: do you approve or disapprove of the Government's decision to allow the Americans to base cruise
missiles on British soil? (See Table 4.3.) Asking a
slightly different question, loaded in its favour, CND
found 58 per cent opposition to cruise in October
1982.
     Women have been consistently more hostile than
men, support for cruise falling to a low of only 15
per cent in January 1983 and recovering to 28 per cent
by March 1984. In this sense there seems to have been
a Greenham 'effect' on women, and the fall of support
for cruise after the initial near equilibrium of opin-

Table 4.3: Guardian Opinion Poll

	April 1981	January 1983	May 1983	October 1983	March 1984
Approve	41	27	34	37	34
Disapprove	50	61	54	48	51
Don't know	9	12	12	15	15

ion might also be attributed to the peace movement.
The Sunday Times in January 1983, round about the time
when opinion seems to have been most sympathetic to
the peace movement, found not only a similar large gap
between men and women but also that 94 per cent of
respondents had heard of the Greenham protests. However, only 32 per cent of women admitted to becoming
more sympathetic to the campaign against cruise as a
result of Greenham, with 50 per cent unaffected.
Nevertheless it seems reasonable to conclude that, at
that stage, Greenham had greatly assisted the peace
movement's impact on the general public. The Sunday
Times found that of the 36 per cent of its sample who
approved cruise (9 per cent more than in the Guardian's
sample) 93 per cent favoured dual key control.
      Opposition to cruise is consistently greater from
the young, although not massively so, usually about
six or seven points. In terms of party affiliation,
at the high point of opposition in January 1983, the
Guardian found that Conservative supporters were even-
ly divided and Labour and Alliance supporters very
hostile (with only 14 per cent and 21 per cent respectively supporting cruise). By October 1983, following
the government's massive propaganda campaign launched
in January and the general election which also helped
to divide opinion on a party basis, Conservative supporters were 55 per cent to 29 per cent in favour of
cruise. Labour and Alliance supporters remained hostile at only 21 per cent and 36 per cent in favour.
The government's campaign was thus partially effective
in helping to consolidate support among Conservatives
who had shown marked lack of enthusiasm for this aspect of their government's policy.
      Opinion on Nato membership and existing American
bases, nuclear and other, is less sympathetic to the
peace movement. In February 1982 CND found strong
support for Nato membership, 69 to 18 per cent, but
among those favouring membership hostility to nuclear
bases, 49 to 43 per cent hostile. In January 1983 the
Sunday Times found opposition to closing all American
bases at about 2:1 (exact figure not given) with Labour supporters opposing closure by 47 to 45 per cent.
At the same time there was considerable distrust of the
Americans and a tendency to lump the Americans and the
Soviets into the same basket. Only 16 per cent trusted the Americans and 5 per cent the Soviets. Only 9
per cent considered the Americans possessed sound
judgement and 3 per cent the Soviets. In May 1983 the
Sunday Observer found opposition to cruise, by 55 to
32 per cent, in line with other polls, but equally
opposition to closing all existing American bases, by

55 to 36 per cent. In October 1983 the _Guardian_ found
strong support for continued Nato membership, by 73 to
8 per cent, but that 37 per cent considered Britain
followed American policy too closely, 65 per cent considered America and the Soviets equally to blame for
the arms race and 39 per cent considered America and
the Soviets to be equal threats to world peace. On
each of these issues, Conservative supporters were
less hostile to the United States, though not markedly
so; while women were, in contrast to men, markedly less
anti-American, more anti-Soviet and less fearful of
imminent nuclear war. These findings on women are
difficult to reconcile with their greater oppositon to
cruise.
     Consistent opposition to cruise and consistent
support for Nato and existing American nuclear bases
(which have not of course been subject to the same
intensive discussion by the media) appears consistent
with a good deal of specialist defence opinion in
Britain. On the whole the strategic studies professionals are pro-Nato but markedly cool towards the
logic behind the twin-track decision.
     Public opinion towards British nuclear weapons is
probably more difficult to measure because the word
'unilateral' tends to provoke a hostile response.
However it is clear that opinion distinguishes between
the existing nuclear capability, which is normally
taken to refer simply to Polaris, and expenditure on
Trident to acquire a greater future capability. In
February 1982 CND found opposition both to Polaris,
53 to 34 per cent, and to Trident, 63 to 23 per cent.
Most polls however have found support for Polaris, including CND itself in October 1982, at 51 per cent.
In September 1982 the _Guardian_ found 51 per cent
favoured maintenance of Britain's nuclear capability,
31 per cent abandonment and 15 per cent improvement.
By October 1983 63 per cent favoured maintenance and
only 16 per cent abandonment, including only 28 per
cent of Labour supporters. By November 1983, asking a
slightly different question, Labour support for abandonment had risen to 45 per cent. The _Sunday Times_ in
October found 23 per cent support for unilateral disarmament and 72 per cent opposition, though rephrasing
the problem to ask about the British nuclear deterrent
produced a higher figure of opposition, 34 per cent,
and less support, 59 per cent. Labour voters were
hostile to unilateral disarmament by 58 to 37 per cent.
The _Sunday Observer_ in May 1983 found support for
Britain retaining independent nuclear weapons, at 74
to 20 per cent, including clear support from Labour
voters, 62 to 30 per cent.

96

The Development of the Peace Movement in Britain

Support for abandonment of British nuclear weapons thus seems confined to a minority, and the figures could be interpreted to indicate some success for the government propaganda drive in 1983. Unilateralism is thus unpopular and in fact less popular than in the early 1960s when for a while it commanded majority support. However, while opinion may reasonably be interpreted as hostile to unilateral renunciation of existing capability, it is also hostile to Trident. In April 1981 the Guardian found opinion on Trident 32 per cent favourable, 53 per cent hostile, 13 per cent undecided. By January, 1983 support had fallen to 25 per cent and opposition increased to 56 per cent with little support from women, Labour and Alliance supporters and with Conservative supporters barely in favour, by 40 to 38 per cent. The government's propaganda campaign was ineffective on Trident; by October 1983 opinion was still only 26 per cent in favour and 50 per cent against while undecideds had increased from 19 to 24 per cent. Compared with cruise, the undecideds have consistently been higher, particularly among women who in October 1983 were 17 per cent favourable, 50 per cent hostile and 33 per cent undecided.

On the general question of defence expenditure, the Sunday Observer in May, 1983 found that 69 per cent considered it 'dangerous' to cut spending (55 per cent of Labour supporters) and in September 1983 the Guardian found that 46 per cent favoured spending the same amount, 30 per cent favoured spending more. Amongst Labour supporters only 32 per cent wanted to spend less. Only one poll has attempted to distinguish between spending on nuclear and conventional weapons. The Sunday Times in January 1983 found a clear distinction.

Table 4.4:   Sunday Times Opinion Poll

	Nuclear expenditure	Conventional expenditure
Current spending is:		
Too high	51	17
About right	29	39.5
Too Low	5	30
Don't know	20	13.5

There is clearly much more support for conventional than nuclear weapons. If these figures were correlated with party affiliation then the largest single pairing of the two sets of expenditure among Conservatives was that nuclear and conventional were about right. With Labour voters the largest single pairing was nuclear too high and conventional about right. (33)

These figures as a whole reflect CND's partial success in mobilizing opinion against cruise and Trident, but an almost complete failure in gaining support for unilateral abandonment of British weapons and for removal of American bases. Opinion reflects, perhaps naturally, support for the status quo and opposition to increased armaments. There is a 'Gaullist' effect in the sense that there is more support for British national weapons and some concern about American deployments, with very strong support for dual key control of cruise. By 1983 many Conservative MPs were expressing concern for dual key. The SDP leader David Owen favoured dual key which would almost certainly be the minimum condition for support for cruise from Atlanticists in the Labour Party such as Healey.

The Press

The peace movement has not been supported by the British press which is in its editorial policy unsympathetic to the Labour Party. In terms of extensive news coverage, features and letters the Guardian most fully reflects the peace movement's activities. Its editorial policy is anti-Trident, though not anti-Polaris, and it is pro-Nato. However, its line on cruise has been ambiguous, though certainly not enthusiastically in favour, and it has given some support to ideas for restructuring Nato so as to give a stronger European role to balance the American influence. If cruise is necessary, and it now reluctantly concedes that inevitability, then it favours dual key. The rest of the quality press is hostile both to the broader aims of the peace movement and to its specific immediate objectives (Financial Times, The Times, Daily Telegraph, Sunday Times). The Sunday Observer shares some of the Guardian's views on defence but is more strongly pro-Nato and opposed to British nuclear weapons as detracting from Britain's faith in the alliance.

The popular press is hostile to the peace movement though there is a persistent current of anti-Americanism in British life to be tapped. The editorial line of the popular press, for what it is worth, has been especially hostile towards the Greenham Common women.

CONCLUSION

Four major problems now confront the peace movement and its ability to overcome these will determine in large part whether its remarkable growth over the past five years leads to success. The first is the problem of securing a stronger base in the unions and the working-class to parallel its remarkable integration with middle-class values. CND is a middle-class organization but as it itself notes, its chief political support has to come from the working-class because of the class alignment of voting behaviour in Britain. A similar problem of course confronts the Labour Party which is in danger of becoming an army of middle-class generals without any working-class infantry. The second problem concerns its relationship with the Labour Party which offers the only realistic hope of seeing some of its goals secured. Labour's election defeat, following on the split with the SDP, actually consolidated CND support in the parliamentary party. Before the election CND claimed the support of 122 Labour MPs, after the election it claimed 99 out of the smaller total of 209. On the other hand, Neil Kinnock is attempting to reconsolidate the defence programme of the party around a platform of no cruise and no Trident together with continued American conventional bases and conventional rearmament to raise the nuclear threshold. CND thus can at best hope for only part of its programme to be fulfilled even with a Labour government, and at the October, 1983 rally Kinnock fudged even the issue of unconditional renunciation of Polaris. On the other hand of course, the Polaris issue will decline in salience as the submarines near retirement within a decade or so. One of CND's difficulties is that while it can generate general support for the goal of disarmament it depends on the Labour party to put a detailed programme into operation.

The third problem confronting CND is that its programme of unconditional disarmament by Britain is, quite simply, still very unpopular with the public. In the 1983 election the Conservatives enjoyed, according to one poll, a 54 per cent lead over the Labour on defence, the highest ever recorded. On the other hand, only 7 per cent regarded defence as the most important issue in the election. Nevertheless, defence and disarmament hindered rather than helped Labour in 1983. (34) The government's campaign against CND, and appointment of Michael Heseltine to rally support for its defence programme, can be interpreted as revealing the success of CND but one can equally argue that the government overreacted to the situation.

The fourth problem is the strategy to be pursued by the peace movement in Britain in the light of its failure in the 1983 election and the government's successful initiation of the cruise and Trident pro- grammes. CND now faces the same dilemma that con- fronted it in the early 1960s. Should it continue with mass demonstrations and propaganda or should it initiate direct action and civil disobedience and so cross the uncertain line between legal and illegal activity? The 1982 conference went some way towards endorsing direct action, but so far in a cautious and limited way essentially confined to support for the peace camps. The decision of the national council to organise neither an Easter demonstration in 1984 nor a demonstration during the Western summit in June (though one was eventually organised) dismayed some radi- cals within CND. A group calling itself Action 84' decid- ed to organise some direct action protest during the June summit. The potential for division thus exists and CND undoubtedly runs the risk of losing both the support of activists and the existing level of public support that it enjoys if it goes down the road of civil dis- obedience.

NOTES

(1) For pacifist opinion see the journal <u>Peace News</u>.

(2) <u>Sanity</u>, November 1983.

(3) <u>CND National Membership Survey 1983</u>, <u>END Supporters Survey Report 1982</u>, <u>Together We Can Stop the Bomb: London Demo 6th June 1982</u>. I am grateful to Peter Nias for his assistance. The 1982 survey of members' backgrounds was confirmed in a further, less detailed, report undertaken in 1983.

(4) Frank Parkin, <u>Middle Class Radicalism</u> (Man- chester, 1968).

(5) Ibid., p. 34 <u>et seq</u>.

(6) Ibid., pp. 176-85.

(7) Lord Carver, <u>A Policy for Peace</u> (London, 1982).

(8) The declaration is published in Dan Smith and E. P. Thompson, <u>Protest and Survive</u> (London, 1980).

(9) See his essay 'Notes on Exterminism, the Last Stage of Civilization' in <u>Zero Option</u> (London, 1982).

(10) See Mary Kaldor and Dan Smith (eds), <u>Disarming Europe</u> (London, 1982).

(11) See in particular the articles on the civil liberties of nuclear power published regularly in <u>New Statesman</u> by Duncan Campbell and, on American bases,

his <u>Battleship Britain</u> (London, 1984).

(12) <u>The British Nuclear Deterrent</u>, British Council of Churches (London, 1963).

(13) The Bishop of Salisbury (Chairman), <u>The Church
and the Bomb</u> (London, 1982).

(14) See the reports in the <u>Guardian</u> and <u>The Times</u>
of 11 February 1983.

(15) On industrial conversion see Mary Kaldor,
'Disarmament: the Armaments Process in Reverse' in Smith
and Thompson, <u>Protest and Survive</u>. On Lucas see Hilary
Wainwright and Dave Elliot, <u>The Lucas Plan</u> (London,
1982). For CND's view see Tim Webb, <u>Arms Drain: Job
Risk and Industrial Decline</u> (London (CND), 1982).

(16) House of Commons Committee of Public Accounts,
<u>Chevaline Improvement to Polaris Missile System</u>, House
of Commons paper 269, 1981-2.

(17) <u>Report of the Labour Party Conference</u> (1972
and 1973) and <u>Let us Work Together: Labour's Way out
of the Crisis</u>, p. 14.

(18) See, for instance, the <u>Statement on the Defence Estimates 1975</u>, Cmnd 5975, HMSO, London.

(19) <u>The Times</u>, 4 December 1979. A civil servant
working on defence planning has confirmed to me the
accuracy of the report by Peter Hennessy.

(20) 'In 1974, we renounced any intention of moving
towards the production of a new generation of nuclear
weapons or a successor to the Polaris nuclear force;
we reiterate our belief that this is the best course
for Britain. But many great issues affecting our
allies and the world are involved, and a new round of
strategic arms limitation negotiations will soon begin. We think it is essential that there must be full
and informed debate about these decisions in the
country before any decision is taken.' <u>The Labour Way
is the Better Way</u>, published in <u>Labour Weekly</u>, 20 April
1979, p. 21.

(21) <u>Statement on the Defence Estimates 1976</u>, Cmnd.
6432, HMSO, London.

(22) <u>Statement on the Defence Estimates 1979</u>, HMSO,
London.

(23) <u>Sense about Defence: the Report of the Labour
Party Defence Study Group</u>, London, 1977.

(24) Memorandum by John Gilbert, John Tomlinson
and James Wellbeloved (later an SDP defector) published in Mary Kaldor <u>et al</u>., <u>The Report and Papers of
the Labour Party Defence Study Group: Democratic Socialism and the Cost of Defence</u>, London, 1980.

(25) <u>The New Hope for Britain: Labour's Manifesto
1983</u>, p. 36.

(26) Fourth Report from the Defence Committee
1980-1, House of Commons paper 36, 1980-1.

(27)   See the speeches by George and Gilbert in the debate on the 1983 defence estimates, criticizing Labour's defence policy in the election manifesto: Hansard 6, vol. 40, columns 430 and 448, 20 July 1983.
(28)   The Sunday Observer, 23 October 1983.
(29)   Among many criticisms of current strategy from a fairly orthodox background, and confining the list to Britain, one would note: Lord Carver, A Policy for Peace, which opposes British nuclear weapons and argues for greater conventional strength for Nato deployed under the American nuclear guarantee.   Elmar Dinter and Paddy Griffiths, Not Over By Christmas (London, 1983), which argues for increased conventional strength to maintain a forward defence for Germany without recourse to battlefield nuclear weapons; Lord Cameron (chairman), Diminishing the Nuclear Threat: Nato's Defence and the New Technology (London, 1984), a report of a British Atlantic Committee working group of military and bureaucratic establishment figures which argues in favour of employing the new technology to strengthen the power of the defence over the offence and thus to raise the nuclear threshold, though without renouncing the possibility of first use of nuclear weapons; European Security Study; Strengthening Conventional Deterrence in Europe: Proposals for the 1980s (New York, 1983), which takes a roughly similar line to the report by the British Atlantic Committee group; Gerald Segal et al., Nuclear War and Nuclear Peace (London, 1983), reflects the view of academics close to the SDP.
     From a left-wing and peace movement perspective there has been an enormous flood of literature. Most of it calls for disarmament and does not directly address the question of alternative security policy. However there are discussions in Gwyn Prins (ed.), Defended to Death (London, 1983), Chapter 18; Kaldor and Smith, Disarming Europe.
(30) Frank Barnaby and Egbert Boeker 'Non-Provocative, Non-Nuclear Defence of Western Europe', Armament and Disarmament Information Unit Report, vol. 5 (1), 1983; Ken Booth, 'Unilateralism: A Clausewitzian Reform?' in Nigel Blake and Kay Pole (eds), Dangers of Deterrence: Philosophers on Nuclear Strategy (London, 1983); John Baylis (ed.): Alternative Approaches to British Defence Policy (London, 1984),
(31)   Alternative Defence Commission, Defence without the Bomb (London, 1983).
(32)   Jeff McMahan, 'Nuclear Blackmail' in Blake and Pole, Dangers of Deterrence.
(33)   See the Marplan polls published in the Guardian on 23 September 1982, 24 January, 22 October

22 November 1983 and 29 March 1984; the Harris poll in the Sunday Observer on 22 May 1983 and the MORI poll in the Sunday Times of 23 January 1983. CND commissioned an ORC poll, Sanity, February 1982 and a Gallup poll, Sanity, December 1982.

(34) Bruce George and Curt Pawlisch, 'Defence and the British Election', Armament and Disarmament Information Unit Report, vol. 5 (4), 1983 and Ivor Crewe's analysis of the election result in the Guardian, 14 June 1983.

(35) After the 1983 conference, and at Kinnock's initiative, the party attempted to work out a compromise policy on defence which would be internally broadly acceptable and at the same time be publicly more acceptable and less ambiguous. The result was Defence and Security for Britain, approved by party conference in 1984. The report reemphasised a non-nuclear defence strategy, including closure of all American nuclear bases in Britain and immediate decommissioning of Polaris. At the same time, much stronger sympathy was displayed towards NATO. Two important recommendations exemplifying this attempt to reconcile Labour's Atlanticists were explicit support for American conventional military bases in Britain and support for British forces assigned to NATO, including additional reserve forces for the British army in Germany if these were needed to enable credible defensive deterrents to be established.

Chapter Five

THE WEST GERMAN PEACE MOVEMENT: A PROFILE

Hartmut Grewe

INTRODUCTION

The contemporary peace movement in the Federal Republic of Germany is in the main a reaction by individuals
and groups, backed by some popular appeal, especially
among the well-educated young, against the NATO double-
track decision of December 1979 to deploy new medium-
range nuclear missiles in Western Europe as a response
to the growing Soviet SS-20 threat, unless the Soviet
Union agrees to a negotiated reduction of its nuclear
weapons in Europe. The protest against this NATO policy is directed less at the Soviet Union and its military threat than against the foreign and defence policy of the Reagan Administration and the qualified
support given to it by the Federal Government in Bonn.
This is because popular protest is likely to have more
influence on official policy in open democratic societies than in closed totalitarian states.
    The foreign and security policies of the Federal
Government, as of other Western democratic states, are
aimed at maximizing what is called the 'national interest' and are generally shaped by two forces:

1. external constraints emanating from the NATO
alliance and its regard for vital interests of the
United States as its bulwark;
2. internal constraints arising from the political
situation at home, which dictate that special consideration be given to influential interest groups and
lobbies, so enhancing the government's sensitivity to
public opinion for electoral reasons.

PEACE MOVEMENT MEMBERSHIP

The West German peace movement is a very heterogeneous

movement composed of church and secular groups led by
a handful of individuals who have become well-known
during its development and who serve as rallying points
for a mass following of predominantly youthful sympathizers.
   These individuals come from vastly different
circles: established political parties, specifically
the SPD (Eppler, LaFontaine); trade unions (Benz of
IG Metall); the Protestant and Catholic Churches
(Albertz, Niemöller); the military and defence establishment (Bastian, Mechtersheimer); and last but not
least, the ecologists (Leinen) and the new political
formation of the 'Greens' (Kelly). (1)
   Sympathizers include well-known academics and
journalists and writers with a pronounced political
orientation (Böll, Grass, Jens), dissenters from East
Germany (Bahro), as well as actors, singers and dir-
ectors (Schygulla, Heller, Zadek).
   The established political organizations, such as
the main political parties and the trade unions, hardly
play an institutional role in the peace movement. Instead, the movement is carried from within these by
growing minorities of rank-and-file members. This is
also true for the churches. Although the peace movement claims to represent a broad spectrum of all societal and political sectors in the Federal Republic,
it undoubtedly mainly represents the young, students,
the ecological protest movement, communists and church
activists: in sum, the politically motivated, more
articulate, and left-leaning citizens. (2)

ORIGINS AND HISTORY OF THE GERMAN PEACE MOVEMENT

There has always been in the Federal Republic's young
history a peace movement of sorts which was opposed to
governmental policies in the foreign and security
field. Rearmament became a hotly contested issue in
the 1950s when church groups, pacifists and communists,
as well as trade unions and the SPD opposed the re-
establishment of German armed forces and warned against
the country's integration into the NATO-alliance. In
the late 1950s, their protest turned against NATO-
plans to place American nuclear weapons on German
soil. None the less these were accepted by a majority
vote of the West German parliament, and an SPD-in-
itiated referendum drive on this issue was declared
unconstitutional by West Germany's Federal Court.
   British-style Easter marchers turned up in size-
able numbers during the 1960s to protest against nuclear armament and the practice of deterrence, advo-

cating unilateral disarmament as a first step towards
world peace. Because of widespread allegations that
these protest marches were led by communists, the
German trade unions and the SPD this time refrained
from active participation. The protest movement
swelled its ranks when, in the course of anti-Vietnam
demonstrations in the late 1960s, groups of students
joined and created a more or less permanent extra-
parliamentary opposition to themes transcending the
security realm: anti-capitalism, anti-imperialism and
democratization became issues of ideological conflict.
    More concrete concerns - such as the siting of
nuclear power plants, water and air pollution, and
demands for co-determination - were taken up during
the 1970s by groups of students, intellectuals and
ordinary citizens who initiated drives to stop or re-
vise diverse construction plans and to force political
leaders to reconsider the use of nuclear power and to
take seriously the protection of the natural environment. These ecology-oriented, anti-nuclear lobbies,
together with traditional anti-war groups, became the
forerunners of today's peace movement. They were
joined by groups of the young, feminists, and protagonists of an alternative life style who sympathized
with their cause, to form a rather mixed reservoir of
protest against Western civilization and its dominant
traits and values. They abhorred any form of capital-
istic enterprise, materialistic outlooks and techno-
cratic bias. They came to challenge the traditional
view on economy and security with a gut anti-establishment feeling and a post-materialistic touch of
subjectiveness. Perhaps the peace movement of the
1980s classifies as a counter-cultural phenomenon, as
some observers are inclined to believe. (3)

THE ORGANIZATIONAL STRUCTURE OF THE GERMAN PEACE
MOVEMENT

Decentralized organization is a trademark of the peace
movement in the Federal Republic. Thousands of local
groups attempt to discuss political strategies and to
co-ordinate their activities at regional conferences
for the sole purpose of preventing the installation of
new American nuclear missiles in Western Europe. Since
these conferences are practically open to anyone walk-
ing in from the street without regard to group affiliation or representation, they are usually dominated
by members of communist groups who turn out in dis-
proportionately large numbers and stay to be counted
when decisions are cast after long and heated debates.

The West German Peace Movement: A Profile

Grass-roots democracy has its price, after all.

Until a year ago there had been no central office or co-ordinating committee at the national level. It was only then founded by 26 different organizations in order to usher in the 'Hot Fall' of 1983: to plan and co-ordinate their numerous activities in the few re- maining months before the dreaded implementation of the armament-part of NATO's twin-track decision. The broad spectrum of groups represented in the committee prevents any camp from monopolizing decisions but it also impedes effective decision-making. To search for the least common denominator on the basis of often fragile compromise formulas charaterizes the work of the central co-ordinating committee at its bi-monthly meetings. Consequently a six-member steering commit- tee handles day-to-day decisions and public relations, for media coverage which may sway public opinion in its favour is vital for the peace movement's standing in domestic and international politics.

The peace movement is mainly an extra-parliamen- tary force which only after the Federal elections of March, 1983 obtained a parliamentary leg, the anti- establishment 'Green' party. The mass following stems largely from two sectors: the so-called 'alternative scene' or the 'New Left', and from within the churches, although important elements also come from the tradi- tional Left with the SPD and the trade unions, espec- ially its youth organizations. Last but not least, it includes followers of the small but active Communist Party (DKP) and its numerous 'front (or 'label') or- ganizations'. (4) This latter fact has given rise to the well-publicized allegation of communist infiltra- tion of the West German peace movement.

PUBLIC SUPPORT FOR THE GERMAN PEACE MOVEMENT

The development of a social movement, as evidenced in the mass rallies of the peace movement is not only determined by its active potential (some 10 per cent) and the passive support it receives (between 40 and 50 per cent), but also by the degree to which it is rejected by the public or met with indifference or acquiescence. (5) It is, however, to the groups of activists and sympathizers that we turn for a closer look.

Every second respondent of a youth survey conduc- ted by Infas in North-Rhine Westphalia during the last months of 1981 - still in the early stages of peace activities - affirmed the following statement: 'I think that the worries for peace of the peace movement

are justified; I fully support its demands.' When
taking into account their party preferences, we find
that among sympathizers of the SPD one out of two,
among those of the CDU one out of three, among FDP-
sympathizers two out of five and among those of the
'Greens' and 'Alternatives' four out of five support
the movement, at least verbally. (6)

A Der Spiegal survey conducted in the autumn of
1981 produced similar results. However, while four out
of ten respondents sympathized with the peace movement
in general terms only one out of ten was prepared to
work actively for its cause. As to party preferences,
every third CDU/CSU-voter and every second voter of
the SPD and FDP sympathised with the peace movement,
while only tiny minorities were actively engaged in
its work. Activism increased dramatically within the
ranks of voters of the 'Greens' or 'Alternatives':
three out of four claimed to be actively involved in
the peace movement.

Even more discriminating variables are age and
education. Every second youth in the 18 to 29 age-
bracket sympathized with the peace movement (which is
in line with the normal distribution of attitudes in
the German population), but one out of four in this
group declared to be actively involved in the peace
movement (one out of 10 or 20 in the over-30 generation). Age compounded with education increased the
likelihood (for example, for a person aged under 35
with a higher-level education) of belonging to a group
of peace-activists to a startling 41 per cent. (7) In
other words, nearly every second person with high-
school or college education thought of himself or her-
self as being active in the peace movement.

These figures square with survey data gathered
during the autumn of 1983 - the peak time of peace
activities in the Federal Republic of Germany. When
a representative sample of 2,000 citizens over 18 were
asked to clarify their attitudes towards the peace
movement 14 per cent responded that they were fully
supportive of its demands, 50 per cent declared their
general sympathy, 27 per cent expressed grave concerns
as to its actions and a mere 8 per cent opposed the
movement in fundamental terms. (8) Again age and education discriminate: in the age bracket between 18
and 29 years three out of four responded that they
either actively supported or at least sympathized with
the peace movement, as did two out of three respondents with high-school and/or college education. People
older than 45 years were much more reserved and scep-
tical.

Looking at party preferences, we find that every

second voter of the 'Greens' fully supports the peace
movement, while the other half almost without exception can be counted as sympathetic to its cause, SPD-
voters are overwhelmingly in favour of the peace movement but their support is less pronouced than that of
the 'Greens' electorate. Noteworthy is that partisans
of the ruling coalition partners take a very reserved
position vis-a-vis the peace movement: this is true
for every third FDP-voter and every second CDU/CSU-
voter.

When asked whether they would join the peace movement and participate in its actions, 3 per cent said
that they already were activists and 10 per cent said
that they had the intention to do so. However, 85 per
cent declared that they would not consider such a
move. (9) Providing we accept these survey results
as representative for the 45 million West-German citizens over the age of 18, with every percentage point
counting for 450,000 people, we get an idea of what
these percentage figures mean in terms of real numbers
of peace demonstrators: some 1.5 million activists
presently, plus a potential of 4.5 million for eventual mobilization by the peace movement. These figures
do not seem unrealistic in light of estimates of turn-
out in mass rallies and of the number of people involved in numerous peace activities at the local level.

Again, the young and better educated are overrepresented in this pool of peace activists. Those
who are close to the Greens show by far the greatest
enthusiasm for the peace movement: either they are
already involved in its activities or are inclined to
become involved.

Turning to the focal point of the peace protest -
the NATO twin-track decision - a Der Spiegel survey
conducted in the autumn of 1981 found that there was
no real difference in the degree of support between
voters of the three established parties (ranging from
35 to 38 per cent) and only a slightly higher degree
of opposition within the then governing parties SPD
(22 per cent) and FDP (23 per cent) than within the
CDU/CSU (18 per cent). The Green electorate differed
greatly: a clear-cut majority of 6 per cent opposed
it, while only 17 per cent favoured the decision to
deploy American missiles in Western Europe prior to
disarmament negotiations with the Soviet Union. (10)

When the same question was repeated two years
later, Der Spiegel reported that its opinion poll
showed a different configuration. In the autumn of
1983 a relative majority of 34 per cent opposed NATO
policy, while only 28 per cent seconded it; 35 per cent
were either indifferent or had not yet made up their

minds. The great change occurred within the ranks of
the SPD voters whose majority shifted from a largely
supportive role to a predominantly negative one. The
political spectrum of the Greens remained staunchly
opposed to NATO's security policy, while voters of
CDU/CSU were still its most solid supporters among the
West German electorate. But even here the impact of
the peace movement's activities became evident: support decreased some 3 per cent and dissent picked up
another 6 per cent. (11)

The climate of public opinion during the 'Hot Fall
of 1983' was indeed raised, not only by mass rallies
and activities of the peace or 'anti-missile' movement, as it was often labelled, but because of its
veto stance. An important factor was also the con-
flicting results of numerous opinion polls which were
launched during this period by various institutions,
precisely, one must assume, for the purpose of influencing public opinion.

For instance, a ZDF-sponsored poll saw three-
quarters of the West German population in opposition
to NATO'S twin-track decision, when only the aspect
of missile installation in Western Europe was high-
lighted. Another poll published by Allensbach found
49 per cent in favour, 23 per cent in opposition and
28 per cent undecided, when the question posed mentioned both sides of the coin. Depending on what particular cues were given, responses to differently
worded questions - all touching upon the same subject-
matter - naturally differed, with sponsors having the
final say on what results to disclose and on what information to withhold. (12)

GOALS AND IDEOLOGY OF THE GERMAN PEACE MOVEMENT (13)

The peace movement is guided by a variety of motiv-
ations: moral indignation, pacifist tendencies, political principles and practical considerations. Activists, supporters and sympathizers take issue with
a whole gamut of political developments which they
selectively highlight:

- They despise the general arms race which they
  believe is fuelled by the NATO-deployment resolution and the massive Reagan-style armament
  programme as a dangerous and costly exercise
  of muscle-flexing by the superpowers.
- They believe that the projected Soviet military threat is a ploy by the Western propaganda
  and defence establishment in order to push

through their own parliaments new weapon systems to be installed in Europe.
- They fear that the NATO strategy of nuclear deterrence by 'flexible response' with recourse to advanced nuclear weapon systems is less likely to prevent wars than to facilitate nuclear warfare at the expense of the European peoples, especially the German people in East and West. The nuclear 'threshold' is believed to have been lowered by the availability of nuclear weapons with limited range and selective use.
- The absurdity of risking to destroy what is considered worth defending at any cost has created an unresolved crisis of identity with American interests and loss of credibility on the part of the American allies.
- Many feel that German national interests are better served by a policy of detente, East-West collaboration (even in the security realm), a softening of the alliance systems, and unilateral renunciation of nuclear arms. They distrust the Reagan Administration's policy of renewed military strength which might lead to a new era of global confrontation between the superpowers and risk eventual nuclear holocaust. Some even advocate the 'uncoupling' of Europe from America.
- They feel strengthened in their views and positions by an emerging American peace movement which under Edward Kennedy's leadership advocates the bilateral 'freezing' of nuclear armaments, in order to brake the 'insane' arms race between the superpowers and their respective allies.

Activists of the peace movement are seen to pursue ends:

1. They want to put an end to the constant arms race which they consider not only as a dangerous 'play with fire' but one which swallows huge sums of financial, human and material resources that could be utilized more productively to solve the problems of scarcity and development in Third World countries.
2. To this end they want to press on with armaments reduction of limitation talks between the superpowers and the two military alliance systems in order to reach negotiated and observable settlements.

111

3. They want to rid Europe of all nuclear weapons and outlaw their use ('atomwaffenfreie Zone') - if necessary, even by a unilateral declaration of intent.
4. They want to outlaw the transfer and export of military hardware to Third World countries.
5. They want to continue with a policy of detente in order to further East-West co-operation in all fields and better to serve German national interests.
6. They want to abolish the division of Europe by a purposive demantling of the Eastern and Western military alliance.
7. They want to create a lasting peace without the help of weapons by creating an interdependent system of security partnership.
8. They claim that their ultimate aim is to prevent the premature use of nuclear weapons by the Western allies in Central Europe simply by the force of military of technological constraints. They stress the desirability to upgrade conventional military forces, which is a costly but worthwhile exercise since it seeks to exclude the explicit use of nuclear weapons.
9. They want a more plausible alternative to the still valid security doctrine of deterrence by 'flexible response' which threatens the first use of nuclear weapons by the Western alliance (especially the US-Armed Forces) against a communist aggressor even when operating with conventional warfare.

TYPES OF ACTIVITIES OF THE GERMAN PEACE MOVEMENT

NATO's so-called twin-track decision of 12 December 1979 - initiated by (the then) Chancellor Schmidt's warnings of a dangerous 'missile gap' due to the Soviet SS-20 threat in Europe - called for the stationing of new American middle-range nuclear missiles in several West European countries after a four-year moratorium, in case the ongoing arms-reduction talks in Geneva between the United States and the Soviet Union should fail. It was the point of departure for the contemporary peace movement. A first step to demonstrate its opposition to that policy was taken in November, 1980 by the so-called Krefeld Appeal, a DFU-sponsored subscription campaign to pledge resistance against the stationing of American Pershing II and cruise missiles in Western Europe. The sponsors claim that by now some six million signatures have been gathered.

The West German Peace Movement: A Profile

    In June 1981 the 19th National Assembly of the
Protestant Church in Hamburg was the first site of a
mass rally for peace with some 50,000 to 80,000 participants. In September, 1981 the visit of General
Haig (then US Secretary of State) in West Berlin witnessed 50,000 protesters, some of whom clashed with
police forces. On 10 October 1981, the biggest peace
demonstration to date in the Federal Republic's history assembled some 300,000 people in the centre of
Bonn to call for a revision of NATO security policy
and to advocate a Europe without nuclear arms. Roughly
an equal number of demonstrators was mobilized several
months later on 10 June 1982, on the occasion of the
NATO summit conference in Bonn. Throngs of young
people marched in sunny weather through the city to
meet in a large park on the outskirts of the city to
listen to folk music and speeches by prominent peace
activists. The atmosphere resembled that of a Wood-
stock-type 'happening'. (14)
    Mass rallies of this scale did not recur, even
during the peak of 'Action Week' in October, 1983.
Instead numerous decentralised activities were planned
and co-ordinated at local and regional levels, such as
blockades of military installations and sit-ins on
railway tracks to stop munition convoys. Human chains
were formed to link or encircle symbolic sites such as
military bases, embassies or parliament and government
buildings. Information and propaganda stands were put
up in nearly every town square to coax people into
accepting the peace movement's arguments and to confirm their position by signing diverse political
appeals and proclamations which were to be used by peace
activists to put pressure on party and government
leaders.
    The activities of the peace movement reached a
peak during the so-called 'Action Week', between 15
and 22 October 1983. Organizers expected some three
million people to take part in about 100,000 separate
demonstrations, ranging in size from very small local
events to very large central rallies in Hamburg, West
Berlin, Stuttgart and Bonn. A spectacle of extraordinary dimension was undoubtedly the formation of a
human chain linking Stuttgart and Neu-Ulm - more than
60 miles apart - involving more than 150,000 people.
    Violent actions aimed at destroying or damaging
public property, such as cars and buildings, and
actions resulting in the injury or even death of pol-
icemen in action have already occurred during activities of the peace movement, for instance at the 1982
swearing-in ceremony for young draftees in Bremen, and
during Vice-President Bush's courtesy visit to Krefeld

during the summer of 1983. There is no guarantee that
peace demonstrators will always be peaceful, especially when groups of radicals, the so-called autonomous
peace groups, participate in mass rallies. Their
purposive actions may get out of control, despite great
care taken by organizers and other groups to prevent
the outbreak of violence.

Acts of civil disobedience, which are advocated
by the peace movement as a strategy to keep the movement alive after missile installation, often cross the
borderline between legality and breach as of the law.
Frequently, the courts are called upon by political
officials to arbitrate in disputed cases. Officials,
police forces and political leaders themselves have
had to cope with unaccustomed situations produced by
unconventional behaviour on the part of peace activists. They have had to learn when to be law-enforcing
hardliners and when to be flexible and pragmatic,
overlooking illegal actions on the part of protestors
in order to avoid large-scale confrontations. The
official side was as much in the limelight of national
and international news media as were the masses of
young protesters.

ACHIEVEMENTS OF THE GERMAN PEACE MOVEMENT

The peace movement has put pressure on political leaders and institutions to take seriously its arguments
and demands. The leadership of political parties,
trade unions, Protestant and Catholic churches have had
to deal with the peace movement since large numbers
of their members became actively involved in its activities.

The peace groups were forced in a short space of
time to make two crucial adjustments: firstly, they
had to cope with the change of government in October
1982 which turned the SPD out of office and put in its
place the CDU/CSU, with the FDP staying on as coalition
partner. This political change was subsequently
approved by popular vote in the Federal Elections of
March, 1983 which also for the first time gave the
extra-parliamentary representation through the party
of the 'Greens'. In light of this a dual strategy of
action was devised.

Secondly, the fact that new American nuclear missiles were actually being stationed in the Federal
Republic despite massive-scale protests and the mood
of the public apparently against this as expressed by
a majority of the West German population - if opinion
polls are to be believed - necessitated deliberation

114

The West German Peace Movement: A Profile

as to what strategy to pursue in order to survive as
a social and political movement and to have lasting
impact on domestic and international politics.

THE POSITION OF THE POLITICAL PARTIES

The position of the Social Democratic Party (SPD) with
regard to the peace movement has been ambiguous. On
the one hand, the official defence and security policy
under Helmut Schmidt's guidance had to be pursued with
due regard for the constraints imposed by the climate
of East-West relations, in particular the global relationship between the United States and the Soviet
Union. This deteriorated after the Soviet invasion of
Afghanistan; developments in Poland, Central America
and Africa; and the Soviet build-up of SS-20 missiles.
     The era of detente has been a frustrating exper-
ience. Due to Soviet exploitation of Western concessions, it is considered 'as good as dead'. A new
realism has supplanted the hopes and aspirations of
being able to persuade the Soviet Union to exercise
self-restraint. Although United States-German relations have been somewhat strained by different evalu-
ations about Soviet political intentions and the necessary Western response, a basic consensus with the
United States Government on the need for nuclear deterrence and military parity is shares by the SPD and
the CDU/CSU.
     On the other hand, the SPD is internally divided
as to what foreign policy and military strategy is
adequate to promote German interests and Social Democratic goals. An articulate minority among the SPD
rank-and-file, representing majority views within the
autonomous youth organization, had gathered around
Erhard Eppler within the peace movement to espouse
views opposed to those of the party leaders. It was
paradoxical, yet also revealing about the state of the
SPD, that while it was in government its foreign and
defence policy enjoyed more support from the CDU/CSU
than within its own ranks.
     Now, that the party is in opposition - endowed
with a new high-ranking candidate for the office of
Federal Chancellor - it has changed course, so to speak,
in mid-stream. Under pressure from party activists and
following prescriptions from regional party conferences the national party adopted a different security
policy at a special party conference at Cologne in
November 1983. The SPD officially rejected the stationing of US missiles and voted against a parliamentary resolution welcoming this move.

The West German Peace Movement: A Profile

The FDP's leader and Minister of Foreign Affairs, Hans-Dietrich Genscher, was for some time wrapped up in internal disputes on what strategy to follow to ensure the liberals' political survival. It could hardly afford to pay serious attention to the views of its two rival youth organizations on defence and security matters. Their membership is believed to be sympathetic to the cause of the peace movement.

The peace movement finds the bulk of its support among the Greens. For the most part they are too young, well-educated, articulate and environment-conscious. These people oppose nuclear power plants, nuclear weapons and the arms race. They work outside the established political parties and have only just begun to organize themselves into the form of a political party, successfully contesting local and regional elections.

Their electoral success in the March, 1983 Federal Elections, which entitles them to parliamentary representation, may lose some of its initial impetus once the test of political office and responsibility gets under way, but this is something the Greens shun. The 'parliamentarization' of the Greens has been held up by political strategists of the SPD as a possible solution to the problem of reintegrating this protest generation into the mainstream of parliamentary politics. Whether this is a realistic assessment remains to be seen.

The Christian Democrats (CDU) and Christian Social Union (CSU) voice strong opposition to the peace movement, (15) which they regard as infiltrated, and manipulated, by communist organizations. This view is shared by 45 per cent of a representative sample of the West German electorate. (16) The movement's purported anti-Americanism and neutralism, its closeness to the SPD youth organization (which has a neo-Marxist orientation) in the view of the CDU and CSU makes it the ideal partner for the Communist Party's political objectives even though many of its supporters are not affiliated to that party's organizations. The CDU rejects the peace movement, especially after taking over government, because of the harmful effect it has on relations between the Federal Republic of Germany and the United States and on the Atlantic Alliance, values which the CDU regards as worth defending and which are the basis of the security policy of the Federal Republic of Germany.

ACCUSATIONS AGAINST THE GERMAN PEACE MOVEMENT

Critics of the peace movement claim that:

116

1. it is a predominantly communist-inspired propaganda exercise to destabilize public opinion
   and the Federal Government's support for the
   NATO-deployment decision, thus serving Soviet
   expansionary goals;
2. it expresses an Anti-American sentiment -
   particularly vis-a-vis the Reagan Administration - thereby creating tensions between the
   two countries and weakening the NATO alliance;
3. by stressing neutralist positions for the
   Federal Republic in order to solve the German
   question by reunification of the two German
   states it endangers the survival of a free
   and independent democratic society and plays
   into the hands of the Soviets;
4. its pronounced pacifism (symbolized by the
   slogan 'freedom and security without the help
   of arms') and its propagation of a unilateral
   renunciation of the first use of nuclear weapons by the NATO alliance is a naive and dangerous utopianism not fit to be realized in
   an international environment characterized
   by the constant use and abuse of power to
   serve nationalistic goals;
5. it constitutes a rear attack against the
   official defence and security policy of the
   Federal Government which will ultimately lose
   its credibility and good standing in the Western alliance.

THE POSITION OF THE TRADE UNIONS

Despite the public stand the trade unions have taken
in support of peace and security, the unions and their
official leaders have been afraid of being identified
as a political organization which formally sides with
a protest movement having supposedly pro-communist
slant and which opposes the Federal Government's official defence and security policy. Initially, the
'Deutsche Gewerkschaftsbund' (DGB, the German TUC) and
some of its member-unions have actually pressured
prominent members not to make official speeches at
peace movement rallies. Those individuals who did
venture to take a public stand for disarmament have
until recently been anxious to stress that when they
speak up they do so as individuals.
    This self-restraint was abandoned after the change
of government. When the SPD went into opposition the
DGB and its member-unions no longer felt obliged to
hold former Chancellor Schmidt's line. They were free

to voice their opposition to the stationing of American nuclear missiles on German soil and to allow their members and functionaries to become actively involved in the peace movement.

However, many unions whose members work in arms production and related industries find themselves in an awkward position when addressing peace gatherings. In principle, the unions oppose the use of force to attain political goals and claim that the arms race wastes money that could be put to better use for social services and national development. On the other hand, they are actually concerned with job security, even if war-related production sectors have to be sustained to do so. Alternative schemes to make the scarce resources now going into research and development of military technology available for peaceful purposes have not yet won solid backing from the unions' rank-and-file.

A similar charge about the ambivalence of trade union attitudes could be made with regard to ecological issues such as the use of nuclear energy and the protection of the environment, raised by the same young people who actively support the peace movement and call for disarmament.

None the less, we observe attempts on both the unions' and the peace movement's sides to form some sort of 'grand coalition', bringing together under one ideological roof demands for international peace through disarmament and demands for introduction of a 35-hour working week, as a means to solve the problem of unemployment and to secure social peace at home.(17) Easter marches and May Day celebrations this year witnessed this incipient coalition of peace and labour activists at work, however fragile it may prove to be.

SUMMARY AND OUTLOOK

The German peace movement is an amorphous alliance of environmentalists (the Greens), Christian initiatives and political Left, groups in which the young and the better educated are overrepresented. They oppose deployment of the new US-built intermediate-range nuclear missiles (INF) in Western Europe. Not surprisingly, communist groups have tried to jump on this bandwagon to convince West Europeans that the United States, not the Soviet Union, is 'fuelling' the arms race and risking all-out nuclear war. (18)

The tiny pro-Moscow Communist Party in the Federal Republic of Germany, the DKP, regularly polls about 0.5 per cent of the vote in national elections. By

118

The West German Peace Movement: A Profile

superior organization, however, and because of ample financial support deriving from the Soviet Union and the German Democratic Republic it has succeeded in infiltrating the peace movement and so making its views public, for instance through the German Peace Union (DFU). It tries to correct the negative impression which the Soviet Union and its aggressive policies have created among the West German public, which distrusts Soviet intentions. Three out of four of those questioned in a recent survey believed in a Soviet drive for military superiority. Three out of five suspected that the Soviet Union tries to exploit the Western policy of detente and conciliation for its own purposes and is seeking to extend its sphere of influence, Soviet aggression in Afghanistan being cited as a prime example. (19)

The continuity of Soviet foreign policy, accompanied by its steady military build-up, has been paying off, it appears. After a decade of negligent US-defence policy and that of their European allies - there seems to be today a Soviet military superiority. The decision of the Reagan Administration to correct this perceived imbalance of power has been interpreted by critics and an alert public opinion as a reversal of detente policy and a return to the cold war period, without any truly perceived necessity to counter a possible Soviet threat. Thus American credibility to conduct a security policy guided by the principle of preventing wars and securing peace has suffered by the apparent lack of continuity in US-foreign policy. Consequently, the hardline foreign and defence policies of the Reagan Administration have polarized public opinion in the Federal Republic according to the results of various polls and have spurred the peace movement, not only here but all across Europe and in the United States as well. However, there continues to be a general consensus on security policy in the adult West German population. Among youth groups, however, a radical departure from the official policy prescriptions is noticeable. To them, peace can only be secured by a policy of detente, preferably without the aid of arms. They reject the logic of deterrence - arming for war in order to guarantee peace - as implausible and dangerous. A new ethos seems to be developing in national security policy: the unilateral renunciation of the first use or of any use of nuclear weapons by the Western nations. This is seen as necessary to deter a conceivable attack - whether nuclear or conventional - by the Soviet Union and its military allies, and seems to have become a moral imperative for many adherents of the peace movement.

The West German Peace Movement: A Profile

'Peace without arms' is proclaimed by many without due regard for the accepted practices of power and
force in international politics which nation-states
continue to engage in. While these pacifists by conviction do not dispute the basic affinity of the Federal Republic to the Western alliance they refuse to
see the Soviet Union as a power threatening the status
quo in international relations by military force and
political blackmail. The implications of a massive
SS-20 build-up in Central Europe was hardly recognized. Disarmament - even by unilateral proclamation and action - is seen as a value per se. It supposedly guarantees international peace by removing the
impending threat of reciprocal physical annihilation
and obviating the need for arms even for the purposes
of self-defence.
        Chancellor Helmut Schmidt's address to the German
parliament (which was also applauded by the CDU/CSU
opposition), just before the peace rally in Bonn on
10 October 1981, clarified the Federal Government's
position vis-a-vis the peace movement.
        That statement is still valid today, since Helmut
Kohl, CDU-Chancellor, is known to share this view.
While expressing his sincere respect for the pacifist
convictions, the Federal Chancellor none the less
stressed the need to uphold a military equilibrium -
though prefereably at much lower levels - and to remain a reliable member of the Western alliance. He
rejected the notion that unilateral steps towards disarmament by the Western nations or the Federal Republic would make peace more secure and help to prevent
wars. Instead he voiced his concern that this policy
would surely create greater insecurity and play into
the hands of those communist-inspired propaganda troops
who claim that Soviet missiles are securing peace while
US-missiles are endangering peace.
        The political effect of the peace movement is
judged very differently. According to survey results,
every second respondent attributed to it little or no
political effect in terms of armament or disarmament.
The rest were equally divided between belief in the
statement that the peace movement was likely to bring
about progress in disarmament negotiations and belief
in the opposite statement that the peace movement was
likely to impede the West in making up its deficit in
conventional and nuclear arms. (20) The issue of
national security - especially when achieved by means
of nuclear deterrence - is a complex one comparable to
the question of nuclear energy use in power plants.
Scientists and self-styled experts can increasingly be
found on both sides of the fence. The force of public

The West German Peace Movement: A Profile

opinion may have given the dissenting view a prominence which further attracts people who respond with
bewilderment, anxiety and fear to seemingly technical
and non-political but none the less existential and
highly controversial questions. Technical expertise
is suspect when emotions run high. Nevertheless moral
indignation and utopian idealism cannot and should not
forsake informed and rational reasoning.

What is worrisome, however, is the fact that the
basic and enduring bipartisan consensus on matters of
defence and national security which is shared by the
great majority of the West German people seems to be
waning, in as far as the SPD approaches positions held
by the ecological and peace movements. We should not
take Gerhard Wettig's apprehension too lightly when he
warns that:

> neither better and more intensive endeavors to
> explain the motivation and logic behind Western
> security policy, nor new concepts in the field of
> security policy that make allowance for the crit-
> ical objections raised are in themselves...enough
> to bring about the integration of the expanding
> alternative-culture core of the peace movement. (21)

Thus, the prospects of the peace movement in the
Federal Republic are that it will not simply fade
away. Rather, the movement will persist, most likely
with reduced size and in different shape, waiting to
be activated for differing motives and political ends.
The political process will have another dimension from
now on.

NOTES

(1) A short biography of names follows: Eppler:
former cabinet member and regional party chairman,
member of the SPD executive committee; Lafontaine:
Mayor of Saarbrücken, regional party chairman, member
of SPD executive committee; Benz: member of the national executive committee of IG Metall - West Germany's
large union of metal workers; Albertz: former Mayor of
West Berlin, Protestant clergyman, member of the SPD;
Niemöller: Protestant bishop, former president of the
National Council of Churches, died in 1983; Bastian:
retired Major General of the German Army; Mechtersheimer: former Lieutenant-Colonel in the German Air Force,
former member of the SCU; Leinen: national chairman of
the BBU-Ecologists' Movement, organizer of the June,
1982 peace rally in Bonn; Mrs. Kelly: national chair-
person of the 'Greens' until November, 1982, member of

the German Bundestag.

(2)   This has been the finding of numerous empir-
ical studies based on poll data. See, for instance:
'Jeder dritte hofft auf eine Null-Losung' in Der Spiegel, 23 November 1981.

(3)   See Gerhard Wettig, 'Die Friedensbewegung der
beginnenden 8oer Jahre', Berichte des Bundesinstituts
fuer Ostwissenschaftliche und Internationale Studien,
9, 1982. English version, 'The New Peace Movement in
Germany' in AuBenpolitik, 3, 1982.

(4)   See Appendix 1 for a list of organizations.

(5)   See Appendix 2 question 5, also supported by
other studies.

(6)   See 'Zur Situation der Jugendlichen in Nord-
rhein-Westfalen (survey among German youth), Infas,
1982.

(7)   See Manfred Kuchler, '18 bis 35 + Abitur =
Aktivgruppe' in Der Spiegal, 23 November, 1981.

(8)   See Appendix 2, question 5.

(9)   See Appendix 2, question 6.

(10)   See Der Spiegel, 23 November 1981.

(11)   See Der Spiegel, September 1983.

(12)   See Elisabeth Noelle-Neumann, 'Drei Viertel
gegen die Raketenstationierung ? Die Wirklichkeit
sieht differenzierter aus' in Frankfurter Allgemeine
Zeitung, 16 September 1983; and 'Hier Mehrheit, dort
Minderheit: Umfragen der Meinungsforscher zum NATO-
DoppelbeschluB und ihre Widersprüche' in Der Spiegel,
29 August 1983.

(13)   Factual information on motives, demands and
activities of the West German peace movement was gathered by means of a careful reading of newspaper clip-
pings, interviews and various documents. The following sources have been particularly helpful: 'Die Friedensbewegung im Herbst 1983', DPA-Dokument 3o85, 5 October 1983 assembled by Edgar Bauer; 'Frieden und Freiheit, Gewalt und Widerstand', Information fur Journal-
isten, Bonn, October 1983; 'Vor der Genfer Entschei-
dung: Friedenspolitische Aktivitaten der SPD im Herbst
1983: Materialien zur Friedenspolitik', edited by Vor-
stand der SPD, Abt. Presse und Information, Bonn,
July 1983.

(14)   This personal impression was also echoed by
news media reports.

(15)   Some of their arguments can be reread in
Playing at Peace, a joint study of the Peace Movement
in Great Britain and the Federal Republic of Germany
by the Bow Group and the Konrad-Adenauer-Foundation,
1983; in 'Argumente fur Frieden und Freiheit', For-
schungsbericht 25 der Konrad Adenauer Foundation, ed.
by Hans-Joachim Veen, Melle, 1983; and Manfred Wörner,

'The Peace Movement and NATO: An Alternative View from Bonn' in Strategic Review, vol. X, 1) (winter 1982).

(16) See Appendix 2, question 7; support for this thesis is found by Gottfried Linn, 'Die Kampagne gegen die NATO-Nachrustüng: Zur Rolle der DKP'in Demokratische Verantwortung, vol. 6, Bonn, 1983.

(17) The line of argument is: The more money is spent on arms, the less money is available for social services and union demands.

(18) See Appendix 2. question 3. While overall 40 per cent of the respondents blame the Soviets, fully 40 per cent of the Green sympathizers believe that the Americans pose a greater threat to world peace than the Soviets. For more thorough discussion see, Gunther Schmid, 'Sicherheitspolitik und Friedensbewegung: Der Konflikt um die Nachrustung' in Akademiebeiträge zur Lehrerbildung, vol. 11, ed. by Akademie für Politische Bildung, Tutzing, 1982; and Heinz-Ulrich Kohr and Hans-George Rader, 'Socio-Political Orientations and the Perception of Military Threat in West Germany Youth'in Forum, vol. 2, Sozialwissenschaftliches Institut der Bundeswehr, München, 1983.

(19) See 'Jeder vierte Pazifist gegen Friedensbewegung' in Der Spiegel, 30 November 1981; and 'Angstlücke und Vertrauensschwund' in Der Spiegel, 7 December 1981.

(20) See for opposing views, Ulrich Albrecht, 'Zur politischen Bedeutung der neueren Friedensbewegung in der Bundesrepublik Deutschland' in Osterreichische Zeitschrift fur Politikwissenschaft, 2, 1983; and Hansjurgen Rautenberg, 'Friedensbewegung und Nukleardebatte in westeuropäischen NATO-Staaten' in Beiträge zur Konfliktforschung, 3, 1982.

(21) Wettig, fn. 3, p. 26.

APPENDIX 1

The main groups and organizations of the peace movement are:

1. church groups
   - Aktion Sühnezeichen/Friedensdienste (ASF) - Protestant
   - Ohne Rüstung leben (ORL) - Protestant
   - Aktionsgemeinschaft Dienst fur den Frieden (AGDF) - Protestant
   - Pax Christi - Catholic, branch of international organization
   - Initiative 'Kirche von uten' (IKVU) - Catholic, laymen's church movement

2. ecological-oriented peace groups
    - the 'Greens' (parliamentary party, extra-par-
      liamentary activities, practising grass-roots
      democracy)
    - Bundesverband Bürgerinitiativen Umweltschutz
      (BBU) (association of more than 1,000 local
      citizens' initiatives, its chairman, Jo Leinen,
      is chief organizer of the peace movement)

3. traditional Left and New Left groups
    - non-dogmatic socialists (Sozialistisches Büro,
      Komitee für Grundrechte and Demokratie, Demok-
      ratische Sozialisten)
    - Third World groups with an anti-imperialist
      tinge (Bundeskongreß entwicklungspolitischer
      Aktionsgruppen - (BUKO)
    - Women for Peace (Anstiftung der Frauen fur den
      Frieden)

4. communist groups (with some 100,000 members, lar-
    gest and most active grouping)
    - German Communist Party (DKP) - 0.5 per cent of
      the national vote, (50,000 members)
    - orthodox communists
      Sozialistische Deutsche Arbeiterjugend (SDAJ) -
      young workers, Marxistischer Studentenbund
      Spartakus (MDB) - Marxist Students
    - Deutsche Friedensunion (DFU) - sponsor of the
      Krefelder Appeal
    - Deutsche Friedensgesellschaft/Vereinigte Kriegs-
      dienstverweigerer (DFG-VK) - conscientious
      objectors, 25,000 members
    - Komitee für Frieden, Abrüstung und Zusammenar-
      beit (KFAZ) - committee for Peace, Disarmament
      and Co-operation

5. various anti-missile initiatives
    - Krefelder Initiative (DFU-sponsored, three na-
      tional meetings (Forum) so far)
    - professional groups against nuclear armament
      (physicians, lawyers, teachers, journalists,
      scientists, sportsmen, artists and entertain-
      ers)
    - autonomous groups (Bundeskongreß Autonomer
      Friedensinitiativen (BAF) - anarchists, mili-
      tants, terrorists)

The West German Peace Movement: A Profile

APPENDIX 2.

Question 1: What do you think, are the prospects for a lasting peace in Europe?

	excellent	good	less than good	poor	no answer given	excellent/ good	less than good/ poor
all respondents	5	47	39	8	1	52	47
age groups							
18-24	6	37	43	12	1	43	55
25-29	4	42	46	7	1	48	49
30-44	6	48	38	8	1	54	46
45-59	4	55	35	5	1	59	40
60 and older	5	46	39	7	2	51	46
educational level							
lower	5	50	39	6	1	55	45
intermediate	4	46	39	9	1	50	48
higher	7	37	42	12	2	43	54
party preference							
CDU/CSU	6	57	32	4	2	63	36
FDP	11	52	29	8	1	63	37
SPD	5	43	43	9	1	48	52
Grüne	4	25	54	16	1	29	70
no preference stated	3	39	48	9	1	42	57

Source: survey of a representative sample of the West German electorate conducted during the autumn of 1983 by the Social Science Research Institute of the Konrad Adenauer Foundation.

Question 2: Do you believe that, in the case of the Federal Republic of Germany, the military threat emanating from the East has in recent years increased, decreased or has not changed?

	has increased	has decreased	has not changed	no answer given
all respondents	38	6	55	2
age groups				
18-24	46	4	49	2
25-29	41	6	52	2
30-44	33	6	61	0
45-59	36	8	54	2
60 and older	38	5	54	3
educational level				
lower	35	7	56	2
intermediate	42	3	54	1
higher	41	5	51	3
party preference				
CDU/CSU	45	4	49	2
FDP	51	4	45	0
SPD	32	7	60	1
Grüne	16	11	71	2
no preference stated	36	5	57	2

Source: survey of a representative sample of the West German electorate conducted during the autumn of 1983 by the Social Science Research Institute of the Konrad Adenauer Foundation.

Question: Considering the nature of contemporary East-West relations, especially relations between the United States and the Soviet Union, which side, do you believe, poses a greater threat to peace – the Soviet side, the American side, or can this be seen differently?

	Soviet threat	American threat	has to be seen differently	no answer given
all respondents	40	13	47	1
age groups				
18-24	32	18	48	2
25-29	33	17	50	1
30-44	34	15	51	1
45-59	44	11	44	1
60 and older	47	8	44	1
educational level				
lower	43	11	46	1
intermediate	37	15	48	1
higher	30	19	49	3
party preference				
CDU/CSU	53	6	41	1
FDP	28	14	57	1
SPD	29	19	51	1
Grüne	13	40	46	1
no preference stated	37	9	52	2

Source: survey of a representative sample of the West German electorate conducted during the autumn of 1983 by the Social Science Research Institute of the Konrad Adenauer Foundation.

The West German Peace Movement: A Profile

Question 4: Do you think that the existence of the Western defence alliance - e.g. NATO - has made world peace more secure, less secure, or has NATO not made a difference?

	more secure	less secure	no effect	no answer given
all respondents	63	9	25	3
age groups				
18-24	59	14	22	5
25-29	61	10	24	6
30-44	64	8	26	1
45-59	67	7	23	2
60 and older	61	8	28	3
educational level				
lower	61	8	28	3
intermediate	63	11	24	3
higher	71	10	17	3
political interest				
high	69	9	20	2
medium	62	8	27	3
low	54	10	31	5
party preference				
CDU/CSU	76	5	18	3
FDP	70	15	15	0
SPD	57	11	29	3
Grüne	43	27	23	6
no preference stated	48	5	43	4

Source: survey of a representative sample of the West German electorate conducted during the autumn of 1983 by the Social Science Research Institute of the Konrad Adenauer Foundation.

130

The West German Peace Movement: A Profile

Question 5: Do you consider becoming actively involved in the peace movement or is that out of the question?

	I am already active	I intend to be active	I do not consider such a move	no answer given
all respondents	3	10	85	2
age groups				
18-24	6	25	65	4
25-29	7	18	73	3
30-44	4	12	83	1
45-59	2	6	92	1
60 and older	1	3	96	1
educational level				
lower	1	6	92	1
intermediate	4	15	80	1
higher	10	21	67	2
political interest				
high	6	15	77	2
medium	2	9	88	1
low	1	6	92	2
party preference				
CDU/CSU	1	4	94	1
FDP	3	11	85	2
SPD	4	14	82	0
Grüne	21	35	41	3
no preference stated	2	9	84	5

Source: survey of a representative sample of the West German electorate conducted during the autumn of 1983 by the Social Science Research Institute of the Konrad Adenauer Foundation.

The West German Peace Movement: A Profile

Question 6: It is sometimes asserted that the peace movement in the Federal Republic of Germany is infiltrated by Communists. Do you share this view or do you not?

	I share this view	I do not share this view	no answer given
all respondents	45	49	6
age groups			
18-24	25	69	6
25-29	36	60	4
30-44	42	52	6
45-59	57	38	5
60 and older	52	41	7
educational level			
lower	46	48	6
intermediate	46	48	6
higher	43	53	4
political interest			
high	52	44	5
medium	43	51	6
low	38	55	8
party preference			
CDU/CSU	61	33	6
FDP	53	40	7
SPD	35	61	5
Grüne	20	75	6
no preference stated	35	56	9

Source: survey of a representative sample of the West German electorate conducted during the autumn of 1983 by the Social Science Research Institute of the Konrad Adenauer Foundation.

131

Chapter Six

THE PEACE MOVEMENT IN FRANCE

Joel-Francois Dumont

ORIGINS AND HISTORY OF FRENCH PACIFISM

The word 'pacifisme' first appeared in France at the end
of the nineteenth century when the world was deeply
imbued with nationalism. By this time, it had both
philosophical and political meanings. The former de-
noted a belief in the establishment of a universal
peace and the latter that peace be attained at any
cost.
      When the French army was defeated at Sedan in
1870, conservative forces wanted to reach a peace
agreement while a liberal and Republican coalition condemned this effort. French pacifism suffered an additional setback from enthusiastic reactions to the
announcement of the declaration of war in 1914. With
the condemnation of pacifism by an Emile Faguet work
in 1908, the concept took on overtones of defeatism,
cowardice or even treason.
      At that time, pacifists could be found in both
left and right political parties. The cleavage was not
between the Left and Right as much as between warmongers and pacifists in each camp. The opponents of war
were known as minoritaires de guerre (war minority)
and the warmongers called union sacrée (war supporters).
The First World War, however, gave rise to a revival
of pacifist thought. The so-called 'Great War' was
supposed to be the 'des-der-des', that is, the very
last of all wars. The search for peace had now become
almost an obsession for large segments of the French
population. War seemed to be absurd. Once again,
however, the revival of pacifism was shattered by the
rise of the Nazi regime in Germany, the growth of
facism in Italy, and by the signing of the French-Sov-
iet mutual assistance treaty in 1935. With surprising
speed, pacifism underwent a metamorphosis in which
anti-militarists were transformed into warmongers: in

132

Europe against Germany, in Africa against Italy, and in Spain where they fought side by side with the republicans.

As a result, a confrontation took place in France between the supporters of rearmament efforts represented by Léon Blum and the anti-militarists led by Paul Faure, the undisputed socialist leader. However, rearmament came too late to prevent the humiliating defeat of France in the Second World War and occupation by a totalitarian regime. After 1945, pacifism held relatively little meaning. There was only a modest revival within the human rights movement which produced no significant achievements. General de Gaulle was to have a decisive impact on French pacifism by creating an independent national nuclear force in France; the well-known force de frappe. Eventually, all political parties, some even as late as 15 years after the establishment of this agency, were supportive of this project. This helped to establish a national consensus in France with regard to national security which has largely excluded pacifism.

GOALS AND IDEOLOGY OF THE FRENCH PEACE MOVEMENT

There is dispute and/or rivalry within the French peace movement over goals and ideology, with differing viewpoints held by two major organizations; the movement for peace and the independent movement CODENE. Despite their different ambitions, however, some similarities do exist.

Both movements view the struggle for peace as an integral part of the struggle for democracy, equality and the defence of human rights. This struggle is, at the same time, considered to be a tool of social transformation and an ideological tool in the fight against the ruling class. Despite their ideological differences, all pacifists share the belief that peace will become a reality. Therefore, it can be said that their ideology is grounded in eschatology which is based on the tenets of the 'final catastrophy'. The goals of the French peace movement are quite similar to those of other European peace movements. The primary aim is to prevent the deployment of new nuclear weapons in Europe. The French movement also shares the idea of a freeze and unilateral disarmament with its European and American counterparts. In addition to these goals are a few unique to the French. The most important goals of the communist pacifists are to separate West Germany from France and to stop the development of the neutron bomb in France. The socialists in the French peace movement campaign for the reconversion of armament industries, while the confessional groups try to despecialize defence problems. Overall, the most important goal of the movements is to erode the credibility of the French nuclear forces by using every opportunity to frighten the public.

THE ORGANIZATIONAL STRUCTURE OF THE FRENCH PEACE MOVEMENT

In general, it can be said that the French peace movement consists of three groups:

1. The Communist front organizations
2. The independent movements.
3. The confessional movements.

The Communist Front Organizations

This category represents 70 per cent of the organized French peace movement. The most important groups of this type are the 'Mouvement de la Paix' (the Movement for Peace) and the 'Comité des Cent' (the Committee of One Hundred). Both of these groups belong to the World Peace Council (WPC).

The Movement for Peace was founded in Paris in April, 1949. This first congress for peace was attended by famous communist dissidents and other non-communists such as Christians, Protestants, artists and intellectuals. The Movement for Peace became famous a year later with the Stockholm Appeal of March 1950, which called for the absolute interdiction of atomic weapons. The fact that this appeal was signed by 14 million people points to the considerable public support the movement had at that time.

The organizational structure of the movement consists of the Secretariat (the administrative office) staffed by twelve members, the national board of 86 members, and a national council. The secretaries are members of both the secretariat and the national council, working on a permanent basis given the lack of a general secretary. By controlling the administration and co-ordination of all activities, the Secretariat is the major organ of power in the movement. Correspondents of the movement are decentrally located in 82 French départements or districts. The organization benefits from the logistical support and mobilization capacity of the French Communist Party and is financed by the BCEN, the trade bank of Northern Europe and the most important bank in France. The leadership of the

movement is drawn from a variety of sources. For example, Jaques Denis and Michel Laugignon are members
of the French Communist Party, Bernard Lacobe and
Bernard Boudouresque represent the trade unions, and
Pierre-Luc Seguillon is a journalist. There is also
at this time representation of Socialist Party leftists and the Progressive Christian Party in the Movement for Peace. In addition, there are two former
generals in the leadership elite.

The activists of the movement see themselves
neither as pacifists nor neutralists, but rather as
'soldiers for peace'. Their campaign and activities
have focused on four grand themes:

- the termination of the arms race and safeguard-
  of detente;
- the search for a new international economic
  order and condemnation of the arms trade;
- support for movements of national liberation
  and independence;
- opposition to the neutron bomb.

Given the fact that the Movement for Peace has supported Soviet foreign policy line in almost every case,
it has lost credibility with the French electorate.

The second of the two communist front organizations is the Committee of One Hundred. About 50 per
cent of its members are considered communist militants
while the remainder are socialists, revolutionaries,
trade unionists and progressive Christians. This new
peace movement concentrates their efforts on public
appeals against nuclear weapons, such as the famous
appeals of Stockholm and Krefeld. Overall, it can be
said that these two communist front organizations have
not succeeded in turning French pacifism into a mass
movement.

The Independent Movement
The independent part of the French peace movement developed from three main strands:

- The pacifists' Union of France which is the
  French section of the 'Resistants to War Internationale'; they advocate unilateral disarmament
  by the West.
- MDPL (Movement for Disarmament, Peace and Freedom) is an anti-militarist movement which was
  founded in 1968 as the successor to the MCAA
  (the Movement against Atomic Armament). This
  organization focuses on French atomic weapons

and proposes the reconversion of the armament
industry as well as alternative defence postures.
- MAN (Movement for a non-violent alternative),
created in 1974, sponsors about 40 small study
groups. Instead of calling for immediate unilateral disarmament, this movement seeks the
development of a credible civilian resistance
based on non-armed techniques. They see this
as essential in order to cut the old link between armament and defence and establish a 'non-
violent' stand to current defence postures.
The 200 members of this movement, one not considered communists, are known frequently to
attack French nuclear forces and especially its
naval component.

After 1981, these three main groups were among
the 27 organizations which created the independent
movement CODENE (Committees for Disarmament). The
main goal of CODENE is the demilitarization of Europe
by the elimination of all nuclear weapons. The members of CODENE are usually former opponents of the
civilian use of nuclear energy who have now focused
their criticisms on the use of nuclear power in the
military sphere. The movement convenes the European
Convention for Peace every year and also callaborates
with the group 'Defence and Peace' and 'La Forge'. In
addition, it has intensified its contacts with other
European and American peace organizations as well as
with the International Peace Communication and Co-ordination Centre (IPCC).

The Confessional Movements
The most famous of these various French denominational
peace movements is 'Pax Christi', the French contin-
gent of the international Catholic peace movement.
Other groups in this category include the following:
the Justice and Peace Commission, founded in 1923 and
whose members are closely linked to MAN, the MIR
(International Movement of Reconciliation); the COE
(Conseil Oeucuménique des Eglises), which is engaged
in helping East European churches; the JOC (Christian
Worker Youth), which has close ties to the Communist
Party; and finally, the Federation of Protestant
Students, which has close ties to the Movement for
Peace. None of these denominational movements have had
great impact given some of the prior activities of its
leaders, particularly during the Algerian War. This
has caused them to lose credibility in the eyes of the

The Peace Movement in France

French public.

THE ELECTORATE OF THE FRENCH PEACE MOVEMENT

A specific or well-defined electorate as such does not
exist in France. Apart from the ecologists who represent a negligible portion of the electorate and the
traditional communist electorate of one-third which
might favour pacifism, there is only marginal support
for the peace movement among socialist, liberal and
Gaullist voters. Taking this fact into account, along
with the general stability of voter alignments and
recent voting studies, one can see that specific groups
like the young and women are particularly attracted to
the peace movement. In this respect, the social basis
of the French peace movement does not differ from that
of other European peace movements. However, the fact
that 20 per cent of the French populace does not have
an articulate view regarding the issues raised by the
peace movement distinguishes it from other European
countries. In fact, recent studies have demonstrated
that 22 per cent of the French public can be labelled
as anti-militaristic because they are 'unconcerned'.
This lack of concern is associated with negative attitudes toward the use of nuclear energy; studies show
that 49 per cent of the French public distrusts the use
of nuclear energy. These preferences do not, however,
translate into support for the French peace movement.
Therefore, it can be said that in contrast to other
European countries, the French peace movement does gain
significantly from public anti-nuclear sentiments.

ACTIVITIES OF THE FRENCH PEACE MOVEMENT

One of the main activities of the French peace movement
is the public distribution of magazines, booklets,
pamphlets and posters. Magazines and booklets serve as
the main link between supporters and members. Quite
often, the leading articles are translated from English
or German peace movement publications. The organization of demonstrations and rallies is another important
activity of this group. In June, 1982 the Movement for
Peace and the Committee of One Hundred organized a
demonstration of 250,000 people which was considerably
more than the rally organized by CODENE two weeks
earlier. Recently, the peace movement organizations
have tended to call only a small number of activists
together rather than organize large public demonstrations. The yearly congress of the various organiza-

tions is an example of such an activity. In addition
to national contacts, the various peace movements have
developed forms of co-operation with similar foreign
pacifist movements. This has not, however, resulted
in the establishment of a greater European network.

MEDIA COVERAGE OF THE FRENCH PEACE MOVEMENT

An important fact to consider in assessing the media
coverage of the French peace movement is that the per-
sonnel and structure of the state-run radio and press
have changed dramatically since the Socialist and
Communist parties assumed power in 1981. For example,
the most important positions at the operational level
and the heads of the various radio and television
stations have been occupied by supporters or members
of the parties in power. This is particularly true
of the news departments in those stations. These
changes have worked to the benefit of the arguments
and activities of the French peace movement. Overall,
the movement receives rather extensive media coverage
which is characterized by a slanted selection of news
and interviews, as well as a somewhat one-sided inter-
pretation of the facts.
    Newspaper coverage is quite similar to that of
radio and television. Le Monde and Libération comment
extensively on the activities and ideas of the peace
movement, and L'Humanité even reserves a daily selection for peace movement views. Despite this extreme
and one-sided media coverage, pacifism has been and
still is rejected by the French public. Instead of
being positively affected by the peace movement, the
public has become disenchanted with the peace movement
and its media coverage.

NATIONAL CHARACTERISTICS OF THE FRENCH PEACE MOVEMENT

In contrast to other European peace movements, the
French movement has never enjoyed high public support
for their ideas or significant participation in their
activities. In this sense, France can almost be regarded as a counter-model of pacifism. This is due to
the fact that there has always been, and still is, a
strong public consensus on the necessity of a defence
posture based on nuclear dissuasion. It is this consensus upon which the policies of General De Gaulle
were based. Another reason is that the French public
firmly believes that the defence of vital interests
cannot be assumed by a foreign nation. There is, how-

ever, a specific distinction drawn by the French public between the defence of France and the security of
Western Europe: while only 6 per cent of the French
population considers the American nuclear umbrella as
essential for the security of their own country, 67
per cent believe this umbrella is the only way to as-
sure the security of Western Europe. Both attitudes
are not receptive to pacifist ideals.

A third reason may be that anti-nuclear attitudes
are not as prominent as is the case in other European countries. This is particularly true of the military application of nuclear energy. The <u>force de</u>
<u>frappe</u> and its air, sea and land-based systems are not
the focus of criticism let alone protest, but rather
a matter of French national pride.

A fourth reason is certainly that pacifism historically has a negative connotation in France and that
past experiences of the French have discredited pacifism. Overall, one can say that both the broad
national consensus with respect to foreign policy and
defence in France coupled with the traditional French
view of pacifism has not changed significantly, which
has therefore limited both success and public support
for the French peace movement. The general rejection
of pacifism in France, which has been brought about by
these specific national characteristics, is even shared
by the socialist electorate, for which Soviet expansion
and totalitarian dictatorship are sill considered to
be the prominent threat. This view of the Soviet
Union and its foreign policy as the main threat to
French and European security is also shared by an overwhelming majority of the French populace.

Finally, the weakness of the Greens and the predominantly catholic orientation in France constitute
other reasons for the low impact of the peace movement.
One should keep in mind that the French bishops distinguish between the possession of nuclear weapons for
deterrence purposes and for aggressive use. Only the
latter is rejected as immoral. For all of the above
reasons the pacifist movement in France, which includes
various peace organizations, has not succeeded and is
not likely to succeed in the foreseeable future.

Chapter Seven

THE PEACE MOVEMENT IN ITALY

Sergio A. Rossi and
Virgilio Ilari

INTRODUCTION

During the late 1970s and early 1980s, Italy was not
spared from the wave of criticism and self-doubt over
national security and defence priorities which were
precipitated notably by the Nato dual-track decision
of December, 1979 on Intermediate Nuclear Forces or
INF. In many Italian streets and cities, as elsewhere
in Europe, we have witnessed familiar scenes of anti-
nuclear protest and peace demonstrations staged by
various organizations, from leftist political parties
to Catholic movements.
     Two particular examples may give a better idea of
this situation. Several Italian town councils, (especially in smaller or provincial cities, where leftist
parties and above all the PCI (the Italian Communist
Party) have the political majority) have voted specific
motions or deliberations that ban the deployment of
missiles and the installation of nuclear power stations
within their territorial boundaries. These deliberations sometimes produced large road signs, placed at
the entrance of the town, saying 'Denuclearized Zone'.
Although they have no real juridical value, they sym-
bolize a political initiative and a movement of opinion (1)
     On the other hand, on 12 February 1983 the Court
of Sondrio, a town in Lombardy (Northern Italy) acquit-
ted 14 pacifists, among them several catholics and
even a clergyman, who had deducted from their annual
tax declaration exactly 5.5 per cent, that is, a per-

          1. Paper presented at the Conference on the
          International Peace Movement, organized by the
          Institut fur Politische Wissenschaft of the
          University of Kiel, Germany, 11-13 May 1984)
          (revised September, 1984).

centage equal to the amount of the state budget allo-
cated to defence expenditures. Instead of paying this
sum to the Internal Revenue Service, they devolved it
to peace initiatives or to charity organizations. (2)
    However, in spite of all these and other activi-
ties, there is a striking difference between Italy and
the situation in other European countries, notably
West Germany, The Netherlands and Belgium, where the
pacifist and anti-nuclear movements have had a serious
impact on government attitudes and policies. It is
widely acknowledged that the pacifist movement in
Italy, although it has received considerable attention
from the media and a certain support from some political quarters, have failed to reach a 'critical mass',
that is, the intensity and the political weight necessary to affect the government's foreign and defence
policies.
    The principal reasons of this failure are on the
one hand, the lack of genuine cultural roots in the
Italian peace movement (IPM) whose behaviour and objectives are often perceived as imported or borrowed
from foreign models and experiences; (3) and on the
other, the decreasing credibility due to the growing
internal politicization of the peace movement and to
the struggle between the Radical and Communist parties
for its control and leadership.

ORIGINS AND HISTORY OF THE ITALIAN PEACE MOVEMENT

We do not have a comprehensive written history of the
Italian Peace Movement (IPM), whose origins may be
traced to the socialist campaign against the Libyan
war in 1912, and to the socialist and catholic movements against Italy's participation in the First World
War. The Italian Peace Movement developed largely
after the Second World War, and has known three different seasons or stages.
    The first stage occurred in the years 1948-1952,
during the debate on Italy joining NATO and CED (the
aborted European Defence Community). The Communists
were the protagonists, while the catholics under the
leadership of Pope Pius XII were strictly in favour
of military defence, even nuclear, in the case of
aggression, according to the traditional doctrine of
the 'Just War'.
    The second stage came later in the 1960s, and was
linked to East-West detente, to Kennedyism and the
'New Frontier', and to the catholic reforms of the
Ecumenical Council. There was also strong influence
from the French experience in the Algerian War and

American protests against the Vietnam War. Here again the Left is in the vanguard, but particularly in cultural terms we now see the emergence of a catholic protagonism, underlined by Ecumenical and anti-militaristic trends. These were the years to which conscientious objection, that is, the right to refuse military service on the grounds of conscience, was widely debated and acknowledged, especially after the papal encyclical, 'Gaudium et Spes', of late 1965. There was at that time strong influence from American pacifism, as people sang songs such as 'John Brown', 'We shall overcome' and 'I care', etc. A new cultural framework for the Italian Peace Movement was emerging, where the dominant theme was not so much peace, but anti-militarism. The leading political force became the Radical Party, notably throughout the 1970s.

The third stage of the IPM is now just beginning. From 1967 to 1981 the Radical Party organized 14 anti-militaristic marches, the last six of which had an international character, with protesters marching through the principal Italian, French, German and Benelux military bases. In 1979 the 4th International March from Paris to Warsaw involved even the Polish Peace Committee.

The trigger of this third stage was the NATO decision on INF (Intermediate Nuclear Forces) of December 1979, which once again brought to the fore the theme of peace. But this time, pacifism, it was decided, must be exported to the East; and a debate erupted among Italian pacifists on this issue: pacifis need not be only an anti-Western movement. This third stage of the Italian Peace Movement can be subdivided into three further stages. From 1979 to 1981 the Radical Party was predominant in various initiatives, marches and demonstrations. These took place against a background of relatively soft attitude towards INF adopted by the PCI, which in this period tried to demonstrate its right to enter a hypothetical Government coalition.

From 1981 onwards, the communists began to intervene more directly and to take control of the peace movement, especially with the formation of the first local peace committees. This was prompted by the official announcement of Comiso (Sicily) as the site chosen for the deployment of cruise missiles, an announcement made by the Italian Government in August, 1981. There is now a precise political goal (avert INF deployment) and a need for the PCI to 'recover electoral ground on its left'. Large marches with the participation of thousands of people were organized in Rome and elsewhere, with the aid of the trade unions

The Peace Movement in Italy

and the participation of the catholic Left, and even
of some US congressmen (November 1982). However, the
military 'coup d'etat' in Poland at the end of 1982
had a noticeable impact on the direction of the Italian
Peace Movement, opposing to some extent its dominant
themes of anti-Americanism and anti-Westernism.
    'After Poland, Pacifism changes gear' declared an
editorial in a February, 1982 edition of the weekly
L'Espresso (by A. Gambino). 'Side by side with the
sentimentalists and the utopians and with those resigned to an agreement with the USSR (better red than
dead) a more realistic form of pacifism is emerging.'
    1982 and 1983 witnessed the growing control of
the PCI over the IPM. It was a delicate political
operation by the communists, trying to lead the IPM
without pushing it too far, for fear of being accused
of pro-Sovietism and thus losing electoral ground.
This fact did not prevent the PCI from organizing a
huge mass rally in June, 1982 during the visit of
President Reagan to Rome.
    Despite these efforts, including an attempt to
persuade the socialist-led government to declare a
temporary moratorium on IMF Deployment, the Italian
Peace Movement failed. This was already clear during
the general elections of June, 1983 when the INF question as an electoral issue was avoided by almost all
parties. This amounted to an unspoken agreement between the parties, in order not to frighten off an
electorate already overwhelmed by other domestic
issues. By the end of 1983, INF Deployment in Comiso
had begun, and according to many observers this was the
end of the Italian Peace Movement.
    Although we tend to agree with this statement, we
would prefer to say that since January 1984, a new
phase in the life and activities of the IPM has begun,
a phase in which the IPM, and especially the PCI, is
looking back at the experience of the last few years,
assessing strategic and tactical mistakes, and above
all looking to the future for a more comprehensive and
long-range strategy for the Italian Peace Movement.

GOALS AND IDEOLOGY

The declared goals of the Italian Peace Movement in the
late 1970s and early 1980s were first of all to avert
INF deployment in Europe and to fight against the
decision by the Italian government to deploy nuclear-
tipped cruise missiles in Comiso. When the decision
was made the peace movement tried to delay its implementation and to call for a moratorium on missile de-

ployment.

A long-range goal was the establishment of nuclear-free zones in Europe and in the Mediterranean.
Another and more immediate goal was to freeze, or better still to reduce defence spending, and to allocate
these resources to social expenditures. A corollary
of this was to call for a policy of no-export of armaments abroad, starting with a tighter control on arms
sales and with a gradual reconversion to civilian production of the booming Italian arms industry.

The ideology of the peace movement contains two
principal components:

1. Pre-political component, entirely 'Western-
   ised'. similar to other peace movements,
   especially in the USA and West Germany. Its
   salient characteristics are ecologism (although the Italian 'Greens' are much less
   powerful and politically organized than the
   Germans), anti-militarism and anti-nuclearism
   This is an ideological background particularly favourable to the radical culture and activities of the Radical Party.
2. A more political component, with peculiar
   national characteristics: anti-Westernism,
   nationalism, anti-Americanism, and even pro-
   Sovietism. This is the ideological component
   more open to the communist hegemony. The
   Italian Communist Party is in fact neither
   pacifist, anti-nuclear, nor anti-militarist.
   We find here also a catholic component, which
   has rediscovered some old themes of the 1950s
   Catholic 'integralism' or dogmatism is indeed
   anti-Westernist and anti-illuminist, and
   imitates (but only to a limited extent) the
   models of behaviour of US pacifism.

We shall analyse now in more detail the attitude
of the church, and the problem of its refusal of nuclear deterrence and nuclear war as contrary to the
traditional concept of the just war.

The Attitude of the Italian Church

The position of the church on pacifism and war must
not be confused with the position, sometimes quite
different, taken by such activist Catholic groups and
movements as the Christians for Socialism, the Popular
Movement, Pax Christi, FOCSIV (the Catholic Volunteers),
etc. This official position is determined by the declarations of the Italian Episcopal Conference (CEI),

by the Pope himself, by the Vatican policy (led by
Monsignor Casaroli) and by authoritative articles and
essays, especially by Father Sorge, editor-in-chief of
the influential Jesuit monthly, La Civilta Cattolica.
    Clearly, the church is conducting an in-depth
revision of the traditional concept of the just war,
theorized some centuries ago by St. Augustine in De
Civitate Dei and later by St. Thomas Aquinas. As
early as 1963, the encyclical 'Pacem in terris' of Pope
John XXIII had affirmed the need to overcome the concept of peace based upon the balance of forces, expec-
ially nuclear ones (the balance of terror). The Second
Vatican Council and the Encyclical 'Gaudium et Spes'
confirmed the legitimacy of 'defensive war', but also
said that in the nuclear age, military actions conducted with means capable of generating huge and indis-
criminate destruction 'go by far beyond the limits of
legitimate defence' and therefore the problem of war
must be considered with 'an entirely new mentality'.
    This kind of war (mass destruction), continued
the text, 'is a crime against God and Mankind, and must
be condemned firmly and without hesitation'. (4) The
immorality of nuclear war (and therefore, of the doctrine of nuclear deterrence) was then indicated in a
remarkable editorial in the monthly Civilta Cattolica
in January, 1982.(5) However, even under Pope Wojtila,
the official Catholic milieu in Italy has showed until
now a rather cautious attitude on such thorny issues
as INF and nuclear deterrence, and in any case is much
less 'militant' than the attitudes adopted, for example, by Catholic movements in the US.
    Such prudence on the part of the powerful 'Italian
Episcopal Conference' and of the Movement 'Justitia et
Pax', was confirmed during a 'summit' in the Vatican
in January 1983, where Italian Bishops discussed with
representatives of the Episcopal Conferences (or of the
Bishops) of France, Belgium and Britain, the more recent
initiatives and actions on Nuclear Disarmament organized by the American Bishops.
    The national daily La Stampa of Turin explained
the reasons for Italian prudence (19 January 1983) with
the observation that 'the Nuclear debate in Italy does
not seem, until now, to have penetrated the popular
conscience and has not provoked reactions comparable to
those of other European countries'.
    A full discussion on this issue was then conduct-
ed, with a lively and controversial debate by the
Jesuit Father Bartolomeo Sorge in an invited lecture
at CASD, the Centre of Highter Defence Studies of the
Italian Armed Forces on 30 March 1984 in Rome.
    The immorality of using nuclear weapons, and

therefore of building and deploying them was clearly
stated before the entire Italian military establishment, lined up for the occasion. However, Father
Sorge mitigated his statement, recalling the message
of Pope John Paul II to the Second UN Special Session
on Disarmament on 11 June 1982 that said: 'In the
present conditions, a dissuasion based upon the [nuc-
lear] balance, surely not conceived as an end in itself, but as a transition stage on the road to gradual
disarmament, may still be considered as morally acceptable.'(6)

In this way, the position of the church remains
in priniciple against nuclear missiles, but shows a
substantial flexibility and a tacit acceptance of INF
deployment. But this time the Roman Catholic Church
also took an active step, when Pope John Paul II
charged his 'foreign minister', Monsignor Casaroli,
to mediate between the US and the USSR, inviting them
to resume the interrupted Geneva negotiations on
nuclear weapons.

A more autonomous position has been taken by the
Franciscans, which have opened up on the Left, receiv-
ing in Assisi in 1983 the then Secretary of the PCI,
Enrico Berlinguer, for a dinner-conversation with
their Father-General. Moreover, the Franciscans sent
a delegation on peace missions to Washington, where
they were received personally by President Reagan,
and to Moscow, where they were equally well received
at the Kremlin, although not by President Chernenko
himself, who ordered instead that a personal message
be delivered. At the same time, the Franciscans are
building a meeting centre, in Assisi called the 'Cita-
del of Peace'.

THE PROTAGONISTS OF THE PEACE MOVEMENT: ITS ORGANIZA-
TION, STRUCTURE, AND NATIONAL CHARACTERISTICS

The Protagonists
Among the many groups and organizations that form the
Italian Peace Movement, the more noteworthy are:

     1.   Communist party and affiliated organizations:
     -   Democratic Proletarian Union Party
     -   Independent left-wing MP (elected in PCI's
        lists)
     -   Christian Socialist (PSI's MP)
     -   ARCI (Association for Cultural Relations),
        Environment League, Gramsci Institute, Ital-
        ian Women's Union (UDI)

2. Religious Organizations:
-   Protestants (Ecumenical, Waldensian
    Churches)
-   Pax Christi
-   Catholic Volunteers
-   ACLI (Catholic Italian Workers' Association)
-   Parish Organizations
3. Environment (Ecological) and Cultural Organ-
    izations:
-   Local governments (usually left-wing)
-   Universities (prevailing physics, medicine,
    biology and philosophy departments)
4. Rival peace groups:
    a. Radical Party: its main aim is to diver-
        sify the ideological mainstream, which
        is monopolized by the Communist Party.
        The Comiso missile base is not of vital
        importance; the Radical Party tries to
        shift the discussion towards anti-milit-
        arism rather than simply towards anti-
        nuclear pacifism, in the West as well as
        in the East (Warsaw, Prague).
    b. The Catholic 'Popular Movement' and
        'Comunione e Liberazione': its main con-
        cern is to push the Catholic pacifists
        away from communist hegemony. It stres-
        ses the moral and theological aspects of
        pacifism rather than its political im-
        plications. 'True' and 'noble' is how
        their pacifist attitude is termed, be-
        cause it is free of political implica-
        tions and is well respected. It is more
        right-wing than the official church pos-
        ition.

Problems of Co-ordination

The Italian Peace Movement has had a problem of central
co-ordination for many years. Gianni Baget Bozzo, a
Catholic columnist close to the Socialist Party, was
the first (L'Unita, 6 October 1983) to propose a central co-ordinating structure. He considers it a 'fundamental mistake' to have expanded such an effort on
the 'last battle' against missile deployment in
Comiso. He points out that the PCI's embarrassment is
an obstacle to the peace movement; the party fears to
be excluded in the future from any possible participation in government because of its position on the INF
issue.

The peace movement, therefore, should be free of
its 'purely political and ideological features', and

should rather stress its political component; the
debate should be directed at the Euro-American relationship (as with the German peace movement) and not
simply on Euro-missiles. Berlinguer (the then PCI's
leader) replied that 'the peace movement should not be
monolithic, otherwise its autonomy would be alienated,
and so would its different social components, such as
religious associations, trade unions, political parties and representatives of scientific and cultural
associations' (the 'greens', the 'Womens' movement'
etc.).

The PCI has in fact two good reasons for not becoming the 'peace movement' party. Firstly, according
to Gianni Baget Bozzo, the PCI fears accusations of
its taking a pro-Soviet position (despite the clear
division between the PCI and the 'Fight for Peace'
group, openly financed by the USSR) which would risk
undoing the positive effects of political choices made
in 1973 and 1983 (Eurocommunism and open criticism of
the USSR).

Secondly, the peace movement is a popular issue
especially among youth groups and may attract votes.
It is then seen as important not to alienate the different components of the peace movement, and to keep
its structure and organization as open as possible.

Structure
A partial co-ordinating body is the Office of Peace and
Disarmament, created by the PCI and placed under the
direction of Senator Renzo Gianotti (September 1983).
There is also a Unitary Committee for Peace and Disarmament, directed by Mr A Cagnes and a Mrs Caccio: this
body, however, does not have real co-ordinating ability.

Locally, the official bodies that should co-ordinate are city districts and the office of the councillor
responsible for a municipal department. The ARCI and
Gramsci Institute (PCI area) are very efficient, and
the local PCI offices operate in this field when local
authorities show signs of indifference.

More research-oriented are the following centres:
Archivio Disarmo, Disarmament File, (Independent left-
wing MPs); CESPI (PCI), IRDISP (Radical party). The
remainder divides into: Religious organizations: ACLI,
Pax Christi, FOCSIV; The Scientists' Union for Disarmament, created in 1983, attracts academics and intellectuals. Medicine for Peace also exists, but only in
public meetings; The International Meeting Against
Militarization and cruise Missiles is stationed in
Comiso and organizes meetings to protest against the

missile base (police have twice intervened, wounding
on one occasion an MP).

National Characteristics
The salient national features of the Italian Peace
Movement are summarized below, taking also into account
some interesting remarks recently made by Senator
Renzo Gianotti. (7)

    1.   Italian Pacifism has suffered, along with
other Mediterranean and south European peace movements,
from what may be called the 'peripheral effect',
especially related to the nuclear disarmament issue,
but far stronger in Central Europe.
    2.   The roots and motivations of pacifism in other
European countries are mostly 'extrapolitical', stemming from religious movements, from a demand for more
participation in public life and in policy decisions
by certain social groups, such as the Greens, etc.
But in Italy, the road to pacifism leads predominantly
through the mass political parties, and these have
acted in order to block, or at least to control and
direct the peace movement for political use in domestic
policy.
    3.   Especially in Central Europe, pacifism has
been strictly linked to the crisis of political identity of the Social Democratic parties, as it has been
demonstrated particularly in the West German case.
(The SPD split on the nuclear issue and on the deployment of NATO cruise and Pershing missiles.) We have
witnessed a certain identity crisis within the Communist Party (that continues after Berlinguer's death
and even after the recent electoral successes) and at
the same time the relative consolidation of the Socialist Party (PSI) of Bettino Craxi, who leads the present
coalition government. The Socialist Party has displayed no love for the peace movement, and has tended
to assert its legitimacy as newly pro-Atlantic.
    4.   There is a peculiar relationship between pac-
ifism and nationalism, again especially if compared
with the German case. A weaker or incomplete 'national
conscience' stemming from only a century of national
unity of the Italian State, the preservation of this
unity after the Second World war, the lack of an imperial tradition (unless we go back to the Roman
Empire), all these factors make Italy different from
the other European countries.
    5.   There has been a certain weakness in the re-
lations between the peace movement and the trade unions. Admittedly, some mass demonstrations for peace

and against nuclear missiles were staged by the trade
unions, such as on Christmas eve, 1983, and on 31 October 1981, when several local trade union demonstrations took place in various Italian regions. On the
other hand, the same trade unions leaders have publicly
acknowledged some definite limits to these initiatives
pointing out the difficulty of developing a peace
culture as an integral part of trade-unionism, and of
strengthening the relations between the trade unions
and the peace committees. Briefly, the main issue
seems to be the overcoming of the partial or special
politico-economic values peculiar to the trade unions
as an interest group, and the adoption of a more glo-
balistic 'peace culture' that implies a more comprehensive view of the need to reform socio-political and
economic relations.

6.   There has been, as we have already seen, a
remarkable lack of unity and purpose in the Italian
peace movement. This kind of fragmentation, politicization and fluctuation has ruined, from the inside,
the overall image and credibility of the movement in
public opinion, in spite of a generally sympathetic
'attitude towards peace values and ideals'.

7.   Except in a few cases, notably represented by
some Italian physicists and scientists, connected with
the Pugwash Movement (the ISODARCO group), there has
been a significant lack of an adequate cultural-scien-
tific background to arms control and disarmament issues in the peace movement. This naivete has been only
lightly balanced by some studies and publications cir-
culated by the communist and radical study-centres on
peace and security issues. The consequence has been
the apparent inability quickly to find new issues likely to provoke widespread social and political mobilization.

PUBLIC SUPPORT

If we can link neutralism with pacifism, opinion polls
conducted in 1982 and 1983 by the Doxa and Makno In-
stitutes (8) showed an average level of neutralists
of 32 to 33 per cent. This figure is quite close to
the percentage of Italians who think that military
force should never be used under any circumstances (the
group known as 'unconditional pacifists').

The Makno survey of 1983 also showed quite different levels of 'neutralism', a factor which was more
pronounced among young people in the 20-24 age group
(41 per cent), but weaker among teenagers (28 per
cent), who were also the least pro-NATO (only 36 per

cent), and even weaker among older people in the 44-55 age group (25 per cent). However, other polls conducted by the Doxa Institute on behalf of the United States Information Service showed a sharp gap between the percentage of 'passive pacifists' who declared themselves to be against nuclear missiles, and the percentage of 'active pacifists' who admitted taking part (at least once) in some kind of peace demonstration or activity or who signed petitions in favour of disarmament. This group consisted of no more than 3-5 per cent.

It will be useful now to review briefly the type of support given to the Peace Movement by the main Italian political parties.

The Christian Democrats

The Christian Democratic party (DC) which dominated, at least until recently, every government coalition in Italy since the Second World War, has always maintained a firm pro-NATO position. This has been confirmed, to the surprise of the other NATO allies, by the smooth decision on INF deployment made by the Cossiga government in 1979-80.

This pro-Atlantic attitude of the party was then reconfirmed in early 1983 by the then Minister of Foreign Affairs. Emilio Colombo, with particular reference to the debate and the doubts on the political viability of the 'Zero Option' proposal made by President Reagan. The present Foreign Minister and past Premier, Giulio Andreotti, a leading Christian Democratic and national politician, also expressed his diffidence towards pacifism on several occasions, saying, for example: 'In the Peace Movement there are people who are marching, and people who are exploiting those who are marching.' (9)

However, the pro-Atlanticism of the Christian Democratic Party has never prevented its left-wing or certain militant Catholic movements and intellectuals from expressing pacifist leanings or participating in peace initiatives. But this is on the condition that these initiatives would not necessarily degenerate into unilateralism and anti-Americanism.

The Socialist Party

The Socialist Party's position regarding the peace movement and the missile deployment in Europe was relatively vague in 1979-80. But this became clear in 1981. The Socialist Party, in parliamentary debates, insisted on the 'dissolution clause', that is, if the negotiations with USSR were successful, the deployment of missiles would not be started. In fact this afterwards became the 'zero option' proposed by President Reagan.

The PSI had to take into account the opinion of its left-wing, whose representatives had already taken part in several peace marches. However in 1981, the PSI position became more clearly pro-Western and Atlanticist, according to the line of the PSI leader, Bettino Craxi (who went to the USA to meet President Reagan) and of the then Defence Minister Lelio Lagorio a socialist as well, whose nick-name significantly, was, 'the Duke'. The attitude towards the peace movement changed considerably. As a member of the International Affairs bureau of the Party stated: 'It leaves us quite indifferent'. The PSI also make a distinction between true pacifists and those who are instruments of Soviet propaganda. According to the Socialist, Daniele Moro (November 1982):

> The PSI has a special interest which concerns the peace movements and does not consider them simply an instrument of Moscow, but the Party will never stop to watch out for the 'one-way' pacifism, which is not acceptable and, in the long term, dangerous. (10)

Actually, the position of the Italian Socialists would be influenced more by the German Social Democrats, rather than by the Pacifists. A proposal for an 'intermediate solution', for example, leaving some missiles on both sides (East and West) was considered and discussed by Paolo Vittorelli, President of ISTRID (Institute for Study and Research and Information on Defence) and a member of the Trilateral Commission, in the socialist daily, L'Avanti in January, 1983.

The Lay Parties

The main lay parties, that is, the Republican Party, which in 1983-4 held the defence portfolio, with Giovanni Spadolini; the Liberal Party and the Social Democratic Party (which in Italy is much more to the right than in Germany) have never shown much liking or support for the peace movement, except in a few isolated cases involving some youth sections or groups.

The Communist Party

Going now into more details on the communist support for the peace movement, the PCI positon on the Euro-

missiles is rather interesting. The PCI in the parliamentary debate on the approval of the NATO deployment of missiles in Italy, held in 1979, showed itself
very reasonable. It pursued a restrained opposition,
stressing the importance of negotiation and the necessity of a preliminary freeze by the USSR on the deployment of SS-20 missiles (without much success, however). This attitude of the PCI stems from its efforts to closely align itself to the 'majority area'
of the Italian political spectrum.

In Italian political terms, it implies, in an un-
defined future, the possibility to take part in a
leftist Government (with the PSI) or in a 'National
Solidarity coalition', that is to say a new 'historical
compromise' between the communists and the Christian
Democrats. On the other hand, the Communist Party
does not want to be outflanked on the left by the Radical Party and the Party of Proletarian Democracy,
which have a stake in the peace movement and the young
ecologists (or 'environmentalists'). It therefore
organized - in connection with the trade unions - popular rallies and peace marches on this issue. Such
a position dates from 1981-2, when relations between
the parties in power and the PCI became increasingly
cold. This ruled out even an indirect possibility of
the PCI co-operating with the government. However,
the PCI seems to be flexible on the INF issue, and its
pro-NATO position was not substantially changed from
the time of its former Secretary, Enrico Berlinguer,
and his declarations.

A certain ambiguity has been noted in a document
prepared for the XVI Party Congress (L'Unita, 24 November 1982) that criticized the loss of national sovereignty to another country (the USA) and claimed a
more independent role for each nation, even within the
existing international alliances. However, Paolo
Bufalini, member of the central committee of PCI, is
quoted by John Vinocur, of the New York Times as saying that 'the deployment of Euromissiles is theoretic-
ally possible'. (11) The PCI is certainly paying close
attention to the new Soviet and Swedish proposals,
concerning a denuclearized European zone, but the Party
is now in a transitional phase. Enrico Berlinguer, its
leader for many years, died last summer (1984). Therefore, under the new Secretary, Alessandro Natta, previous political positions are under reconsideration
even though a fundamental continuity with the past can
be recognized. Concerning Euromissiles, the public
is awaiting new documents or ideas.

TYPES OF ACTIVITIES

There have been several types of initiatives and activities organized by various groups within the Italian Peace Movement. These can be listed as follows:

- Cultural and scientific meetings organized by by Archivio Disarno, USPID, Universities' Department, National Research Committee (anti-independent research organizations), local government.
- Exhibitions, conferences, debates, concerts, films, organized during several 'Festival dell' Unita' (PCI sponsored).
- Meetings in front of the Comiso base.
- Peace marches (Milan, Como, Palermo, Geneva).
- PCI delegation to the USSR, withdrawal of PCI observers from the Prague Peace Conference, because of police action against local dissidents.
- Referendum or public collection of signatures to abrogate the deployment of missiles in Comiso (This will not have any real effect, because the Italian constitution does not consider the case of an international agreement repealed by popular referendum.)

The Radical Party organized:
- The public collection of signatures against arms
- An attempt to invade a military airport in Northern Italy (Ghedi)
- A peace march in Prague, 1983
- Publications on military expenditures: L'Italia armata (Armed Italy), Quello che à Russi gia sanno e i concittadini non devono sapere (What the Russians know already and you do not have to know), Per il Disarmo (For Disarmament), Le armi della Repubblica, (The Army of the Republic) published by Gammalibri 1982-3); on PCI hegemony of the peace movement: La guerra non violenta (The non violent war), Gammalibri, 1983, and Fate l'amore non la guerra (make love not war), ibid., 1980.

The Catholic movements organized the following events and took the following positions:

- They were at the peace march in Rome, October 1983 organized by the Italian left, which created some polemics.

- They disputed what they called the 'one-way' pacifism of the Left.
- A peace march was organized in Milan by 'Comunio ne e Liberazione', 5 November 1983.
- A pilgrimage to Geneva (March 1984) was organized to present a petition for the resumption of nuclear negotiations between the US and the USSR.
- The Vatican Academy of Science published a document which stated its position on nuclear weapons.
- A volunteer organization was created, called Italian Volunteers' Movement, by more right-wing elements in November, 1983.

CO-OPERATION (NATIONAL/INTERNATIONAL)

We have already seen that the degree of co-operation among the various groups of peace organizations at national level has varied considerably according to the occasion. If there have been several mass demonstrations with broad participation, in other circumstances the peace movement has clearly shown its internal fragmentation and even rivalries between its different political and ideological components.

Secondly, we have also discerned a certain weakness in co-operation with the trade unions. The latter have participated in peace demonstrations, but only to a limited extent, because they were more absorbed with facing the problems of high unemployment and of industrial-technological restructuring and conversion at a time of general economic crisis.

Coming to co-operation at the international level, that is, with peace movements in other countries, the overall impression is that, on balance, the Italian Peace Movement has tended passively to receive and accept support and direct participation from other national groups and movements, rather than actively seeking their co-operation. Of course, there are exceptions, when representatives of the Italian Peace Movement, for example, took part in international marches and demonstrations throughout Europe, but in many cases various Italian groups and organizations took individual action at international level, such as the Franciscan Missions in the USA and the USSR, or the demonstrations staged by Italian Radicals at the European Parliament and even in East Berlin, where they were quickly suppressed by local police.

On the other hand, it was common to see in a large number of peace demonstrations and initiatives

in Italy the presence and the active participation of
foreign pacifists, coming especially from the more
activist countries of Central and Northern Europe -
The Netherlands, Britain, Germany and Scandinavia -
and even from the US. A good example of this phenomenon was that when the Italian authorities arrested
some 15 peace activists, who were particularly tireles
in operating near the Comiso missile base, only two o
three among them turned out to be Italian, and not of
local origin. This means, among other things, that a
good deal of the peace demonstrations staged in Sicil
or near other NATO military bases in Italy, were 'imported' from outside, rather than based on truly spontaneous reactions by the local communities.

Finally, there is another aspect to consider, an
this is the touchy issue of the relations of pacifism
with illegal organizations or sources, sometimes clos
to foreign interests or to international terrorism.
Although it is widely believed that the majority of
peace movements are 'genuine', even when openly linke
to some Italian political party or ideological 'area'
the above-mentioned risk was officially evoked quite
recently by the Italian Prime Minister, the socialist
Bettino Craxi. In his 'Report on information policy
concerning national security' (Relazione sulla politica informativa della Sicurezza) prepared by the
Italian security services, and sent by the Prime Minister himself to the House of Representatives and to
the Senate in early September 1984, a specific passag
in the text warns of the danger of infiltration in
anti-militarist, Greens, and peace movements by agent
and provokers. They might corrupt these areas and
provoke incidents with police forces, transforming th
peace movements - 'in fertile ground, ripe for subver-
sive action' (12) Although this report provoked angr
reactions by leftist intellectuals and leaders of the
peace movement, it would be unwise to dismiss it as
entirely unfounded.

MEDIA COVERAGE

Although there is no detailed survey on this particul
aspect, a few observations may easily be made. First
of all, there has been an unprecedented, continuous an
extensive coverage by the mass media of the activitie
of the Italian Peace Movement. This kind of coverage
has been frequently linked to increased public awareness for other national security issues, not just INF
Deployment, but also the Italian peacekeeping mission
in Lebanon, Mediterranean security, etc. Nevertheless

media coverage of the peace movement displayed the same characteristics as the general coverage of other security issues, namely, sensationalism. There has been a significant lack of in-depth analysis of pacifism, and only on rare occasions have the principal daily newspapers and periodicals published special surveys or more than occasional articles on the subject. One exception was <u>il Resto del Carlino</u>, the Bologna daily, and <u>Rinascita</u>, the PCI weekly.

Media coverage of the peace movement in Italy sharply decreased in intensity after the beginning of cruise missile deployment in Sicily in 1983. It would appear that the media, like the public, has perceived the failure of the peace movement's main objective and it has therefore ceased to be news. An example of this attitude was the national conference on 'Cultures and Strategies of Pacifism', jointly organized in April, 1984 in Milan by the three main study and research centres of the Italian Communist Party: CESPI (Centro Studi di Politica Internazionale), CRS (Centro Studi per la Riforma dello Stato) and Instituto Gramsci. Coverage of this event by the media, in spite of its importance as a 'soul-searching exercise' for the Italian Peace Movement, was minimal.

The third European Convention on Nuclear Disarmament, held in July, 1984 in Perugia received rather more attention from the media (and not only from the communist press), mainly because of its international character and of the open confrontation between Western 'spontaneous pacifism', (although rather fragmented) and Soviet and East European 'official pacifism'. Speeches and interventions by East European representatives were indeed the object of sharp criticism and protest.

ACHIEVEMENTS AND PROSPECTS

After the failure in any way to reverse or influence the decision by the Italian Government to deploy INF in Comiso, many observers declared the Peace Movement dead. Stefano Malatesta, for example, wrote in the daily <u>Repubblica</u> (a sort of Italian <u>Le Monde</u>) on 22 September 1983: 'The Intelligentsia does not march any more. The intellectuals, after having marched for thirty years following any slogan and pass-word, sometimes decent, sometimes less decent, now prefer to stay at home in bored silence.'

Others ascribed the disengagement of the intellectuals from the peace movement to the fear of being manipulated and to widespread anti-Sovietism, or even to the feeling of having jumped on the wrong bandwagon (the PCI), and to the consequent trend of adopting a less 'leftist' attitude.

But for a clearer perception of the evolution of the peace movement in the general context of Italian society, we also have to consider that in these same years some entirely opposite trends emerged, such as a growing awareness of national security interests and a more active and self conscious role for the Armed Forces in society as a whole. These trends have slowly surfaced and have increased, especially during and after the mission of Italian troops in Lebanon. It is significant that an opinion poll published by the daily Repubblica showed that the first source of national pride was found to be in Italy having won the World Soccer Cup in Spain. The excellent performance of Italian troops in Beirut came a close second. The results of this poll even provoked some ironic comments on a supposed Italian 'new nationalism'. But the fact is that enrolment applications for Military Academies have increased and not only because of economic reasons, such as the difficulty of finding jobs at a time of high unemployment. Another aspect is that popular awareness of growing risks and threats of instability in the Mediterranean was naturally fuelled by traumatic experiences of national and international terrorism (the killing of premier Aldo Moro by the Red Brigades in 1978, the kidnapping and rescue of the US General Dozier, etc.) and by such events as Gaddafi's boisterous and adventurist policy, and the discovery of Soviet submarines in Italian territorial waters (in the Gulf of Taranto, near an important naval base), etc.

But if pacifism and nuclear disarmament have appeared as new ideals for the young generation, after the fall of many myths of the 1960s and 1970s, from Vietnam to Maoism, in many respects we have today a more mature and better-educated generation. In this context, the temptation of neutralism, or even worse, defeatism (better red than dead) must be assessed with a certain realism. If those who declare themselves in favour of a neutral attitude in the East-West confrontation reach 30 to 35 per cent, that is one-third of the electorate, this percentage drops sharply to only 3 to 5 per cent of those who have actually participate in any kind of peace demonstration, or taken the symbolic action, for example, of signing petitions agains nuclear weapons or defence-spending.

Thus, a greater interest is a perceptible trend towards constructive criticism of the present national and Atlantic defence arrangements, or rather a

'Reformism' of NATO in favour of some kind of more active and autonomous European defence system. This attitude is perhaps surprisingly widespread even among communist supporters. (13)

To sum up, it could be said that pacifism in Italy has been and still is for many people a kind of escape or ready-made solution to the daunting problems of peace and war in the nuclear age. In practice this may mean an unconscious rejection or psychological crisis when confronted with nuclear responsibility, the concept of balance of forces and the more and more difficult and complex problems of arms control and reduction. Leon Wieseltier, in a stimulating essay published in The New Republic writes that one of the gravest faults of the 'Party of Peace' is that it preaches an escape from responsibility and a hate for all military affairs. But this is a symptom that 'we do not believe in what we are, and we do not believe that we have something to lose' (freedom, security, etc). (14)

However, in Italy some think that even the Left and the Communist Party are slowly learning this lesson, although they are still plagued by many oscillations and perplexities. A meaningful example was that given by the Conference on the Italian Peace Movement organized by the PCI in Milan in April 1984. The Conference attempted to analyse the past experiences of the peace movement, to indicate the tasks ahead, and to elaborate a more comprehensive political strategy, articulated in the following five guidelines:

a. To rethink Italy's role in a reformed NATO in connection with the present debate on the Rogers Doctrine, on the revitalization of the Western Peace Movement.

b. To work for the gradual establishment of 'de nuclearized zones' in Europe, an idea partially borrowed from the Scandinavian peace movement.

c. To strengthen the international connections of the peace movement, and to consolidate a New European Dimension of the IPM.

d. To face real problems, more closely linked to such national realities as the growing Italian defence industry, the political and institutional control of the military-industrial complex and of the arms trade, the issue of reconversion of military production, the problem of a new Italian defence model, and the law on military service.

e. To adopt a less idealistic and naive approach to arms control negotiations, and while not indulging unduly in Realpolitik, to rethink at least much of the old - until now a largely ineffective approach to the whole issue. (15)

The tasks outlined for the Italian and European peace movements are by no means easy ones. It remains to be seen whether the Communist Party, in its present state of uncertainty over its future course in Italian politics, will decide to continue riding the horse of pacifism, in spite of past failures, or whether it wil be able to push the peace movement towards a new and more effective stage of development and popular consensus, likely to influence the Government's defence and foreign policies.

This dilemma between idealism and realism may be underlined by the recent remarks made by Marco Fumagalli, National Secretary of the FGCI, the Federation of Communist Youth:

> Are we facing today a pacifist generation or not? If we think 'pacifist' means a definite choice of life, the repudiation of any form of violence, if we adopt abstract or old-fashioned models, then our answer is no. If, however, for pacifist we mean a generation that is against war and its logic, that wants to affirm the value of everybody's life, that wants to give back to mankind the possibility to decide upon its destiny, that thinks of politics not only in terms of power, bu also in terms of values, then, yes, this is a pacifist generation. (16)

NOTES

(1) 'Con quel cartello spaventapasseri Robassomero fa la guera al nucleare', La Stampa, 12 January 1983.
(2) G. Zizola, 'Detraete le armi', Panorama, 29 February 1983.
(3) C. Sottocorona, 'In guerra per la Pace: Movimenti intelletuali e pacifisti', Panorama, 19 April 1982.
(4) Papal Encyclical, 'Gaudium et Spes', n.80.
(5) 'Per evitare la guerra, prepariamo la pace', La Civilta Cattolica, n. 3157, Rome, 2 January 1982.
(6) Quoted in Padre B. Sorge, SJ, La Chiesa, la Guerra, La Pace, conference held at CASD on 30 March 1984. Quaderni del CASD 83/84, Roma, Supplemento al N. 11 del Bollettino, 'Ut Unum Sint'.
(7) R. Gianotti, 'Tendenze e Problemi dei Movimenti in Italia', Paper released at the Conference on

Pacifism organized by Istituto Gramsci, Milan, 6-7 April 1984.

(8) For more detailed data, see the chapter on Italy by the same author in, The Public and Atlantic Defence, Rowman & Allanheld Totowa, New Jersey, and Croom Helm, London, 1984.

(9) From a speech pronounced at a Seminar of the Italian Atlantic Committee in Mondello (Palermo) on 29 October 1982.

(10) D. Moro, 'La posizione del PSI: pace, sicurezza, indipendenza', IPD Informazioni Parlamentari Difesa, no. 29, 16/19 Novembre 1982, ISTRID, Roma.

(11) J. Vinocur, 'Rome Shows Interest in Cutting NATO Deployment', International Herald Tribune, 17 January 1983.

(12) See the article 'Provocatori infiltrati tra i gruppi pacifisti', published on the front page of the national daily, Il Corriere della sera, Milan, 3 September 1984.

(13) Poll taken by Doxa in May 1983 on behalf of Louis Harris and the Atlantic Institute of Paris, and published in Italy by the daily Il Sole 24 Ore of Milan.

(14) Leon Wieseltier, 'The Great Nuclear Debate', The New Republic, 10-17 January 1983, pp. 7-37.

(15) R. Gianotti, 'Tendenze e Problemi dei Movimenti in Italia'. (Also see Note 7).

(16) M. Fumagalli, 'Una generazione pacifista?', Paper presented at the Conference on Cultures and strategies of Pacifism, organized by Istituto Gramsci, Milan, 6-7 April 1984.

Chapter Eight

THE PEACE MOVEMENT IN THE UNITED STATES

James Finn

The peace movement in the United States is a protean
creature; it changes its size, shape and coloration
according to the particular issue it addresses and the
political climate of the time. When it is quiescent,
it is hardly visible to the general public, but when
it is activated it can mobilize impressive numbers of
people and mount dramatic displays.
    The most recent opportunity to see the United
States peace movement in full array was the rally that
gathered in New York's Central Park on 12 June 1982 to
protest against the nuclear arms build-up. Estimated
to be three-quarters of a million people, this was the
biggest single political rally in the history of the
United States. It was a remarkable testimony to the
ability of the peace movement to unite people under the
banner of a single issue. A combined description and
analysis of that event will tell us a great deal about
the peace movement in the United States today.
    The banners and the addresses revealed the pres-
ence of groups with the widest array of affiliations;
religious, political, professional and miscellaneous.
There were the 'peace churches' in the United States,
generally considered to include the Mennonites, the
Friends or Quakers, and the Brethren. There, too, were
representatives from the Fellowship of Reconciliation,
an international, interdenominational peace organization started in England in 1914, shortly after the
start of the First World War. (1) The American branch
of Pax Christi, the international Catholic peace organization was also visible. There were also organizations such as Clergy and Laity Concerned that came into
existence during the anti-Vietnam protest during the
1960s and groups formed more recently still, for example, those that are focused primarily on the conflicts
in Central America.
    What is true of the religious groups was also

true of groups that might more narrowly be described
as political. There were long-standing organizations
with well-developed policies and others newly sprung
up. Anyone familiar with the anti-war movement of the
1960s would have recognized familiar names, slogans
and faces on the day of that rally and would have en-
countered more that were fresh to the movement. In
addition to those accurately described as religious
or political there were others that were self-designa-
ted as professional (for example, the Physicians for
Social Responsibility); environmental groups (for
example, the Environmental Defence Fund); womens'
groups (for example, Women Against Military Madness and
Women Strike for Peace); anarchist groups (for example,
the War Resisters League); and miscellaneous groups
such as Grandparents for Nuclear Disarmament.
     As anyone who saw the rally had the opportunity
to observe, the diversity of the participants extended
beyond their organizational affiliation, for their
banners showed that they came from almost every region,
class and ethnic group in the United States. And anyone who followed the planning of the rally would have
seen that it both fed upon and nourished smaller rallies, conferences, town meetings, seminars, lectures
that extended across the country - from California to
New England, from the state of Washington to Florida.
The professionalism of the accompanying movies, slide
shows and publications showed that the movement could
raise considerable financial support and enlist people
eminent in their respective fields - science, art,
education, politics, entertainment, etc. The movement
is thus pervasive.
     The movement is also significant. Its energies
can sometimes be translated into political leverage.
For example, in the mid-term elections of November,
1982, the biggest referendum on a single issue in the
history of the United States was on a nuclear freeze
resolution. Nine states and the District of Columbia
voted on the resolution and only one state voted it
down. Previously, 275 city governments, 12 state leg-
islatures, and 446 New England town meetings were on
record as supporters. A freeze resolution was defeated
in the House of Representatives by only two votes.
Given such widespread support for a nuclear freeze,
even candidates who were opposed to it were reluctant
to meet the issue head-on. Not all of the opposition
to the nuclear freeze can be attributed to the peace
movement, but the apparent degree of political success
has attracted additional converts to the movement, encouraged various elements within it and has led to
plans for present and future political action. For

example a number of organizations are now directing their attention to the forthcoming elections of November, 1984 and - no matter what the outcome - beyond that election.

The Nuclear Weapons Freeze Campaign, claiming about eleven million supporters - in reality, a conglomeration of different existing organizations - plans an educational campaign based on publications, teach-ins, small conferences, demonstrations, and citizen exchanges with people from the USSR. SANE, an anti-nuclear organization whose fortunes and membership have waxed and waned over the last three decades, will focus on the defeat and election of selected candidates for Congress. The Council for a Livable World was formed with the specific purpose of focusing on elections to the Senate and of defeating candidates whose views on nuclear arms they consider unsatisfactory. Women Strike for Peace is trying to insert into the political debate its own specific plank: the impeachment of any president who orders an invasion of another country that has not first invaded the United States. It is at least arguably true that arms and disarmament issues play a bigger role in the 1984 presidential campaign than they would have without the pressure of the peace movement.

This view of the peace movement in the United States - that it is a movement able to motivate people and organizations of highly diverse backgrounds and divert their energies to a particular issue - is accurate, but by itself it is highly misleading. It suggests a movement that is more formidable, more directed, more sustained, than it actually is. For although the diversity of the individuals and groups in the movement is often described as its strength, it is also its great weakness. Not all of the people that participate in the movement come to it with the same goals, information, degree of sophistication, perseverance. In fact, like most peace movements, the one in the United States is misnamed. It is less a peace movement than a protest movement, that is, those who participate in it are more united in what they <u>oppose</u> than what they <u>propose</u>. As long as the goal is something as desirable and vaguely defined as 'peace' they are joined in opposition to what seems to threaten that peace. However, as soon as the nature of that threat is broken down into a consideration of particular nuclear weapons, specific policies shifting strategies, the nature of the adversary, then the inevitable divisions in the movement begin to appear. And as the plans intended to counter that threat grow increasingly specific, the usual predictable splintering begins.

164

The Peace Movement in the United States

For the leaders of the movement have highly differentiated views, analyses and goals that often run at
cross-purposes. I will give three different kinds of
examples to illustrate this process by showing how the
movement deals with 1. unilateral disarmament, 2. no-
first-use of nuclear weapons; and 3. the nuclear
freeze proposals. All of these are prominent issues
in the present peace movement.

The peace rally of June 12 was impressive. It
gave the impression of people united in their efforts
to promote peace. But before that rally took place
the committee responsible for organizing the rally had
to be restructured to exclude extremists. Nevertheless, some organizations almost withdrew and some
individuals actually did. And some people who thought
they were marching to show support for a freeze proposal were shocked to find they were marching side by
side with people who favoured unilateral disarmament.
These, in their turn, drew away from those who supported total disarmament. There was still further division between those who wanted to speak only to Western
policies and those who wished to address the Soviets.
That still leaves a number of people who could supposedly unite on the other two issues. But here, too,
the cracks appear. In the Spring, 1982 issue of
Foreign Affairs, McGeorge Bundy, George F. Kennan,
Robert McNamara and Gerard Smith urged consideration of
a nuclear policy of no first use. In their article,
they were careful to say that 'it is obvious that any
such policy would require a strengthened confidence in
the adequacy of the conventional forces of the
Alliance...' But 'no-first-use' has now become a slogan, a sentiment embraced by many in the movement who
do not wish to consider the alternate provisions and
the considerable expense necessary to develop such a
policy. If the debate on no-first-use continues it
will continue to divide those in the movement who
grasp its manifold complication and wish to pursue
them, and those who refuse to acknowledge them.

But that still leaves supposedly widespread support for the freeze resolution. It has, after all,
gained the support of the Democratic Party, Senator
Edward Kennedy and presidential candidates. It has
strong support within Congress and, as we noted, it is
a factor to consider in elections. Some polls indicate that over 70 per cent of the American people
favour a bilateral and negotiable freeze on nuclear
weapons. The actual resolution that most of them are
familiar with - for there are more than one - is that
sponsored by Senators Kennedy (Democrat; Massachussets)
and Mark Hatfield (Republican; Oregon). This calls for

a 'mutual and verifiable freeze on testing, production, and further deployment of nuclear warheads, missiles, and other delivery systems'.

However, the apparent widespread support for this resolution conceals attitudes that could rapidly alter this perception. A CBS/New York Times survey of May, 1982 showed the expected support for the freeze. But when the questions were further defined, the divisions, the splintering again appeared. For example, over 70 per cent said verification was essential for such an agreement; of those who favoured the freeze (or had no opinion) 80 per cent said they would oppose it if either side could cheat without detection, and almost 70 per cent would oppose a freeze if it would result in greater Soviet strength. Over 80 per cent said that it would be better to fight than accept Soviet domination.

It is evident that here, too, what is being supported is an attitude, a sentiment, not a policy that has found its programme. If a freeze seems to promise greater safety and stability, people will support it. If it endangers or reduces security, they will question or reject it. As the proposed resolution moves towards the necessary issues of verifiability, trust in Soviet agreements, and the present balance of nuclear and conventional forces, the present supporters of freeze will find themselves taking different paths. The apparent consensus will begin to unravel.

In addition, the apparent size of the present peace movement is misleading. There are a number of organizations almost heroically devoted to pacifism and arduous peace efforts in good times and bad. Their policies and their long-term membership are fairly consistent. The membership rolls of other organizations shift with the political tides, particular issues rousing intermittent, lively interests. For example, like its counterparts in Europe, the peace movement in the United States peaked just before the US began employment of Pershing IIs in Europe and declined somewhat after that. The Nuclear Arms Educational Service at Stanford University has identified about 1,250 anti-nuclear groups. Only a few of these are engaged in the kind of electoral politics that could have long-term effects; others are planning activities that will have possibly dramatic but definitely ephemeral impact during political campaigns; most are merely quiescent.

The peace movement also finds it difficult to remain focused on a single issue, such as the nuclear freeze. Both because of the pressure of events and the interests of some of the leaders, attention is

necessarily diverted to other issues, other areas.
Many who marched in the nuclear freeze rally of 1982
are now concentrating their energies and attention on
Central America and what they regard as the nefarious
role the United States is playing there. They have
been very successful in working with peace activists
in Europe, and are pleased to see Central America in
terms of another Vietnam - a grave mistake. Still
others have emerged - or re-engaged - themselves in the
familiar debate between the virtues/faults of capitalism vs the virtues/faults of socialism and are applying their findings to the relation of advanced, in-
dustrialized countries to the developing countries.
And there is one contingent that sees the issue of
arms, environmental protection, economics and poverty
as one single issue of 'peace and justice' that demands one overarching response. For example, in the
autumn of 1983, a new journal, World Policy, was published with the hope, according to its editor, Sherle
R. Shwenninger, that it would become a voice for peace,
church and environmental activists. In the first
issue Mary Caldor, a founder of END (European Nuclear
Disarmament), argued that, in effect, the West created,
in psychological terms, the new Russian menace, and a
member of the editorial board wrote an article entitled
'Why is There No Green Party in the US?' According to
one account, Mr Shwenninger said the journal will be
supportive of Third World revolutions and praised
Cuba for fulfilling America's ideals. This is not an
editorial course that everyone in the peace movement
would endorse or follow. (2)
     Although it would be possible to add many more
particulars to this overview of the peace movement -
more accurately described as a protest movement - they
would not change the general contours that already
allow some summarizing judgements.
     First, the peace movement is not a cohesive, un-
ited monolithic group that can be described and praised
or dismissed with an easy descriptive label. People
in the movement exist on a very wide spectrum, differing in goals, intentions, dedication, political sophistication, and tactics. It would be a mistake not
to discriminate, a mistake to dismiss what is positively valuable along with what is positively harmful or
merely misguided. (3)
     Second, the extensive activity and widespread
publicity that the movement has generated - the professional movement people know how to get media attention - disguise but do not hide the fact that much of
its support is soft and transitory. Many of the most
active participants in the peace movement of the 1960s

are now critics of the present movement.

Third, there is an idealism that is proper and necessary in political life. This is present in the movement, but so also is an abstract idealism that, impatient with the resistant realities, attempts to vault over them to some fancied utopia. Refusing to recognize the moral principles must be incarnated in particular policies before they can be realized, these idealists attempt to bypass the order of politics. This idealism is particularly dangerous when it proposes itself as the solution to the fear engendered by nuclear weapons. This is exactly what Jonathan Schell did in The Fate of the Earth - for a short time the bible of the movement for many people - when he described a nuclear holocaust, rejected deterrence, proclaimed the need to invent a new politics, and then said he could not presume to tell us how to go about it.

Fourth, some people in the movement have clearly defined goals and are pleased to instruct others. But many who say they want to forgo politics, who say they simply want 'to take a stand', also want to be a political force. These contrary ambitions lead to clumsy and dangerous propositions. For, given present realities, the efforts of the peace movement in the United States are directed at and felt by those responsible for the policies of the US and of NATO, not the Soviet Union. What is offered as neutral or balanced criticism is, thus inevitably biased in its effect.

Fifth, there is a group in the movement that significantly ignores or sympathetically misreads Soviet behaviour. Some do this out of a developed analysis that has anti-Western, anti-capitalist overtones, others out of simple ignorance about or disbelief in the massive arms build-up in which the USSR has been engaged and the deployment of many of those arms in Europe.

Many of these people are in positions of leadership in the National Council of Churches (NCC). This partially accounts for how a delegation of 266 church leaders under NCC sponsorship could conclude a two-week visit to the Soviet Union in June, 1984 praising the state of religion in that country and simultaneously condemning the role of the United States in the arms race.(4) They do not acknowledge, therefore, that a declared policy of no-first-use, a nuclear freeze, or a policy of rapid denuclearization - at this time - would seriously favour the Soviets. (5)

Sixth, some in the peace movement are familiar with and concerned about the weaknesses and excesses of the movement. Since its founding in 1967, the

the World Without War Council has attempted to put peace activities on a sound realistic basis. Recognizing the problems of both American military involvement and disengagement, the reality of Soviet military and political power and the dangers of a nuclear arms race, it offers specific policy proposals and initiatives to achieve the declared goals. Because it also monitors the activities of other peace organizations, it is the frequent recipient of harsh counter-criticism. In addition, some peace organizations remain aware and critical of limitations on authentic peace groups in the Soviet Union. For example, in August, 1982 over a dozen major peace groups organized a demonstration at the Soviet Mission to the UN in New York City in support of a new, independent peace group in Moscow and one of its founding members, Sergei Batovrin, then being held in a Soviet psychiatric hospital.

Seventh, a most important point, the attitudes of the American people on matters of nuclear defence have remained almost constant over almost four decades. The rise and fall of successive peace movements have not altered this basic fact. Conclusion: what is needed is engagement with and discriminate response to the peace movement, not total opposition.

I have left to the end of this brief analysis one factor that I do not regard simply as a coda, but as a factor of real importance - the new role of the Catholic Church in the peace movement. There have been traditional peace churches whose stance is known and anticipated, and particular religious leaders who speak from a biblically grounded pacifism. But Judaism, the mainline Protestant Churches, and Roman Catholicism have not, historically, been peace communities in this sense. Their adherents have, in fact, been criticized in the past for upholding all too unquestioningly the foreign policies of the various countries in which they live. This is no longer the case. The most dramatic example of this is the Roman Catholic Church. For a number of historical reasons the Church as it is represented by Catholic bishops in America has taken a public stance highly critical of US strategic policies. In their Pastoral Letter on War and Peace, issued on 3 May 1983, the bishops say that they are led to a 'strictly conditioned moral acceptance of nuclear deterrence'. The letter itself supports no-first-use, the nuclear freeze and measures that some see as a step towards unilateral nuclear disarmament. Some critics of the pastoral letter say that while it formally accepts the deterrent system, it actually subverts it by driving a wedge between the actual weapons and the declared will to use them, the twinned elements that together make up the deterrence. Those who argue with this criticism would probably agree with John P. Lehman, Jr, who in his role as Secretary of the Navy, said 'the bishops reduce deterrence itself to an empty incantation'.

While most bishops are content to let the pastoral letter speak for itself, some others have taken more active measures. For example, twelve bishops in the West have urged their parishioners to join a 'prayer vigil' along the route of trains carrying nuclear warheads to various submarine bases. In a joint statement they said:

> Our stand in the pastoral letter is that no further deployment of nuclear weapons can possibly be justified. Every missile and nuclear weapons shipment is both a significant step toward a first-strike holocaust and a violation of the moral stand we have taken, with the support of many other US citizens, especially people of faith. (6)

The importance of such confrontation should be obvious. Many elements of the peace mvoement will fade away; some people, dedicated and ideologically situated, will continue to work, often at the fringes of politics; still others will be absorbed into working in the political process itself, making the kinds of compromises that are essential.

The official Catholic Church, however, does not fit this pattern. This is the first instance in which it has seriously challenged US foreign policy. It plans to be around for some time, it has moral stature, it is respected not only by Catholics but other Americans. It has extensive channels of communication that extend beyond the United States, it has considerable resources if it wishes to draw upon them. It is capable of pulling other religious communities and even secular organizations in its wake.

It has entered as a formidable factor in the peace movement. It may help shift the terms of the debate on peace issues. What are not changed by the attention the American Catholic bishops are belatedly paying to nuclear deterrence and nuclear response systems are the issues themselves. The bishops are a new factor in the debate, but they have not produced new arguments. And in terms of the public debate the overall task remains the same: to persuade the American people by the presentation of dependable information and reasoned argument that the security of the United States and her allies rests upon a deterrent system

The Peace Movement in the United States

that is strong and is perceived to be strong, that this
security is diminished as the deterrent is weakened,
and that many 'peace' proposals would weaken that deterrent system. The present wave of the peace movement should not lead anyone to think that the American
people will not support - as they have in the past -
what they regard as sound measures to secure their
freedom and that of their allies.

NOTES

    (1) The Fellowship of Reconciliation lists the
following as having pacifist fellowships affiliated
with it: Catholic, Baptist, Disciples, Episcopal, Ethical Culture, Liberal (Unitarian-Universalist), Luth-
eran, Methodist, New Church and Presbyterian.
    (2) Other examples could easily be added. For
example, in the New World Review, which celebrated the
twenty-fifth anniversary of the Cuban Revolution, the
Rev. Paul Dinter, regional representative of Pax Christi, reported on a trip to the USSR arranged by the US
Peace Council. In an article entitled 'The Russians
Aren't Coming', he wrote: 'Although lacking an advert-
ising industry like ours that colorfully yet subtly
foists its wares on consumers, Soviet society has a
counterpart that proclaims a different product: the
glory of the party, the people, and the dignity of
labor.' January-February 1984, p. 27.
    (3) On occasion, a number of different organiza-
tions can, of course, co-operate on some particular
programme. For example, on one programme devoted to
discussing 'The Threat of Nuclear War', The Union of
Concerned Scientists co-sponsored it with the Arms
Control Association, Coalition for a New Foreign and
Military Policy. Council for a Livable World, Council
on Economic Priorities, Federation of American Scientists, International Physicians for the Prevention of
Nuclear War, National Council of Churches, USA and
Physicians for Social Responsibility.
    (4) The New York Times, 21 June 1984.
    (5) According to at least one critic, this atti-
tude has penetrated the presidential campaign: the
editor-in-chief of the liberal New Republic reported:
'I am in receipt of a brochure from a group called
Peace Activists for Jackson, among them the silliest
Nobel/Laureate of them all, George Wald. The Peace
Activists are remarkably candid about what Jesse Jack-
son means to them. He reminds them of W.E.B. Du Bois
and Paul Robeson, who played an "inspiring role" in
the US peace movement. That's one way of putting it.
Another way is to tell the truth, that Du Bois and

Robeson were Communist Party members and enthusiastic apologists for the cruelties they knew Stalinism was inflicting on the peoples of both the Soviet Union and Eastern Europe. There are elements in today's peace movement which also think peace activism means support for the aims of the USSR, and these elements have turned to the Jackson campaign as a congenial effort. Jackson has done nothing to dissuade them. In fact, virtually every time he opens his mouth on foreign affairs, he bolsters the confidence of tyrants and terrorists around the world that they have plenty of friends in America.' The New Republic, 7 May 1984, p. 43 (Martin Peretz, 'Washington Diarist'.)

(6) The New York Times, 24 February 1984, p. A10. According to the New York Times the leaders of this effort 'are Archbishop Raymond G. Hunthausen of Seattle, who has compared the trains that move nuclear weapons to Bangor to the trains to the Nazi death camps and Bishop Leroy T. Matthiesen of Amarillo, Texas'.

Chapter Nine

THE US NUCLEAR FREEZE CAMPAIGN: FACTS AND FALLACIES

Jacquelyn K. Davis

In the United States the anti-nuclear movement has
manifested itself in the form of a campaign 'to
freeze' nuclear weapon deployments and modernization
programme. Established as a national movement in
1981, the US nuclear freeze campaign has its origins
in a proposal put forth in 1962 by US Representative
to the Geneva Disarmament Convention, Adrian Fisher.
As originally conceived, the notion of a nuclear freeze
provided for a verifiable halt on 'the number and
characteristics of strategic offensive and defensive
vehicles'. (1) The rationale underlying the freeze
concept was, as it is today, related to a conception
of the strategic balance in which US and Soviet forces
are judged to be equal in terms of their destructive
potentials. Based on the naive and mythical theory
of overkill, freeze supporters argue that there has
been apparent, since the decade of the 1960s, a real
requirement 'for a bold move to halt the arms race as
a clear indication of resolution to reduce the nuclear
terror to which all our populations are subjected'.(2)
     Central to the concept of a nuclear freeze is the
notion that war, in the nuclear age, is no longer an
effective instrument of policy. By this premise, the
United States and the Soviet Union have entered a
'post-Clausewitzian' era in which the classic bond
between war and politics is considered to be badly
frayed'. (3) The nuclear freeze movement is regarded
as an important step in the process of 'transcending
war', of converting military economies into peacetime
societies devoted to enriching the lives of all people.
As explained by Jonathan Schell:

     even in the face of the threat of annihilation,
     nations have as yet shown no willingness to sur-
     render their sovereignty, and conventional arms
     would be one support for its preservation. While

the abolition of nuclear arms would increase the margin of mankind's safety against nuclear destruction and the peril of extinction, the retention of conventional arms would permit the world to hold on to the system of nation-states. (4)

Adopted by the national movement, the concept of a nuclear freeze, beguiling in its simplicity, 'provides the average citizen with a common sense handle on a complex issue'. (5) By comparison, the highly technical nature of debate over SALT, START and INF was confusing to the public at large and, as a result, attracted little general interest. In support of the ultimate objective of banishing nuclear weapons from the face of the earth, freeze proponents argue that the United States, as a gesture of good faith, and the expectation that the Soviet Union will follow suit, should implement its own, unilateral moratorium on the modernization of US strategic systems. Some participants in the US nuclear freeze movement even insist on including conventional weapons in the expectation of 'turning every last sword into a plowshare'. (6) Most proponents, however, restrict their campaign to nuclear weapons and see a bilateral US-Soviet nuclear freeze as a practical first step towards general and complete disarmament.

While still in inchoate mass in the United States, the nuclear freeze movement has, nevertheless, emerged as a well-orchestrated campaign whose initial representation of student groups and service institutions (such as the American Friends Service Committee) has blossomed to attract a broader base of support. Today, the US nuclear freeze campaign draws upon a broad coalition of pacifists, environmentalists and arms controllers who oppose the Reagan Administration's defence policies. Of the well-established groups which make up the nuclear freeze coalition - and they number in the hundreds - many have in common a remarkably consistent socio-political outlook, not the least significant aspect of which is a perception of the United States as an aggressive world power. As expressed by the Women's International League for Peace and Freedom 'All life on earth is threatened by US imperialism'. (7) At the same time, this avowedly pacifist Women's League is an enthusiastic supporter of the Palestine Liberation Organization.(8) Likewise a pamphlet written under the auspices of the Quaker American Friends Service Committee identifies the United States as an 'outlaw nation'. (9) On that basis the author of the document builds a rationale in support of progressive movements and warns against pas-

sing judgment on the violence perpetrated by 'liberation movements'. (10)   The worst violence, it is further contended, 'begins with those who "control weapons
and institutions of repressive violence"'. that is,
the United States. (11)   The Soviet Union strangely
enough, is seldom criticized by freeze supporters.   Of
the Soviet military offensive against Afghanistan, the
Women's League (for Peace and Freedom) stated 'that
while intervention was always regrettable, it was none-
theless "understandable", given the Soviet interest in
having close relations with a neighbouring country with
which it shares a 2,000-mile border'. (12)
    The congeniality of views between some involved
in the US nuclear freeze movement and the Soviet Union
is not a coincidence.   Soviet exploitation of the
'peace' issue can be traced to the 1950s and the
Stockholm Peace Appeal, the earliest in a series of
campaigns to play upon Western fears of nuclear war.
The principal outlet for Soviet activity in this area
has been the World Peace Council, a global organization
enjoying the support of the Moscow-based USA Institute
which provides speakers, fluent in English, for participation in a wide array of pro-freeze activities. (13)
In his definitive expose entitled The Peace Movement
and the Soviet Union, exiled Soviet dissident Vladimir
Bukovsky suggested that Moscow's interest in the US
nuclear freeze goes far beyond its apparent desire to
codify a strategic balance that favours the USSR. (14)
The US nuclear freeze campaign is regarded by the Soviet Union as an important tool contributing to change
in the global correlation of forces by driving a pol-
itical-military wedge between the United States and its
principal allies.
    To not an insignificant degree, militant elements
within the freeze movement, including its Soviet supporters, have played upon popular fears in the United
States of the dangerous state of US-Soviet relations
and hence the prospect of nuclear war.   The result has
been the development of a grass-roots movement which
is susceptible to manipulation by the more militant
anti-nuclear activists in the United States.   In this
regard, the nuclear apocalypse as portrayed in such
popular literature as Jonathan Schell's The Fate of the
Earth and in graphic pictorial representation like ABC
television's 'The Day After' and the movie Testament
have contributed greatly to the anti-nuclear cause both
in the United States and abroad where anti-nuclear
groups, including the West German 'Greens' and the
British Campaign for Nuclear Disarmament, reinforce
American fears of the increasing probability of nuclear
war.   To the most ardent proponents of the freeze con-

cept, that is, those who support a unilateral US freeze or disarmament, the only hope for the United States and indeed the entire world, lies in the utopian conception of world government. The catch-all slogans of proponents of this view, 'One World or None', has emerged as a popular theme of the anti-nuclear 'left' in the United States.

Even so, the chimera of one world has its critics within the nuclear freeze coalition, especially among those in the political arena who are not so naive as to assume that the nation-state system is in demise. This, the more pragmatic element of the American anti-nuclear movement, while wistful of the desirability of unilateral disarmament, nevertheless, recognizes the enormity of the task at hand. It is this branch of the nuclear freeze campaign which accepts the reality of the existence of strategic weapons by espousing a course for disarmament based upon a minimal deterrence concept. According to this perspective, the US deployment of a minimal deterrent capability based on the existence of a few strategic submarines is adequate for the purpose of war deterrence. As expressed by former US President Jimmy Carter, one Poseidon submarine alone deploys enough weapons to destroy all major cities in the Soviet Union. Consistent also with this perspective is opposition to President Reagan's Defence Initiative based on the absurd notion that to protect oneself or one's military assets is destabilizing and threatens to undermine the putative superpower strategic relationship. While such a perspective obviously fails to take into account the nature of Soviet strategic thinking, its most serious fallacy rests on the presumption that the 'population hostage' concept is sufficient to deter Soviet conventional and nuclear aggression against the United States and/or its allies in Europe or Northeast Asia.

Prominent in the nuclear freeze campaign are prestigious professionals, notably physicians and clergymen, who hold that nuclear weapons are immoral and should be banned from the face of the earth. The American Catholic bishops, standing in a long moral tradition which condemns the threat to destroy innocent civilians, have attempted, with their Protestant counterparts, to give intellectual respectability to the nuclear freeze concept. (15) Ironically, as has been pointed out by Albert Wohlstetter, 'the view dominating all their (Catholic bishops) revisions (of the pastoral letter) reflects an evasive secular extreme which, instead of speeding improvements in the ability to avoid by-standers, has tried to halt or curb them'. (16) Contrary to humanist dogma and the 'just war' thesis, both of which emphasize the need in war to avoid civilian casualties and restrict combatant fatalities the American Catholic bishops support a freeze concept which would leave population centres undefended, facing the threat of annihilation. While the US Bishops in the third and final draft revision of their Pastoral Letter acknowledge that nuclear weapons have not been used since the Second World War, they refuse to credit the deterrent posture of the United States as contributing to this fact. Instead, the American Catholic bishops, like others in the freeze movement, consider that stability built upon the deterrence concept is not 'an infallible way of maintaining real peace'. (17) Deterrence, from this perspective, is thus considered to be a temporary expedient, 'a tactic whose purpose is to set in motion the process leading to complete disarmament'. (18)

To some extent, the contradictions apparent in the bishops pastoral letter as well as those in the nuclear freeze concept itself result from the mistaken notion that the Soviet Union shares Western values and strategic conceptions. Such may be the inevitable result of the 'lay strategist's' attempt to infuse a particular conception or morality into military thinking. To a far greater extent it is the result of a massive disinformation campaign which presumes that the Soviet Union values the legalistic norms of Western society. From this conception flows the view that Soviet strategic programmes are intrinsically defensive in nature, the result of provocative military developments in the United States. What proponents of the so-called 'action-reaction' thesis fail to understand is the time-cycle inherent in weapons development programmes and the symmetry between the characteristics of Soviet strategic deployments with the declared objectives and operational concepts of a Soviet military doctrine that is offensive in nature.

If religious leaders involved in the freeze movement are prone to emphasize moral considerations, their counterparts in the scientific community, including the medical profession, have made a point of dwelling on pragmatic considerations. Groups like the American Federation of Scientists - which, by the way, is sponsored by anyone who cares to 'donate' as little as 15 dollars, regardless of profession - and Physicians for Social Responsibility, emphasize the fatality ratios of nuclear-exchange scenarios and the environmental devastation that would ensue. Psychotherapists discuss the emotional dangers of living with nuclear weapons, while astronomers speak of the 'nuclear winter' that allegedly will ensue as a result of a US-Soviet strategic exchange. Lending credibility to the freeze campaign is the support of 'nuclear experts', like Nobel physicist Hans A. Bethe, and military professionals such as retired Admiral Eugene LaRocque, who contend that the Soviet Union would participate in a nuclear freeze if the United States took the initial step and at the same time forswore the 'first-use' of any nuclear weapon.

Unfortunately, however, there exist fallacies in the nuclear freeze concept which are likely to have the effect of rendering less likely the attainment of real and equitable reductions in the strategic arsenals of the United States and the Soviet Union. At the very least, the notion of a nuclear freeze is incompatible with the Reagan Administration's zero option proposal which seeks the dismantling in Europe of all long-range theatre nuclear forces. For the Soviet Union this would mean the drawdown of its 378+ triple-warhead, European-based SS-20 IRBMs as well as its older arsenal of SS-4s and SS-5s which are targeted against Western Europe. The United States would be required, under the zero option proposal, to discard plans for its deployment of 108 single warhead Pershing II IRBMs and 464 ground-launched cruise missiles. To 'freeze' now would mean the codification of a European theatre force imbalance that would erode the credibility of the extended deterrent concept and hence the Flexible Response strategy which has provided the basis for the defensive posture of NATO Europe since its adoption in 1967 by the Atlantic Alliance. At the Eurostrategic level a nuclear freeze would foster the interests of the Soviet Union which has long sought to decouple the United States from its European allies. A Western Europe, denuded of its US deterrent protection, may seek to provide for its security by means of accommodationist policies towards the Soviet Union. Nuclear freeze advocates seldom discuss the implications of their proposal for US allies; most attention is focused on the United States where it is contended that there already exist enough nuclear weapons deployments to cause the destruction of the earth if used.

Proponents of the nuclear freeze rely overwhelmingly on the mythical notion of 'overkill' as the intellectual basis of support for their concept. In the real world, however, the use or threatened use of nuclear weapons would not occur in a vacuum, but within a complicated context of relative strengths, advantages, weaknesses and vulnerabilities. Numbers of weapons, in combination with their particular characteristics and in light of a nation's military doctrine, could mean the difference between peace and the out-

break of war. The Soviet Union espouses a military
doctrine based on the concepts of surprise, pre-emptive
attack and damage limitation (strategic defence)
against the USSR. Fundamental to the Soviet strategic
conception is a conviction that nuclear weapons may be
used and used effectively in breaking the essence of
an enemy's defensive or retaliatory measures. From
this perspective, nuclear weapons are not regarded, as
they are in the West, as awesome capabilities, never
to be used; but rather as a means of effecting decision
on the battlefield or to extract political leverage in
a crisis situation.
     The concept of deterrence as embodied in Western
strategic thinking is not shared by the Soviet Union
and on this basis Soviet leaders reject out of hand
notions which would require Soviet disarmament. Negotiations to limit offensive nuclear deployments are
more promising, especially if Moscow thinks it can
extract significant political concessions from the
United States. Unfortunately, a nuclear freeze would
be incompatible with the idea of negotiating real reductions in intercontinental nuclear weapons as embod-
ied in the Reagan Administration's negotiating approach
to the Strategic Arms Reduction Talks (START). What
will be the incentive for the Soviet Union to engage
in such negotiations if the United States has already
committed itself to abandoning the deployment of such
systems without gaining equivalent concessions from
the Soviet Union? In this regard, one of the major
problems that the United States confronts is the asymmetry between US and Soviet strategic forces which are
the result of the unprecedented (in peacetime) investment in the build-up and modernization of Soviet strategic forces over the last decade and a half, especially since the signing of the Strategic Arms Limitation
Accords (SALT 1) in 1972. The United States, in its
strategic modernization programme, is seeking to alter
the adverse trends in the strategic balance which resulted from the relentless modernization of Soviet
strategic forces. Without the successful completion
of its strategic modernization programme, the United
States would be faced with a situation in which the
deterrent potential of US retaliatory forces was
jeopardized because of the obsolescence of all three
legs of the US strategic triad and, more importantly,
given their growing vulnerability to pre-emption by
virtue of the Soviet containment of a counterforce
capability.
     At one time, the concept of arms control embodied
the notion that it should aim for the sensible goal of
reducing the danger to demographic centres. Today,

however, arms control generally is equated with disarmament and hence of increasing the risk to civilian
population centres. The modernization of US offensive
nuclear forces which could increase their survivability
and provide more reliable safety mechanisms, together
with the development of stragetic technologies, would
be forestalled by the adoption of a nuclear freeze.
In this sense, the nuclear freeze campaign is regarded
by some of its proponents as an important political
tool for use in moderating the Reagan Administration's
security policies and defence spending. For this
reason, too, the freeze campaign has adopted a new
sense of urgency, no doubt an indication that nuclear
arms issues have taken on greater political significance. Minimal deterrent advocates have jumped on the
freeze bandwagon as a means of criticizing everything
from the budget deficit to MX deployment. The prospects for Congressional passage of a binding nuclear
freeze are, however, limited because of the lack of
unity within the US anti-nuclear movement over the
nature of a 'freeze' and the extent to which the Soviet
Union can be expected to act in concert with its objectives. In 1982, at the time of the US mid-term
elections, a quarter of all US voters were offered nuclear freeze resolutions. Nine states and 27 local-
ities put the issue on their ballots. All passed, with
one exception, indicating the extent to which the
campaign touched the fears of ordinary citizens over
the nature of the US-Soviet relationship.

Typically, the freeze resolution that was found
on a state ballot called for a 'mutual, verifiable
freeze' on the testing, production and deployment of
all nuclear weapons. Opinion polls in the United
States consistently show that the American public favours a moratorium on the modernization and deployment
of nuclear weapons provided that by such action the
Soviet Union does not gain a military advantage. In
other words there is little support for a nuclear
freeze which would codify a strategic balance in which
the United States remains vulnerable to the threat of
a Soviet pre-emptive strike, while its retaliatory
capacity is jeopardized by Moscow's deployment of a
redundant array of strategic defensive (active and
passive) technologies.

In May 1983, the coalition of supporters for a
nuclear freeze successfully pushed passage of a non-
binding resolution through the US House of Representatives. By the resolution, which purports to represent the sentiment of the House of Representatives, the
United States and the Soviet Union are encouraged to
consider a mutual, verifiable freeze on the deployment

of nuclear weapons. A similar proposal, referred to
as the Jackson-Warner resolution, was adopted in the
Senate. While the bilateral nature of these resolutions attracted greater support than an earlier draft,
which called for a unilateral US nuclear freeze, it
was the provision for verification that won over an
undecided block of Congressmen who questioned the potential for compliance by the Soviet Union. The most
ardent of freeze supporters tend to assume that the
good faith of the Soviet Union is enough, although
they also believe that US and Soviet interests are
more compatible than competitive and that, as a result,
both nations have an express interest in maintaining
peace and global stability. The Marxist-Leninist
dialectic is dismissed, if understood, by freeze supporters who also see no Soviet involvement in North-
South conflicts, particularly the rise of insurgency
movements in Third World areas. Endemic problems of
poverty and development are considered by freeze advocates to be the primary source of Third World instability, not Soviet of Soviet-sponsored proxy activities.

Together with the advocacy of the World Council
of Churches, the US Catholic Bishops, and the Physicians for Social Responsibility, the Nuclear Freeze
Coalition is attempting to generate popular support
for its position by means of influencing the national
platform positions, particularly of the Democratic
Parties in the United States. While it is generally
recognized that for the near term, the prospect for
adoption of a national nuclear freeze is remote, the
campaign has served to generate pressure on the Reagan
Administration for arms control negotiations with the
Soviet Union. In this regard, it has served to encourage the US government to commit itself to negotiating positions, such as the 'build-down' proposal, which
may be less than prudent for the United States at
least until there is demonstrated a willingness to
explore reciprocal concessions on the part of the Soviet Union. In contrast, current US arms control proposals - both at the START and INF - are designed to
reduce substantially US and Soviet nuclear deployments.
The effect of a nuclear freeze would be to place a
moratorium on further weapons deployments, while offering no incentives for reducing the current levels of
US and Soviet nuclear stockpiles. In this concern to
stop production of new weapons systems, a nuclear
freeze would result in dependence on less reliable and
more vulnerable nuclear systems, a sure recipe for global instability.

Proponents of a US nuclear freeze express the view

that if the United States takes the initiative in this area, the Soviet Union will follow suit because its apprehensions about US aggressionist tendencies will have been alleviated. In the tradition of Urie Bronfenbrenner's 'mirror image' conception, nuclear freeze coalition members assume that Soviet values and objectives ultimately correspond to those of the United States. Both nations, it is argued, have a vested interest in peace and global stability. What is overlooked or suppressed, as described in Leon Festinger's cognitive dissonance theory, is the abundance of evidence to the contrary - evidence which demonstrates beyond reasonable doubt that conflict remains intrinsic to the dialectic process whereupon the emergence of a socialist world order is predicated. From this perspective conflict is endemic in an international system where the forces of capitalism exist in opposition to the socialist state. 'Mir', the Soviet word for peace, has as its primary definition 'the triumph of world socialism' and not 'the absence of conflict' as is the case in the West. Nevertheless, Soviet apologists dismiss such differences as unimportant in an era when both the United States and the Soviet Union deploy enough nuclear weapons to destroy the world. The subjective nature of the nuclear freeze campaign, with its prejudices against rational analysis of the strategic balance, fails to provide convincing evidence in support of a conception of national security that denies the need for a stable nuclear relationship between the United States and the Soviet Union. For some involved on the nuclear freeze campaign, it is the case of 'don't bother me with the facts; I've already made up my mind'.

The intellectual heritage of many of those involved in the nuclear freeze campaign can be traced to the decade of the 1960s and the literature of the Civil Rights and Vietnam protest movements. Against the themes of racial oppression and an immoral war they took to the streets, adopting the tactic of mass marches, 'peaceful' rallies, sit-ins, prayer vigils, and even violent demonstrations. Today, while some of the same tactics are employed by activists in the freeze campaign, the movement is channelling most of its efforts towards the election process, seeking to foster changes in US policy from within the system itself. (19) Eric Van Loon, Executive Director of the Union of Concerned Scientists, believes that there is:

> enormous vitality and strength in a grass roots
> movement. There is a distinction in tactics
> involving civil disobedience and risking arrest

and working in a democracy to change laws. As in
the civil rights and antiwar movements there can
be people working toward the same goals - even
advancing them - even though they are at different ends of the spectrum. I see them as compli-
mentary.

In this sense, the US peace movement, like its European and especially its West German counterparts, 'has
crossed traditional socio-political demarcation
lines'. (21)
   The new strategy of the freeze campaign, which is
being orchestrated by a 'national clearing house in
St Louis', (22) is to go beyond anti-nuclear rallies
and voter referendums and, instead, to influence specific legislation on issues such as MX deployment and
INF modernization. More recently, nuclear freeze
supporters are endeavouring to waylay President Reagan's Strategic Defence Initiative and to engender
congressional support for a Comprehensive Test Ban
Treaty. The Council for a Livable World has established a political action committee to help finance local,
state and national congressional candidates who support
the freeze concept. Such efforts will be enhanced by
a wide-ranging media campaign featuring Hollywood
stars like Jane Fonda, Paul Newman and Michael Douglas.
The high visibility of some of America's most renowned
entertainers offers vast potential for fund-raising in
support of the nuclear freeze cause. In addition, a
political action committee, Freeze PAC, has been organized to provide funds for candidates who support the
freeze. More recently, coalition activists have been
engaged in an impressive direct-mail campaign designed
to engender support for what is called a 'Quick Freeze'.
According to supporters, the Quick Freeze would ban
further spending on US strategic modernization programmes within a 90 day period after its approval by
Congress. Because the Quick Freeze is unilateral in
nature, the prospects for its passage are not encour-
aging. Nevertheless, the increased attention given to
the nuclear freeze issue will, it is hoped, stimulate
ordinary citizens to act spontaneously in support of
the concept. Philanthropic support for the nuclear
freeze concept has been forthcoming, with such prestigious organizations as the Ford, Rockefeller and
Stanley Foundations in the forefront. While coalition
leaders admit that this switch in tactics to emphasize
specific election issues risks undermining the universal emotional appeal of the nuclear freeze concept,
they nevertheless regard a shift in tactics as necessary if the campaign is to regain its momentum.

Within the nuclear freeze coalition, however,
there is division over the adoption of new tactics.
The Livermore Action Group, for example, is urging
civil disobedience. 'Action', in their view, 'is the
only thing that can change society.' (23)   Potential
activists are being encouraged to withhold payments of
one-half of their assessed income tax as a means of
protesting against US military policies. Other forms
of protest include resignation from jobs relating to
the nuclear weapons industry. Unfortunately, democratic societies, susceptible to the lures of a nuclear
freeze - that is, lower defence spending, a reduced
national deficit, greater attention to social reform,
as well as the promise of global peace and stability -
have not been provided with articulate and reasoned
analysis of the fallacies of the concept. such an
effort is long overdue in the United States, especially
at the grass-roots level where objective debate over
US security policies and the deterrence concept needs
to be aired. If the majority of the American public,
like its European counterparts, is presented with an
alternative view of the nuclear freeze concept, it is
my view that a pragmatic realism will prevail.

NOTES

(1)   See 'Past U.S. Freeze Proposals', contained
in literature published by Council for a Livable
World (11 Beacon Street, Boston, MA, 1984 and distri-
buted by Council for a Nuclear Weapons Freeze, 456
Massachusetts Avenue, Cambridge, MA).
(2)   William E. Colby, 'Why Reagan Should Go For
a Freeze', Manchester Guardian Weekly, 1 May 1983
(3)   Richard J. Barnet, 'Ritual Dance of the
Superpowers', (afterword) The Nation, 19 April 1983,
p. 450.
(4)   Jonathan Schell, The Abolition (Alfred A.
Knopf, New York, 1984), p. 115.
(5)   Quoted in David B. Richarson, 'On the March -
U.S. Version of Peace Crusade', U.S. News and World
Report, 22 March 1982.
(6)   Ibid.
(7)   Quoted in Dorothy Rabinowitz, 'The Building
Blocks of the Freeze Movement', Wall Street Journal,
10 June 1982.
(8)   Ibid.
(9)   James Bristol, quoted in ibid.
(10)   Ibid.
(11)   Ibid.
(12)   Ibid.
(13)   The relationship between the WPC and the Sov-

iet Union - both the KGB and the USA Institute - is documented in John Barron, 'The KGB's Magical War for Peace', Reader's Digest, October 1982.

(14) Vladimir Bukovsky, The Peace Movement and the Soviet Union (the Orwell Press, New York, 1982).

(15) James E. Dougherty, The Catholic Bishops and the Dilemmas of Nuclear Deterrence, an Institute for Foreign Policy Analysis book (Archon Books, Hamden, Connecticut, 1984).

(16) Albert Wohlstetter, 'Bishops, Statesmen, and Other Strategists on the Bombing of Innocents', Commentary, vol. 75 no. 6, June 1983, p. 15.

(17) Quoted in Walter Berns, 'The Nation and the Bishops', Wall Street Journal, 15 December 1982.

(18) Ibid.

(19) For a treatment of the organizational structure of the 'activist left' in US politics, see John Herbers, 'Grass Roots Go National', the New York Times, 4 September 1983.

(20) Quoted in Jeffrey J. Carmel, 'Antinuclear Ranks Swell with New Professional Coalition', Christian Science Monitor, 13 December 1983.

(21) John Dornberg, 'In the West, Demonstrations Can Sway a Nation', International Herald Tribune, 26 October 1983.

(22) The Nuclear Weapons Freeze Campaign National Clearing House was established in 1981 by G. Randall Kehler, who serves as its Executive Director and Randall Forsberg of the Brookline-based Institute for the Study of Security and Disarmament.

(23) James Wallace, 'Nuclear Freeze Crusade, Gaining or Waning?', U.S. News and World Report, 25 April 1983.

Chapter Ten

TOWARDS A COMPARATIVE ANALYSIS OF THE PEACE MOVEMENTS

Werner Kaltefleiter
and Robert L. Pfaltzgraff

For a comparative analysis of the peace movements it
is first necessary to find a basis of comparison. In
a sense every peace movement is unique because it is
based upon the specific historical and contemporary
circumstances of each of the countries under examination. Before trying to find out the common features
it is therefore a basic prerequisite for any comparative analysis to identify the unique circumstances of
every country that is to be dealt with, because these
unique circumstances have given rise to the characteristics of the various peace movements.

NATIONAL CHARACTERISTICS

The situation in Sweden seems to be especially unique.
The Swedish political situation is a model towards
which many other peace movements outside Sweden would
like to aspire; neutrality, non-alignment, and non-
imperialism in a nuclear-free country. This situation
also represents the goals of other European peace movements which are not in such ideal circumstances as
those in which many Swedes consider themselves to be.
Only Sweden, given its geographic location, given the
configuration of the power balance in Europe, has the
luxury of affording a peace movement which can have all
of those characteristics which are represented in the
Swedish concept of neutrality.
    The case of Denmark and Norway demonstrates that
there can be states which are aligned and nuclear-free
and which are not as satisfied with their nuclear freedom. These states have additional nuclear freedom because of their geographical circumstances. They are a
part of the Atlantic Alliance, which lies behind them.
Geography, therefore, provides one of the very important determinants one must consider in the analysis of

the national strategies and foreign policies of states, as well as the attitudes within those which may give rise to various peace movements. All three Nordic countries are Protestant.

The Netherlands is a state which is aligned, but not nuclear-free. This nation has a history of neutrality and would like to return to this concept which served it so well until 1940. The Netherlands is suffering from a religious split between Protestants and Catholics, as in Germany, and the affiliation to the respective church is of great importance for political orientation. Only a few years ago the Protestant and Catholic parties merged but still today the internal fractions of the Christian Democratic Party follow the traditional religious lines which again became so obvious during the debate on the dual-track decision in 1983 and 1984.

Another interesting fact is the multi-party structure in these four countries. A closer look at this might be useful in providing a structure for relating multi-party political systems in the European context to some of the issues relating to peace movements. By influencing only a faction of one of the parties which form a more or less heterogeneous coalition, the peace movements are able to gain a kind of veto position on the government; this became obvious in Denmark and The Netherlands during the crucial INF debate of 1983/4.

There is also a historical basis for the antinuclear movement in Britain, which has re-emerged in the last few years. The British movements have more immediate antecedents in the campaign for nuclear disarmament of the 1950s. Prior to this, during the period between the two world wars, Britain also had a very strong movement toward pacifism. This word has to be used in the case of the British inter-war experience, because of the consensus which emerged in Britain about the horrors of war in the aftermath of the First World War. There was also the new historic effort in Britain to turn this consensus to an understanding of the problems of the 1930s that Britain increasingly faced as the onset of the Second World War approached.

A point of particular interest about the British situation is the substantial support for retaining some form of a national nuclear deterrent. It seems that the opposition that has emerged is based on the cost of Trident. It is also directed against the cruise missile because of the US-control of those systems. It is this situation which makes the British case unique. One can say that a British nationalism exists, which is probably nowhere more fully represented than in Mrs Thatcher today. There is a certain element of this nationalism which has gone hand in hand with the idea of independence, and in the final analysis the argument for the Trident D-5 is the independence that it would supposedly give to Britain in making decisions concerning her nuclear destiny.

The variables of nuclear independence, of high cost and beyond that the historic roots of the anti-nuclear movements, are therefore of relevance for an analysis of the British case. The historic elements that have gone into a British pacifism are deeply rooted in the British political tradition, which is again deeply rooted in the Anglo-American political tradition. The USA and Britain share a historic aversion to large standing armies and the possession of large capabilities in peacetime, which is differentiated in the case of Britain especially by the navy, but not by land forces.

In contrast to the four continental countries discussed above, Britain has a long tradition of a two-party system which however is challenged today. The split of the Labour Party and the foundation of the new moderate left SDP reflects a very complex problem but it also relates to the fact that the Labour Party has left the foreign policy consensus and taken over several positions of the British peace movement, especially the request for unilateral nuclear disarmament.

The situation in the Federal Republic is also characterized by a very unique phenomenon, the German national question. The Federal Republic of Germany depends heavily upon a broader framework, not only as the very basis for the legitimacy of the Federal Republic of Germany as it was founded in 1949, but also as the core of every European security framework. The German national question is unique in Europe because of the abnormality of the division between the Federal Republic and the German Democratic Republic.

Along with The Netherlands, Germany is divided between Protestants and Catholics, a factor which played an important role in German politics: the Thirty Years (of confessional) War was fought on German soil. But the catastrophy of Nazi-dictatorship helped to overcome this cleavage which is represented by the success of the biconfessional CDU/CSU after 1945. Today religion plays no role in party politics, but the contrast between the Protestant and the Catholic culture is of great importance for the German peace movement.

Towards a Comparative Analysis of the Peace Movements

The German party system started as a multi-party system after 1945, and was then transformed into a nearly two-party system in the 1960s and 1970s. The FDP has served as a third minor party which is always aligned with one of the two major parties: up to 1966 with the CDU/CSU, from 1969 to 1982 with the SPD and since 1982 again with the CDU/CSU.

The German case is unique also because this party system is challenged today by the Greens. Originally founded as an ecological party, the Greens have merged with the German peace movement. Therefore the German peace movement is the only one with a parliamentary wing since the Greens came into Parliament in the Federal Election of 1983.

France is considered by the Americans as the oldest ally of the United States. One of the most important facts for the analysis of West European political phenomenons, especially those associated with security, is the relationship between French nationalism and French national security policy with such broad support based on a very widely shared consensus, not only on foreign policy, but on the need for strategic deterrence. This consensus is grounded very much in French historic circumstances and very much in the desire for independence. It is tempting to ask what the status of the French anti-nuclear movement would be if GLCMs and Pershing IIs were stationed on French territory without a dual-key system or even with a dual-key system with the United States having one of the keys. When analysing the British context with respect to nuclear independence, one must realize that from the French perspective, the British nuclear force is not truly independent. Nevertheless, one might argue that it has many of the same characteristics. In the case of France therefore, there is the phenomenon of strong nationalism which is accompanied by anti-pacifism.

Although France has a long democratic tradition in Europe, it is a tradition of political instability. Not before the Fifth Republic, founded in 1958, were the French able to build working political institutions, political stability and a respective party system. Until 1981, this party system was characterized by an asymmetry in favour of the conservative wing caused by the existence of the strong communist block of about 20 per cent of the total vote of the left wing. Until 1981, the communist block put the socialists in a dilemma. If they tried to run alone, they gained votes in the political centre, but lost the election because their gains could not compensate for the loss of the communist vote. If they aligned with the communists they also lost because in this case they

189

could not attract the political centre. This dilemma was overcome for several reasons after 23 years of conservative government in 1981. Since that time, France has had a socialist government with Communist ministers. This has not prevented President Mitterrand to be more Atlantic-orientated than any of his predecessors. He strongly supported the deployment of the INF in 1983 which caused trouble for his fellow socialists in the other European countries discussed above.

Looking at Italy, what has to be said is just the opposite of what one might want to believe; weak nationalism is linked with a weaker pacifism. This is in contrast to the French experience which is strong nationalism linked to weak pacifism. A number of different comparisons or conclusions could be drawn between Italy and France, but again one comes back to the theme of uniqueness. In the Italian case as well there are no indigenous roots. One can see many indigenous roots in the German case, traced in some instances back to the nineteenth century. One can see from the American case that very powerful indigenous roots exist as well.

The party system in Italy seems to be the most unstable among those countries discussed. More than 50 governments have been in office since 1945 and the Italian Communist Party is the strongest in the free part of Europe. Nevertheless, Italy has been a very loyal ally and the decision to deploy cruise missiles in 1983 was much less opposed than in other European countries. The Italian Communist Party - a 30 per cent party - tries to demonstrate its independence of the USSR and therefore normally avoids the use of foreign policy issues for its domestic political exchange with the Socialist and the Christian Democrats. This competition, however, prevents the socialists, as is the case in France, from taking over issues now dealt with by the peace movements.

One of the characteristics that one has to deal with in Italy and France is the strength of Catholic culture, rather than the strength of the Catholic Church. This could be called one of the unifying elements of these societies one should not neglect.

In the case of the United States, one should also stress the uniqueness of the American case before concentrating on the common features. In the United States one might argue that there is a longer tradition which cannot immediately be characterized as pacifist, although it has elements of pacifism. This tradition is certainly closely linked with isolationism. This isolationism is strongly reinforced by the peculiar

190

geographic circumstances of the United States in contrast to all of continental Europe, and to a much
greater extent, Britain. The American view of America
as a global power in the mid to late twentieth century
is to some extent that of America in Britain's place:
if Britain is the island of maritime power located
adjacent to continental Europe, the United States is
the global maritime continental power located between
the Atlantic and the Pacific Oceans.

An analysis of the contemporary American scene
with respect to militarism and peace must be set in
the historic context in which generations of European
immigrants to the United States came to escape what
they perceived to be the wars of Europe. It was a
nation built upon a society which was different from
the European political scene. It was a nation which
was different from Europe in the sense that it combined
elements of Realpolitik as the basis of foreign policy,
in the first generation of American independence; that
is, during and following the revolutionary war and for
a long time afterward, at least as far as foreign
policy views are concerned. It was the idea of a
country which is too good for the rest of the world in
the Wilsonian sense, characterized by a feeling of
corruptibility through excessive external influences.

This view has been more recently superseded by
the view of the United States as a country not good
enough for the rest of the world, but as a country
which is responsible for most of the world's ills.
This view imputes a degree of power to the United States which they do not have and never had. It is therefore perhaps based upon a certain sense of ethnocen-
trism. According to this view, America is responsible
for the fact that there are, in a large part of the
world today, authoritarian governments which do not
represent the will of the people.

These two elements still coexist today in America.
The result of this situation is the set of current
problems in defining American commitments and in defining the role of the United States in the world.
In the final analysis, it gives rise to a feeling that
there is a certain ambivalence about the role of military power in world affairs. This is a deeply rooted
problem for Americans, even more so for American intellectuals. The statement is often heard that we live
in a world in which military power has little or no
active ability.

This is a view which goes to the core of much of
the anti-nuclear movements in the United States today
in this historic context. One might only add that
there is, as far as the United States is concerned, a

tendency to rely upon egalitarianism as a basis for
the conduct of world affairs in contrast to utiliza-
tion of power, especially power in its military manifestations. The fact that the bloodiest of the wars
of the nineteenth century, except for the Napoleonic
wars, took place on American soil does not properly
belong to this discussion. That was an American domestic affair. It had little to do with American
foreign policy. Instead, one should juxtapose the
American views of the roles that the United States
should play in the world. There is a contending set
of values in the United States.

On the one hand, there is a wish to be strong in
defence policy; on the other, a wish to find alternative means in the conduct of American affairs to either the use of force or the threat of force. In this
sense, Americans are uncomfortable with the possession
of force, but reluctant to give it up in the absence
of an alternative. So one will always find support
for strong defence policies in the USA, tempered by a
very strong interest in the pursuit of means towards
the limitation of armaments. This is why one finds
today in the United States very strong support for
the Reagan Administration's defence build-up and at the
same time a very strong movement towards the control
of those capabilities in one fashion or another;
through nuclear freeze, through START or other means.

With regard to the peace movements it also has to
be mentioned that the United States is characterized
by confessional pluralism. The rigid separation between church and state along with this confessional
pluralism has put the churches in a unique position
which is very different from all the European countries:
they have always served as a platform for different
movements in the history of the United States.

THE COMMON FEATURES OF THE PEACE MOVEMENT

Despite the unique conditions which prevail in each
respective country, it is also possible to discern
common features of the peace movements. First, there
are striking similarities between the kind of support,
the activities and the position of the peace movement
in the political systems of Scandinavia, Germany, The
Netherlands and Britain. The well-educated Protestant
middle class and the lower age-groups are the basis
for the recruitment of peace movement followers. They
co-operate closely with people from the ecological
movement and also the women's movement. In all of
these countries - with the exception of the non-NATO-

country Sweden - the Social Democratic Parties were in
power at the time of the preparation (Britain) or still
at the time of the making of the dual-track decision
in 1979. In all these countries these parties are now
in opposition to the peace movements. In all these
countries no important communist parties exist but,
among the peace movement activists, communists play an
important if not the central role, and are in control
of the organization in most cases.

In contrast to such common features in these
countries is the situation in Italy and France. Both
countries have strong communist parties but in fact no
important peace movements which are independent from
the communist parties. In both countries the peace
movements are controlled by the communist parties which
makes it much more difficult for the movements to
attract the type of person they do in other countries.
In addition to that, the catholic culture seems to be
a much more effective wall against the infiltration of
the peace movement's belief system.

Here it is worthwhile to mention that in the
catholic south of Germany, the peace movement is also
much weaker than is the case in the protestant north.
The same is the case in The Netherlands, where the
catholic faction of the ruling Christian Democratic
Party was in favour of the deployment of cruise, while
the protestant wing opposed this decision.

Finally, in the United States the peace movement
on the one hand is rather similar to the respective
movements in Northern Europe and Britain. On the
other, the American peace movement has a second pillar
of support in the Catholic Church, which is contrary
to the European experience. Here it is even more
important than in the case of France and Italy to make
the distinction between Catholic culture and the
Catholic church. It is the American Catholic church,
not so much the Catholic culture, which is infiltrated
by the peace movement.

Given these obvious parallels, the question has
to be raised: what kind of common variables can be
analysed to explain the rise of the peace movements in
the late 1970s?

First of all, in each of the cases examined, one
can see a series of movements that had their beginnings
outside the formal party structure or structures.
Nevertheless, the movements seek, directly or indirectly, to have an impact upon the party positions, or to
take over those parties (one or more parties, depending upon the structure). With the exception of France
and Italy in each of the instances looked at, the party
or parties of the left centre have become the object

of that take-over, especially after they have been
thrown into opposition. It does not necessarily have
to be a disloyal opposition. However, within the
framework of the policies of the recent past, it cannot be considered a type of loyal opposition within
that consensual framework that was provided earlier.
The second point can only be made with some trepidation, but it cannot be neglected. It seems that
the greater the number of political parties that exist
and the greater the emphasis in a particular country
upon a peace movement, the greater the prospects for
that peace movement having some leverage. Here
Holland might serve as the key case. The Federal
Republic, the United States and Britain are, in comparison, fundamentally different: the Federal Republic
is not a multi-party system in the sense that its
predecessor was. Britain has a single member constit-
uency-system. The American system is also very much
the same in this instance as the British, although
there are at least 100 political parties in the United
States, namely 50 republican parties and 50 democratic
parties. There is, in all these states, at least a
semblance of a two-party structure. There are no
national parties in the US except every four years to
run the presidential election. What might seem to be
a horrendous experience, called the national party
convention, is the only manifestation of the coalition-
building process.
One can therefore conclude that the greatest potential of these movements seems to be in those political systems in which there is a multi-party structure. Here, again, Italy with its catholic culture is
the exception. This multi-party structure is therefore necessarily dependent upon fragile political coal-
itions which do not exist to the same extent in the
Federal Republic or in Britain. There are many nuan-
ces to this. One cannot be sure whether this constitutes a similarity or a difference, but at least it is
one basis for categorization.
Another basis for a unifying element is the tendency that has arisen in a great number of Western
societies in which older social structures have broken
down. That generalization characterizes most of the
societies of the West. The older social structures
were in various ways broken down by two world wars in
Europe. They have been breaking down in all Western
societies for reasons of the mobility of affluent
societies. The impact of the advanced technologies of
the consumer society is also important. These sociological and political-economic phenomena have been
called the post-industrial societies by some analysts.

To say that a series of post-industrial societies has emerged is to suggest that there has been a decline in support for existing political institutions, as well as social institutions, in these societies.

No one can maintain that there has been a decline of respectable political institutions in the United States. The imperial Congress, which may now have superseded the imperial Presidency, enjoys no greater support among the American people than the Presidency did in the recent past. To speak of this post-industrial society as a Western phenomenon is also to make a series of generalizations about the question of support for the movements under examination. In general the support comes from the younger, the more educated, the service-orientated sectors of the economy, the professionals and middle classes. The anti-nuclear idea, for example in the United States, but also in Europe is very strongly embedded in the upper middle classes. Nowhere is this more fully optimized in the United States than by the readership of the New Yorker Magazine.

As far as the activists for the movements are concerned one has to take another phenomenon into consideration: the kind of counter-culture movement. To be sure, the readers of the New Yorker Magazine, or those who would read comparable publications in Europe, are not necessarily the counter-culture. They are just the followers, the activists come from the counter-cultures. This is a much broader societal phenomenon which is very much a part of the post-industrial societies' ethos: 'Small is Beautiful', the idea of an anti-industrial ethic - though one cannot be sure that there isn't a certain form of ottism in this, to use an early nineteenth century British expression. This phenomenon is certainly somewhat bound up in the romanticist idea of the early nineteenth century in the USA, at least if one looks at the ecology and the 'back to nature' idea, the anti-industrialism and anti-urbanism. In the American context it is very interesting to recall that a decade before there were the Greens in the Federal Republic of Germany there was a movement in America which was called the 'Greening of America'. The 'Greening of America' has many similarities with the movements under examination. The Federal Republic does not therefore have a monopoly on this idea with the Greens.

The electronic media are another focus of the analysis. As a part of the post-industrial society they seem to be of tremendous importance. If one combines the idea of political pluralism with the electronic media, one can say that the greater the politi-

cal pluralism in a state, and the greater the technological level of that state, the greater the likelihood
of a phenomenon like the ones under examination here.
One reason for this is the pervasive impact of the
electronic media, that is, the instantaneous communications capability. The idea is that events, whether
they be wars, riots or anti-nuclear protest demonstrations, can be immediately transmitted. The result is
that the effect of those events is magnified beyond
their immediate occurrence and the immediate site of
their occurrence. One could argue that the tendency
to communicate news instantaneously, to acquire news
instantaneously rather than through the introspection
of reflection that necessarily accompanies reading
itself, may have as great an impact upon the value
structures of Western societies as had the 'penny
press' at the end of the nineteenth century and the
rise of mass literature.

There is one more impact of this communication
structure: it favours minorities which are prepared
to use unconventional methods of political participation.
The old saying of Mark Twain - if a dog bites a man
that is no news, but if a man bites a dog that's news -
rings true here since the electronic media bring
events so quickly into living rooms. It is characteristic of the peace movements to use these unconventional methods: demonstrations, human chains, sit-ins,
peace villages of tents, blocking barracks or other
public buildings, peace pop-festivals, etc. The broad
coverage of these events by the electronic media has
created the image of a movement with broad public
support from the very beginning which has mobilized
other people to join the movement: a snowball effect.

The role of the churches has to be considered in
this analysis as well. It seems that there is a tendency in those countries, in which the Protestant
churches are important, to develop movements which even
reject the very notion of deterrence in the nuclear
sense as the basis for prevention of war because of
the immorality, or immoralism of deterrence. This can
be called the immoralism associated with those against
the concept of deterrence because of its immorality.
One can therefore conclude that the movements are
strongest in those societies in which Protestantism in
general and Pietism in particular, if not in the present generation at least in historic terms, have been
a major influence. One only has to comment here upon
the Huguenots in order to give another clue to the
basis for the consensus that could be discerned in
France.

One might say with some trepidation that in pol-

itical matters, though not in threological matters,
the beginning of a protestantization of America is the
acceptance of Catholicism. A possible reason for this
is the fact that the Catholic Church is today accepted
as part of American culture and society in a way in
which, historically, it was not. The fact that John
F. Kennedy was the first Catholic President of the
United States settled an issue that would never arise
again in the United States. The fact that it was an
issue is only mentioned to underscore the point that
is being made here. One can almost say that American
Catholicism was more a part of American society as long
as it was not fully accepted. It is now in a position
to be as critical of that society as those who were
felt more fully to be a part of that society, that is,
Protestants.
    Another point with regard to this question of
religion is the phenomena of secularization of society.
Although one sees churches taking positions on political issues to an unprecedented extent, they do so in
a highly secularized society. The United States has
on its currency 'e pluribus unum', but it also has in
its culture the idea of a nation under God. But it
was meant to be a nation in which God was sufficiently
separate from that society, which is a separation of
church and state. Today one can see a secularization
of society to an unprecedented extent, which is mir-
rored in the Supreme Court's decisions in recent years
and currently in the issue of prayer in school. With
regard to this secularized society, one has to ask
what the basis for a revival of interest in religion
is in a society in which the traditional interest in
theology no longer exists. Evidence is provided by
church attendance in Europe. Churches are empty in
Holland and Germany, but churches are not empty in
the United States. There is furthermore, at least
in the case of the Protestant churches, a substantial
decline in membership. There is a correlation here
between the rise of interest in political movements,
and the decline in the actual attendance in churches
of those Protestant denominations which in historic
terms were the most important ones. With respect to
the peace movements, it is important to note that the
secularization of society may well be accompanied by
a secularization of religion - although it might be
possible to object that religion has, as its basic
purpose, an understanding of the world as it is, as
well as an equally important purpose in understanding
and preparing for the next world, rather than dealing
so much with this world. The secularization of modern
societies has created a temptation for the churches to

use political issues to regain support among people
they can no longer attract with a classical message of
the Christian Church.
    Apart from religion one has to consider the break-
down of the defence consensus in various countries as
an important fact in the analysis of the peace movements. There is a common element that runs throughout
the studies about the Federal Republic of Germany, The
Netherlands, the United Kingdom and the United States.
If anything has happened in the political security
environment, it is the breakdown of the defence consensus. This consensus certainly existed in the Federal Republic from 1960, after Herbert Wehner's famous
speech in the German Bundestag when he accepted the
west-integration as the basis of the SPD's foreign
policy to the late 1970s, to the NATO double-track
decision. There is the same phenomenon in the United
States, which has been quite properly associated with
the Vietnam War more than with anything else. But it
has its historic basis in the roots outlined above, as
well.
    There is also another tendency in each of these
countries. It is the tendency of the parties of the
left, which are in opposition, to cope with the forces
further to the left. This is the case with the British
Labour Party and the American Democratic Party and the
Social Democratic Parties in all northern European
countries including Germany and The Netherlands. As
far as the American Democratic Party is concerned,
this began in the late 1960s. It should be pointed
out that it was the American Democratic Party more than
the American Republican Party which represented the
framework for internationalism that emerged as the
basis for American foreign policy after the Second
World War. The historic isolationism of the United
States was associated more with the Republican Party
than it was with the Democratic Party. To see this,
one only has to go back to the debate following Wilson's abortive effort to get the United States to join
the League of Nations. Furthermore, there was the
juxtaposition between Henry Cavett-Lodge, Chairman of
the Senate Foreign Relations Committee, a Republican
from Massachusetts, vs. Woodrow Wilson, a Democrat,
drawn from a Presbyterian tradition.
    The fragmentation of the American Democratic Party
began in the late 1960s during the Vietnam War. The
interesting parallel is that just as most of the European Social Democratic parties were in power at the
time of the NATO double-track decision of 1979, the
Democratic Party was in power in the 1960s in the
United States. The anti-Vietnam position, which enter-

ed the American political spectrum, contains elements
of the American Democratic Party. It had originally
been a highly cohesive unit in the foreign policy area
and had based its policy upon the loyal support of the
Republican Party as it emerged from the Second World
War. One should keep in mind that in 1948 Harry Truman went around the country on his barnstorming,
whistle-stop campaign, excoriating the do-nothing,
republican-controlled Congress. However, it was this
Congress which approved the Marshall Plan, the Truman
doctrine, and the very basis for the internationalism
which still sustains the basic framework for American
foreign policy in 1984.

The crucial question with respect to the fragmentation of the parties to the left of centre is whether
these parties can return to office without moving
back towards the centre, or whether the political
centre will have to move to the left in order to allow
these parties to come back to power. If the answer to
that question is that the political centre will have
to move to the left and the political centre will not
move to the left, as it may not, then in fact there
is the basis for a long-term rule of the CDU/CSU in
Germany and the Conservatives in Denmark, Norway, The
Netherlands and Belgium and perhaps the re-election of
President Reagan, or even the election of a successor
to President Reagan. It may even be that this is the
reason Mrs Thatcher has already announced that she will
stand for a third term as Prime Minister whenever she
feels the time is appropriate, whether it is in 1988
or any time within her five year term.

If, however, the centre really will move to the
left, the security policy of the Alliance and the
Alliance itself will be questioned. This may be the
main challenge of the 1980s. Whatever scenario will
occur these developments will take place within a
highly politicalized and polarized framework in each
of these countries. If the political spectrum moves
to the left, there will nevertheless remain on the
right of the centre very formidable forces opposing
what the left stands for.

Another topic for consideration, which has not
only been raised by American experts but by Europeans
as well, is the anti-Americanism widespread among
peace movements. It seems that one needs to go beneath
the surface of the anti-nuclear movements in order to
clarify the relationship between Europe and the United
States. Is anti-Americanism in part a phenomenon
which is associated with the dependence of what was
once the centre of the political universe, not only
with respect to ideas, but also with respect to inter-

national power and relations? Is a Eurocentric international system a phenomenon associated with the dependence in various ways upon the United States for
security? Such questions help to understand the differences between France and the Federal Republic of
Germany, because this feeling of dependence is greater
in the Federal Republic of Germany. Is it, furthermore, a feeling of hopelessness, based on the relative
positions of the superpowers? Is that part of what
one has to deal with? Is it a phenomenon in which one
is witnessing a decline in what was once perceived to
be a community of interest with the United States,
which was borne of the experience of the Second World
War, and which is now nearly two generations old? One
of the main reasons for the new anti-Americanism does
not follow from foreign policy as was the case with the
first wave of anti-Americanism during the Vietnam War.
The United States is the symbol for societies which
are rather competitive and achievement orientated;
where economic success is a main criteria for a person's position in the social hierarchy. In the affluent societies of Western Europe this value system is
frequently questioned and rejected especially by
younger, well-educated people. This is the hard core
of the Greens in Germany and broadly reflects the general political feeling of most peace movement followers
in Europe. They will reject American foreign policy,
whatever this policy may be, just because it is American. The United States is the symbol of the type of
society they reject.
 The 11th of May, 1984 was the 35th anniversary of
the end of the Berlin blockade, and 1985 will be the
40th anniversary of the end of the Second World War.
Are we confronting a situation where there is a growing
parochialism with respect to Europe, compared to the
growing sense of global commitment of interest in the
United States? This is true more in politico-military
and defence terms, rather than necessarily in cultural
terms. Are there, furthermore, faltering feelings of
community of interest with Europe on the American part?
Are there, for different reasons, tendencies on both
sides which will mutually reinforce themselves, which
are represented in the societal elements that one has
to consider on both sides of the Atlantic? And, of
course, there is a declining community of interests
across the Atlantic, which is represented in the div-
ergent approaches to security that one can see. However, underlying all this, there is a sense of pluralism on both sides, in which there is a great deal of
commonality more apparent than in some of the similarities that exist in the proposals that they put forth.

Towards a Comparative Analysis of the Peace Movements

CENTRAL ISSUES OF THE PEACE MOVEMENTS

Despite different historical roots, the peace movements
in Europe are inseparably linked with the issue of the
dual-track decision of 1979. This decision opened an
opportunity for the Soviets to use the four years until
the scheduled deployment in 1983 to manipulate public
opinion in Europe. It is, however, unfair to make the
point that all the peace movements are just Soviet
creatures. The strong communist influence on these
movements cannot be denied. The Geneva negotiations
on this issue were a perfect demonstration what arms
control means to the Soviet Union: an instrument to
manipulate public opinion in the Western democracies
in order to change the correlation of forces. To prevent deployment was the major objective of the Soviet
Union because this would have weakened NATO's defence
capability and would have been the beginning of decoupling of America from Europe - the historic objective of the Soviet Union. Whether the installation of
the Pershing II and the GLCMs is coupling or decoupling
of America from Europe is an important question. The
peace movement says that on the one hand it is decoupling, but on the other hand it may be coupling because,
after all, the United States will fight this war from
Europe while holding at reserve its own forces. For-
tunately Marshall Orgakov has come to the rescue of the
West and said that any launch of those systems from
Western Europe against the Soviet Union would result
in retaliation with a Soviet attack upon the United
States, which is coupling.

Another issue of the peace movement is the request
for a nuclear free zone. The problem with the nuclear
free zone is that it does not extend to the point of
launch of the system against the nuclear free zone. In
other words, a meaningful nuclear free zone must be
extended to the SS-18 launch pads in the Soviet Union,
which, of course, has never been proposed. This again
demonstrates that the security interest of the West
never plays an important role in the considerations of
the peace movements. Nevertheless, the nuclear free
zone is an idea which has had its time across the Atlantic.

The nuclear freeze is another common proposal. It
aims at the prevention of NATO nuclear deployments in
Europe and the prevention of nuclear modernization in
the United States at a moment when, due to extended
modernization in the past, the Soviet Union is ahead of
the United States in several systems.

The conversion of military spending to other forms
of expenditure is the fourth basic recommendation.

which of course gets much of applause beyond the rank
and file of the peace movements. The argument that
this conversion has to be realized in the Soviet
Union too is rejected by the argument that unilateral
disarmament would change the international climate,
would take into account the real security interest of
the Soviet Union and therefore make the Soviet Union
follow the example set by the West. This way of arguing is of interest for two reasons. On the one hand
it expresses, as all the other recommendations, the
interest of the Soviet Union which demonstrates again
if not the organizational influence, at least the
intellectual leadership of the Soviet Union on the
peace movements. On the other hand, these arguments
demonstrate that the peace movements base Western security on hopes and wishes about the foreign policy
behaviour of the Soviet Union. Rational calculations
like the worst case assumption are alien to their
thinking.

Given these arguments there are two more points
which have to be given sufficient attention. The first
point is that the movements under examination developed
parallel to the rise of Soviet military power and the
pursuit of the detente policy in the West. The Soviet
Union builds SS-20s and Western Europe creates pacifist
movements. This is a phenomenon which has coincided
in its intensity with the rise of Soviet strategic
military power in all dimensions over the last decade.
Nobody can escape this power relation, though there
are difficulties in changing power relations to positive relationships.

Nevertheless, the West would be amiss in not understanding that. Has the threat to Europe so declined, despite the build-up of Soviet military capabilities, that it is fashionable to speak of the need to
disarm? Has that build-up preceded at such a pace
that the West must not in any way disturb the bear in
a way that would lead it to take action against it
because of its weakness? Of course the answer is no,
but it would be unfair only to blame the peace movements and not to realize the Soviet policy of power
projection. This policy was ignored by Western governments during the 1970s when they tried to convince the
Soviet Union of the prospects of arms control and detente. During these years Western politicians and the
media treated the Soviet Union as a normal superpower
without expansionist ambitions, as a power with ter-
rible internal problems and the desire for 'peaceful
coexistence', a word that was not understood in the
framework of Soviet ideology - even after Soviet governments tried to preserve the image of the Soviet

Union as a 'partner' in European security affairs.
After this experience it is not surprising that young
people are unwilling and unprepared to accept the
existence of the Soviet threat. Soviet intimidation
on the one hand and the Western mirror imaging by the
detente policy on the other may be the psychological
parents of the peace movement.

Finally, a double standard is appearing on both
sides of the Atlantic. There is a tendency to give
the benefit of the doubt to the Soviet Union and to
impute the best intentions to the Soviets and the
worst to the United States, or at least to equate the
United States and the Soviet Union in a way such that
they both constitute a somewhat equal threat to Europe.
If that is not a double standard, it is a single
standard at its lowest possible denominator.

The final point and the question that needs to be
addressed is where the West should go from here? What
is likely to be the future agenda of the movements
under examination? It is appropriate to say that these
are not movements which have simply arisen in the
abstract or even from a political context which is
recent. If one thing is apparent, it is that they have
historic roots in most countries. They are movements
which certainly have antecedents in the early 1950s.
The CND in Britain has been mentioned, the Stockholm
Appeal in the early 1950s, the fight against nuclear
death in the 1950s, the Easter marches. etc. They are
movements which are likely in various ways to manifest
themselves in the future. However, how will they
manifest themselves? What will be the political context? What will be their impact? What will be the
issues they will focus upon? If one believes that they
will manifest themselves, one must address these
issues. If one believes that they are a part of a
broader societal phenomenon, perhaps the post-industrial society, it follows that the issues that they will
address will be those that seem to be central to the
elites of those societies. These issues include on the
one hand, the emphasis upon environment vs. industrial-
ization, work vs. leisure, upon sources of energy, the
relationship between man and the environment, and on
the other hand, in the final analysis, the relationship between domestic priorities and foreign policy
and national security policy. Here we will be confronted with a fact that has already been described
by Alexis de Tocqueville in his famous book on the democracy in the United States more than 100 years ago.
The observation he made there seems to be valid for
all our democratic systems. The basic strength of a
democracy, he argues, depends on the innovative cap-

acity which follows from the competition between government and opposition for new ideas and new approaches. This innovative capacity, however, may become dangerous with regard to foreign policy if the international conflict structure is unchanged over a longer period of time. In such a situation, Tocqueville has pointed out, innovation means discontinuity.

This is exactly what is happening today. Since the Second World War, the systemic conflict between totalitarian dictatorship and pluralistic democracy dominates international relations. Again and again people have looked for a way out of this reality and proposed numerous recommendations to bypass, overcome, or change this conflict. The peace movements are part of this tradition. All these aspects of the so-called post-industrial society create an atmosphere that requests these new approaches. From the Soviet point of view, with Foreign Minister Gromyko in office for more than a quarter of a century, the Western countries may look like playing children who try another toy every day. This, of course, is an invitation to the Soviet Union to stimulate these children to concentrate on these toys even more and neglect the security interest. The peace movement's ideas are such toys.

NOTES ON CONTRIBUTORS

Werner Kaltefleiter	Institute of Political Science, Christian-Albrechts-University, Kiel, FRG
Robert L. Pfaltzgraff	Institute of Foreign Policy Analysis, Cambridge, USA
Jan Andersson	Lund University, Peace Research Institute, Sweden
Kent Lindkvist	Lund University, Peace Research Institute, Sweden
Sten Sparre Nilson	Institutt for Statsvitenskap, University of Oslo, Norway
N. H. Serry	Institute for Public Interests, Ej Waalre, The Netherlands
Peter Byrd	Department of Political Science, University of Warwick, Coventry, UK
Hartmut Grewe	Social Science Research, Instititue of the Konrad-Adenauer-Foundation, St. Augustin, FRG
Joel Francois Dumont	French Television, Paris France
Sergio A. Rossi	Centro Studi e Documentazioni Internationali, Turin, Italy
Virgilio Ilari	University of Macerata, Italy

Notes on Contributors

James Finn   Freedom House, New York, USA

Jacquelyn K. Davis   Institute of Foreign Policy
                              Analysis, Cambridge, Massa-
                              chusetts, USA

INDEX